Behind Every Successful President

The Hidden Power and Influence of America's First Ladies

Alice E. Anderson and
Hadley V. Baxendale

Illustrations by Dale Anderson

S.P.I. BOOKS
A division of Shapolsky Publishers, Inc.

Copyright © 1992 by David A. Boehm Productions, Inc.

All rights reserved under International and Pan American Copyright Conventions. Published in the U.S.A. by Shapolsky Publishers, Inc. No parts of this book may be used or reproduced in any manner whatsoever without written permission of Shapolsky Publishers, Inc., except in the case of brief quotations embodied in critical articles or reviews.

For any additional information, contact:
Shapolsky Publishers, Inc.
136 West 22nd Street
New York, NY 10011
(212) 633-2022
FAX (212) 633-2123

10 9 8 7 6 5 4 3 2 1

ISBN 1-56171-089-X

Design and Typography by Kable News Company, Mt. Morris, IL

Manufactured in the United States of America

FOREWORD

This book undertakes to reveal as clearly as possible the little-known but historically important role of the distaff side of the recent American Presidencies. Many of the Presidential wives of this era were far more influential in matters of public policy than is commonly thought, and many of the Presidents enjoyed a close working relationship with their wives. As a husband-and-wife team, they learned from one another and worked out the complex issues of their times through intense discussion and mutual grinding of minds and polishing of consciences.

Further, the majority of the Presidents relied on their wives to accomplish essential purposes of statecraft through means traditionally defined (and typically underrated) as "woman's work": hostessing the White House, charming the ambassadors, taking certain social concerns and other sentimentally charged matters to their motherly hearts. Some of the Presidential wives, moreover, understood that they exercised an important "office" in their own right—although we have begun to discuss First Ladyship in these terms only recently.

A few First Ladies retreated abovestairs at the White House and left it to their husbands to preside over the man's world in which they as women felt unwelcome. However, the closer we look even at the passive ones, the clearer it becomes that their stories also reveal important glimpses into their effects on Presidential power.

The approach in this book has been to study the most reliable accounts—chiefly, autobiographical memoirs and biographical scholarship—of each woman's life, to absorb her personality and concerns, especially those previously hidden details of her story that make her outstanding and memorable. The authors intentionally avoid rehashing the husband's Administration; readers can find that history elsewhere. We do attempt to reflect the idiosyncrasies of each woman's style and perspective, and attempt to piece together not so much an "interpretation" of her partnership in the Presidency as a literary cameo of her.

Reading the story of each lady's lifetime of struggle, tragedies, deaths, and heroism will prove a surprising and often deeply moving experience. While these stories also include the nonsense of politics, the brilliance of lives well lived, and many a high time—all of which lends to laughter —nevertheless, the overwhelming impression one receives is of the nobility of the First Lady role and the sacrifices it has exacted from them and the individuals closest to them.

Some Presidential wives have not yet found their scholarly biographer; to write about these, we have had to scrape around in the works of their husbands' scholars. Some of the living Presidential wives have been written about too much—or too cheaply. To write about them, we had to sift through gossip to unearth the truth.

Our conclusions reflect a kind of "soft feminism." Many a recent Presidential wife, by reason of her individual character and history's demands, was a resilient, inventive, bright human being. Nonetheless, these First Ladies often felt they had to shine with a derivative light borrowed from their husbands, who were, by popular definition, elected to their positions. This tension between the First Ladies' natural abilities and their respect for their distinguished husbands' office tended to cause some to retire somewhat, while on the other hand prompting others to step forward. This situation has dictated, even for the strongest among them, that most of our Presidential wives have been natural feminists even when they were not outspoken about it.

This book makes an extraordinary political statement in any Presidential election year—or in any year, for that matter—inviting the electorate to a new kind of political discussion. The "office" of First Lady—neither elective nor appointive nor budgeted nor constitutionally defined—still is precisely that: an office. Being a Presidential wife entails for her certain specific duties, places certain expectations on her, and requires in her certain qualifications. The Presidency is a male/female partnership, and would continue to be so even if the President should be a woman.

What surprised us in editing this book is that so many of the wives were more sensible and likable than their husbands. Yet until recent years, the wives have been even less known than the Vice Presidents. They deserved to be brought forward into the limelight.

A survey like this, covering almost 70 years, started out as a work to be shared by a group of historians, each specializing in an era. It turned out that Alice E. Anderson and Hadley V. Baxendale alone were so knowledgeable about the whole period and so perceptive in portraying the women that they carried through all the wives from 1928 to 1991 in entertaining fashion—an achievement defying duplication.

The Editors
New York
1992

Contents

Foreword .... *iii*

BARBARA PIERCE BUSH 3

ANNE FRANCES "NANCY" ROBBINS
    DAVIS REAGAN 29

ELEANOR ROSALYNN SMITH CARTER 69

ELIZABETH "BETTY" ANN BLOOMER
    WARREN FORD 87

THELMA CATHERINE "PAT"
    RYAN NIXON 107

CLAUDIA ALTA "LADY BIRD"
    TAYLOR JOHNSON 131

JACQUELINE LEE BOUVIER
    KENNEDY ONASSIS 167

MARY "MAMIE" GENEVA DOUD
    EISENHOWER 191

ELIZABETH "BESS" VIRGINIA
    WALLACE TRUMAN 229

ANNA ELEANOR
    ROOSEVELT 257

LOU HENRY HOOVER 285

Barbara Pierce Bush

*First Lady of Literacy/
Dog Lover*

*A*T HER husband's Inauguration, Barbara—born Barbara Pierce on June 8, 1925—held two Bibles under his hand: the Bible that George Washington had used 200 years before at his swearing-in, and the Bush family Bible. Then, as George and Barbara were moving down the people-lined avenue from the Capitol to the reviewing stand where they would watch the grand parade, the President and First Lady got out of their bullet-proof limousine and "spontaneously" walked along the street, waving happily and greeting the crowds. Breaking ranks, bringing the procession to a standstill, and giving her Secret Service guards conniption fits, Barbara ran over to the sidewalk where she saw Willard Scott, the jovial NBC morning-TV weatherman. There, the new First Lady performed her first official act: "The Silver Fox" (as her children had nicknamed her) kissed the balding, portly public flirt smack on the lips, in plain sight of the watching nation. A few days later, Willard spiced up his weather report by boasting that he had now been appointed

"Secretary of the Lips," and that he planned to have his lips bronzed.

George Bush met Barbara Pierce when he was 17 and she was 16. Three years later they were married. "I married the first man I ever kissed," she admits. "When I tell this to my children, they just about throw up."

George "Poppy" Bush, a "best-at-everything" senior at Andover, was attending a prep-school Christmas dance at the Round Hill Country Club in Greenwich, Connecticut, in 1941, when he noticed a "laughing girl" in an off-the-shoulder, green-and-red holiday dress. She had large eyes, was full of vitality, and seemed to be having so much fun. He wondered who she was, and asked to be introduced. At the same moment, Barbara—who kept on dressing in bright colors even after she grew up—was being seized by a similar chemistry: "I thought he was the most beautiful creature I had ever laid eyes on. I couldn't even breathe when he was in the room."

The band was playing Glenn Miller tunes; but just as a mutual friend introduced the two, the dance tempo changed from fox-trot to waltz. Handsome George didn't waltz, so he asked beautiful Barbara to sit one out with him. They sat several out together. He learned that the colorful boarding-school junior from Ashley Hall, in Charleston, South Carolina, was the daughter of Marvin Pierce and Pauline Robinson Pierce of Rye, New York. Barbara's and George's families were casually acquainted, but the two teenagers, in love at first sight, had hitherto overlooked one another.

Growing up in the Pierce home made life feel "luxurious." The Pierces were comfortable, although they did not think of themselves as rich. Pauline brought her children up "to look after other people's feelings." Marvin, said his daughter, believed that a parent could give his child only three things: "a fine education, a good example, and all the love in the world." The good example included a positive attitude towards hard work and faith in a Supreme Being. For Barbara, family love and belief in God would remain permanently "intertwined."

Barbara was usually an agreeable and docile child. But she also loved to have fun, sometimes at the expense of her mother's china. "Every time I turned around," said Barbara, "I knocked a piece off the table." Speaking of herself, her sister and two brothers, she said: "We were four rowdy, rambunctious children growing up in a very small household filled with antiques."

For young Barbara, life was a happy time of paper dolls, bicycle riding, and playing "imagination" games. Barbara's chum, Lucille Schoolfield, was the leader of the group of girls, and under her direction they acted out Louisa May Alcott's *Little Women*. Lucille was a devoted reader of Albert Payson Terhune's "Lad" stories about collie dogs; she always took the part of the author. Barbara and her other friends always had to be the dogs.

Dogs were more important in Barbara's life than boys. She had Scotties first, then Cairn terriers, and lots of puppies. "Damn!" shouted Marvin one night as he stumbled through his dark house, "Damn! When do I get my bathroom back? Got up in the middle of the night and stepped on a puppy!" Barbara's love affair with dogs would last forever.

Barbara attended public school through the sixth grade, and then was sent to Rye Country Day School. She grew to be a tall, slender young woman with reddish-brown hair. In September 1941, Barbara followed her older sister Martha to Ashley Hall. Here she continued her education and began to mature into the kind of solidly upper-middle-class American woman who was the *McCall's* ideal. According to Margaret Hemphill, one of Barbara's Ashley Hall schoolmates, a person was considered really mischievous if she took off her hat and white gloves when she got out of sight of the school buildings. Headmistress Mary Vardrine McBee's school rules strictly forbade wearing makeup or dating the same boy two weekends in a row.

Barbara kept busy with activities. She played Beatrice in a school production of Shakespeare's *Much Ado About Nothing*, and Viola in *Twelfth Night*. She was a champion speed-knitter, underwater swimmer, and (unofficially) eater of the most hot buttered biscuits at one meal without getting caught.

December 1941 was when the Japanese bombed Pearl Harbor. Barbara was at a rehearsal for the Christmas pageant (not much of a singer, she had the part of the Speaking Angel), when Miss McBee informed the Drama Club of the attack. The stage emptied as the girls raced for the telephone to call home. During the following summer vacation, Barbara took one of the two paying jobs that she would ever have—a summer job sorting nuts and bolts in Port Chester, New York, helping with the war effort.

Following the Christmas dance in Greenwich in 1942, "Barbi" and her friends started writing prank love letters to George "Poppy" Bush, who was in the Navy's flight training school. However, Barbi's love letters were sincere and quite against Miss McBee's rule of "no love affairs." Barbara wrote to George nearly every day. She knitted him Argyle socks, too. George and Barbara saw one another again briefly during Spring Break. When summer came, Barbara went along for a vacation of boating and fishing with George's family at the Bush family home on Walker's Point, in Kennebunkport, Maine. After eight months of being "serious" about each other, Barbi and Poppy became "secretly" engaged. Their engagement, said George, was "secret to the extent that the German and Japanese high commands weren't aware of it." Barbara was liked by her mother-in-law-to-be. Later, Dorothy Bush told Pauline Pierce that Barbara was a "most wonderful daughter" who had pitched in to help feed the family. Barbara's peanut butter sandwiches were the best.

When Poppy got his Navy wings, he was the youngest flier in the Navy. People thought he looked too young to be engaged.

George saw a lot of action in the South Pacific. Meanwhile, Barbara went to Smith College. When Marvin sent his daughter a subscription to *McCall's,* one of the deans noticed its arrival, and told Barbara: "We do not allow pulp magazines." Barbara called her dad. Marvin was outraged. "You tell that lady you're getting those magazines, and that you wouldn't be there if it wasn't for pulp magazines!"

Barbara stayed at Smith only for a year. She was captain of the soccer team, but a "lousy" student. At the beginning of her sophomore year she dropped out, her mind on George, not books. His mind was on her, too. George had named his Grumman Avenger "Barbara," and painted the name of the girl he loved on the side of his plane. When "Barbara" was shot down in the ocean during a raid on Chichi Jima, both of George's buddies were killed. He narrowly escaped with his life.

Wearing her mother-in-law's wedding dress, Barbi Pierce married Poppy Bush, her twenty-year-old hero of 58 combat missions, in the First Presbyterian Church in Rye on January 6, 1945. Looking back, Barbara said that she never regretted dropping out of school to marry George: he was "the nicest person I'd ever met . . . the least negative person I know . . . and still the handsomest man I've ever seen."

After the war ended in Europe, George was reassigned to the force preparing for the invasion of Japan, the assault that never came. When Japan surrendered, Mr. and Mrs. George Bush were living in Virginia Beach, Virginia. George remembered that "within minutes our neighborhood streets were filled with sailors, aviators, their wives and families celebrating late into the night. We joined in the celebration, then, before going home, went to a nearby church filled with others giving thanks and remembering those lost in the war. After four years it was finally over."

At Yale, 1946–48, while George studied economics and played a lot of college baseball, Barbara, pregnant, kept score from behind the dugout. The more pregnant she became, the more comfortable Barbara found the special double seat (two seats with the middle arm removed) that Yale had once provided a famous baseball fan, the 300-pound President William Howard Taft.

George and Barbara talked about their future, wanting to do something different with their life together, "and we didn't put any limit on our imaginations either," said George. They read Louis Bromfield's *The Farm*, and dreamed dreams of self-sufficiency, basic values, and a family farm. But, lacking enough money to become farmers, they went into the oil business instead.

After graduation, George went to work for a West Texas company run by one of his father's Yale classmates. The following year, Barbara and George Jr. joined him in the boomtown of Odessa, Texas, out in the wide-open spaces of the Permian Basin. Barbara, a New Englander who saw herself more as a nester than a pioneer, said: "I didn't want to go at the time, but a day after I got there, I thought it was really exciting."

Moving so far away from her family, Barbara realized later, was good for their marriage: "When you are a couple all grown up, nobody's son or daughter, nobody's shadow, you are you." Barbara did have to reassure her mother, however. Living in Odessa sounded like Russia to Pauline. Certain that modern conveniences were unavailable in West Texas, she did what she could to make Barbara's life easier, including sending her boxes of Tide. Barbara finally convinced her mother that there were "plenty of grocery stores around and that Odessa was bigger than Rye, New York."

They lived, George reminisced, in a "shotgun house on East Seventh Street, with a makeshift partition down the middle that divided it into two apartments. We had one bedroom, a small kitchen, and a shared bathroom." Their front yard was rocks and dirt and one skinny tree. The Bushes owned the only refrigerator on the street. "An old water-drip window air conditioner that cranked up like a West Texas dust storm drew cool air into the bedroom on hot summer nights. The unit wheezed but wasn't noisy enough to drown out the socializing on the other side of the partition. Our neighbors, a mother and daughter, entertained a long line of male guests every night. We shared one of the few indoor toilets on East Seventh, and the guests kept it occupied from dusk to dawn." Barbara was philosophic: "Everything is relative in life. As we had the only bathroom on the street, we didn't complain."

Over the next few years, while George was working hard making his first million in the sweaty and risky business of selling oilfield equipment, Barbara was busy having kids—George, John (Jeb), Robin, Neil, Marvin, and Dorothy (Doro). In 1949 George's work moved them to

California. First it was Huntington Park, then Bakersfield, then Whittier, then Ventura, and finally Compton, where, in December, Robin was born. Robin, her daddy reflected, had "beautiful hazel eyes, and soft blond hair." (Years later, Robin died of leukemia.) "George and I were with her the night she died. The next day we went out to Rye, New York, and played golf with my father. It was the first day we'd been out. We just got up and went out. Played golf. Didn't tell anyone. I later thought that if people had seen us, they would have said, 'Why are those people doing that?' We just wanted to get away."

After Robin's death, they both felt "enormous physical pain for months afterward." George had been grieving during Robin's illness, but Barbara had been the strong one —"that's the way a good marriage works." George now became strong, and Barbara, who had not cried at all while Robin lived, felt as though she could "cry forever." "I nearly fell apart. . . . I absolutely collapsed. . . . I couldn't put my right foot in front of my left." Her hair turned gray "overnight."

Barbara's mother's death the same year as Robin's birth now fused together in Barbara's mind. Barbara became immobilized. She refused to go out or to entertain guests. She could not open her mouth to speak in public without crying.

Because George traveled a lot, Barbara stayed home with the kids. She became the family disciplinarian. Barbara decided to quit smoking when she saw her children start. Upset, she told George Jr. not to smoke. Father George—who, Barbara has said, never yelled at her a single time during their entire marriage—intervened, saying: "Barbara, who are you to tell your son he shouldn't smoke, as you so deeply inhale your Newport?" That did it. She

BEHIND EVERY SUCCESSFUL PRESIDENT

never smoked again.

In late 1959, when Barbara was pregnant with Dorothy, a reorganization of George's oil business forced the Bushes to move to Houston. George, who liked the sea, proved himself inventive as a pioneer in drilling for offshore oil.

The year 1962 found them on the road, campaigning every night. They stumped precincts together. Sometimes Barbara and a couple of disgruntled Democrats were the only audience George had for the evening. Barbara began taking her needlepoint along. "It was a way of staying awake at ten p.m. while listening to a speech I'd heard 150 times before."

"Bitten by the bug," as he terms it, George resigned from the oil business in 1964 and became a full-time politician. As George's career in public service diversified over the next ten years, Barbara excelled as a political wife —totally supportive of her husband, patient with the fickle winds of politics, dogged and sturdy in the many moves of her family from city to city. In 1970, another attempt on a Senate seat failed when George lost to Lloyd Bentsen. During that campaign year, George and Barbara visited with former President Lyndon Johnson and First Lady Bird on the LBJ Ranch, and were treated to one of Lyndon's famous 80-mph rides across his Central Texas cow pasture in the Lincoln Continental, LBJ himself at the wheel.

In 1971, during the Nixon Administration, George became the U.S. Ambassador to the United Nations; so the Bushes moved to New York, and spent a considerable amount of energy shuttling between D.C. and the U.N. Working for Nixon was politically tricky for George, but Barbara was having a wonderful time: "I'd pay to have this job," she said. They moved back to Washington in 1973, when Nixon picked George (against his and Barbara's wish) to chair the Republican National Committee.

After Watergate, George asked President Ford and received the appointment to become U.S. envoy to China. They departed in September 1974, and the kids, mostly grown, were left at home.

The one Bush "child" who was not left at home was C. Fred. C. Fred Bush was Barbara's golden cocker spaniel, named for Midland and Houston friend, C. Fred Chambers. Knowing that the Chinese savor dog as a delicacy, Barbara asked Chinese Ambassador Huang Zhen whether it would be all right to take C. Fred with them. "A dog? Yes, of course, bring him. He isn't a *sleeve* dog, is he?" The Ambassador was more worried about politics than the menu: a pre-revolutionary decadent elitist Manchu sleeve dog would not have been appreciated in Mao's China, but an American Yuppie puppy was OK.

In China, when Barbara went jogging, C. Fred went along too, as he did also when Barbara and George went out on bicycles to discover Asia. When Barbara drove her moped to the tennis courts, she would stuff C. Fred into a bag over her shoulder. The Chinese were confounded, and C. Fred suffered an identity crisis: blond and pretty, he didn't look like a dog to them. They would point, and instead of saying "Go" (Chinese for "dog"), they would say "Mao!"—not as in Chairman, but as in meow. Little Fred looked more like a cat than a dog. The first sentence that Barbara learned to say in Chinese was: "Don't worry, he's only a little dog, and he doesn't bite." C. Fred was, however, an undiplomatic, Cold War kind of pooch—he chased the Communist cat at the Polish Embassy. To Barbara's dismay, the dust of the city's streets turned C. Fred's coat from gold to gray.

BEHIND EVERY SUCCESSFUL PRESIDENT

Later on, after Barbara had become Second Lady, she acted as "editor" for a book published under C. Fred's name, *C. Fred's Story: A Dog's Life* (1984). This bit of Barbara Bush drollery became her wry way of commenting on Washington personalities through a dog's eyes, and of reporting from C. Fred's perspective the coal-dust air pollution, the shortage of hot water, the limits on their personal freedom, and the constant official surveillance that the entire three-member Bush team had experienced in China.

In a guesthouse provided by the Chinese government, Barbara was writing a letter home. Although the establishment was supplied with everything the Bushes' hosts had anticipated that their guests might require—from toothpaste to house slippers, cosmetics to pen and ink and postage stamps—someone had forgotten the glue with which to paste the stamps on the envelopes (Chinese postage stamps seldom came equipped with glue and required an outside supply). Barbara commented aloud to George: "Everything's here but the glue," but mentioned the lack of glue to no one else. Next day, a bottle of glue was in place on the desk—a lesson in what it's like to be listened to and watched by "Big Brother."

While they lived in Beijing, Barbara studied Chinese, took up T'ai Chi as part of her daily health regimen, and broke a legation taboo by playing tennis with international diplomats of lower rank. She and George rode bicycles, the usual *modus transportandi* of the Chinese populace; and they came to be known as "Busher, who ride the bicycle, just as the Chinese do."

In 1975, Henry Kissinger delivered a message to George from the President: Ford wanted him to become director of the CIA. Barbara quipped ominously: "I remember Camp David." She was remembering that Nixon had been at Camp David in 1973 when he asked George to take the job as Republican National Committee chair, the job that Barbara had wanted George not to take. The CIA job was one more hot seat, and Barbara was hesitant. She liked the life of the diplomat, and had grown fond of China over their 13 months—she had immersed herself in the study of Chinese history, art, and architecture. Now, she was worried about the effect on their children, should George accept the new post: the kids had caught a lot of flak from their classmates during the Watergate scandal—what *would* people say about George, if he were head of the CIA! Worse than that, might not the job at the CIA turn out to be a political dead-end? George and Barbara left China with decidedly mixed emotions.

The negative effect of George's new job was one that neither of them had expected: "For the first time in our married life," said George, "we couldn't speak freely about how things were going at the office." George's CIA work required strict secrecy, and that meant non-communication with Barbara about his work. George said that the positive result was that "Barbara and I spent a lot more time at home talking about family, friends, and personal matters." But Barbara, at age 50, was more negatively impacted.

Stuck in the middle of middle age, left out of her husband's work, with most of her children grown and gone, and with the Women's Movement telling her to expect more out of life, Barbara felt displaced and, as a "mere mother," unaccomplished.

Partly, Barbara's irrepressible good humor came to her aid: "Why would George tell me any CIA secrets?" she joked, "He says that I begin every sentence with, 'Don't tell George I told you this, but. . . .'" But jokes are not enough;

and in 1976, Barbara's native inventiveness began the thoughtful expansion of her self-image. She assembled a slide show on China, perfected it, and toured the country making speeches—a new beginning for a person who had once cried for shyness because she had to give a speech to the Houston Garden Club.

Especially she took on the problem of illiteracy. Son Neil had struggled with dyslexia, and Barbara had helped him. The more she learned about people who could not read, the more she realized that it was one of America's biggest social problems, and was at the root of unemployment, poverty, homelessness, and losing one's share of America's bounty: "One out of five Americans can't read. . . . Illiteracy—the most important issue we have. If we can get people to read, we can get them out of jails and homes and shelters and off the streets, and get them back to work."

After she had been listening in on one of George's briefing sessions with some of his Republican supporters at the rectory of St. Ann's Church in Kennebunkport, she had gone jogging and mulling; and it all came together for her: "I once spent the summer thinking of all the things that bothered me—teen pregnancy, drugs, everything—and I realized everything would be better if more people could read and write."

Barbara set to work, and by the time George became Vice President in 1980, she had already become the Second Lady of Literacy in a field where there was no First Lady. Barbara's friend Janet Steiger said that Barbara was "a great force in helping unite the literacy groups. Always quietly, never with any big show."

Barbara's contribution of her celebrity status as a fund-raiser made her a visible asset to the literacy movement. (C. Fred Bush's celebrity status helped, too: he generously donated the proceeds of his book to the literacy movement —if a dog could write a book, anyone could learn to read one.) At some slow-paced official banquet, Barbara found herself sitting next to Harold W. McGraw, Jr., of McGraw-Hill publishing company; she took the opportunity to convert him to her gospel of literacy. He then established the Business Council for Effective Literacy—Barbara called it "a beacon for corporate involvement in the cause of literacy" —and he helped to form the National Literacy Coalition. By the time she became First Lady, Barbara's trademark white hair and paste pearls had glittered at more than 500 fund-raisers for literacy.

In the re-election campaign of '84, Barbara took umbrage at the Democrats' constant reference to the Bush family wealth. To even the score a bit, she quipped that Geraldine Ferraro, the female candidate for the Vice Presidency on the Democratic ticket, was a "four-million-dollar— I can't say it, but it rhymes with 'rich.'" Barbara's "wicked wit" caused a bigger flurry in the press than anything else she had ever said or done, and Barbara herself deeply regretted having popped off: she called Ferraro to apologize, and even went so far as to issue a claim that she had meant "witch," not "bitch."

After one of Nancy Reagan's stormy encounters with Raisa Gorbachev, Barbara (as overheard by Maureen Reagan) described the meeting with some exasperation, pondering how she might handle Raisa when her turn came: "Nancy invited some of us for coffee with Raisa. Let me tell you, all that woman wanted to do was lecture all of us on the glories of the U.S.S.R. and the shortcomings of the American political system. She wouldn't let anyone else get a word in. She'd just cut you off and keep talking. I've never seen anything so rude. I don't know how Nancy kept her cool." The likelihood of Barbara and Raisa getting along, should the time come, was fairly strong: they had already identified their mutual interest in education, and the Soviet Embassy had even expressed Raisa's preference for Barbara over Nancy as tour guide to the National Gallery of Art—a preference that neither Barbara nor Nancy was willing to accommodate so long as Nancy was First Lady.

When the Princess of Wales came visiting, Barbara found someone to admire and a kindred spirit: "I didn't think I'd like the little princess from England. But Diana is the most outgoing lady. I took her to a hospice. She sat on the beds of people who were in the last two weeks of life, held their hands and asked how they felt. They glowed." Barbara observed that Di raised pointed questions about the people's comfort and care. "She was so mature."

Despite her unmistakable white hair and being the wife of the Vice President, Barbara was still a relatively unknown figure. She told with bemusement of a reception at the Swedish Embassy. One person passing along the reception line frankly asked, "Who are you?" Another greeted her, "Well, hello Mrs. Schultz." A third gave her a hearty handshake: "Welcome to our country!"

While George was winning the Presidency in 1988, Barbara was his most appealing asset. The candidate spoke of "a kinder, gentler America," and the future First Lady seemed to embody the promise. She savored her last few days of relative anonymity. During a photo op, the photographer shooting the candidate yelled for "the woman in the red dress to please get out of the picture." Barbara laughed: "I looked down at my dress and thought, 'My Lord! It's me.'"

Following tradition, First Lady trivia became the pursuit of the media. What was her favorite fast food?

Tacos. Her favorite place to eat out? Chinese restaurants. What White House snacks would she be serving? Popcorn (more healthful than George's fried pork rinds).

Did she wear red, white, and blue as a sartorial Pledge of Allegiance? No, rather because she had always liked bright colors—and she either kept her size-14 dresses till they wore out, or donated them; she was not in the second-hand clothes business, nor did she worry about appearing in public twice in the same gown: "In a world where there's AIDS, the homeless, and drugs, if you wear the same dress twice, it's not important. You shouldn't worry about these things. I owe it to the public to look nice and have a clean mind and a clean head of hair. And that's it."

Would "Barbara blue"—a deep turquoise—become the new national color? Would "Barbara Bush pearls"—she wore them everywhere—replace the stars in the flag? Barbara couldn't care less. Were her pearls real? No, they were "fake," she said, and cost $95; and she wore them, she said, "to hide the wrinkles." She wore the pearls and a "Barbara blue" cloth coat to the Inauguration. The only thing fake about Barbara Bush, said a political aide, was her pearls.

How was her tennis game? A fierce competitor at ladies' doubles, with the "same girls I've been playing with for sixteen years" (including Andy Stewart, wife of Supreme Court Justice Potter Stewart, and Justice Sandra Day O'Connor); but a frustrated loser: "I'm going to fall on my sword." A genteel sexist, Barbara opined that "most girls slow the game down for men." At least she did for George, and he did love so to win; therefore, she usually no longer played doubles with George. "A man is afraid to hit a woman—a nice man is—and my boys and George Bush are all nice men."

BEHIND EVERY SUCCESSFUL PRESIDENT

Did she mind being called "the Silver Fox?" It was "cute," she thought, and "slightly insulting." Reporting on her mail, she quipped that the folks out there seemed to be saying "stay fat, stay gray, stay wrinkled, we love you." Barbara laughed: "My mail tells me that a lot of fat, white-haired, wrinkled ladies are tickled pink!" She pronounced the color of her hair "a boring subject," and dictated to the chief media advisor of the Bush campaign: "I'll do anything you want, but I won't dye my hair, change my wardrobe, or lose weight."

Truth was, Barbara was slightly offended at, and considerably bored by, the constant discussion of her looks. Looking at a bad photo of herself taken in Detroit, she moaned: "You could have planted a whole potato field in the rows of wrinkles." She had dyed her hair for ten years, she admitted, but stopped in 1970. However, as she says, "I wish I hadn't let my hair go white. It makes me look older than George. . . . People can be so rude about the fact that George looks so young and I look so old. It's not nice."

As a Presidential election cannot take place without at least the hint of scandal, when the rumor went round that George had had affairs with a widowed family friend and a longtime aide, Barbara was "hurt and angered." She called the rumor "a large, fat smear, and I didn't like it one bit."

Meanwhile, other people were wondering about a couple of Bush saplings, and whether they might turn out to be weeds in the White House lawn: George, Jr., had become a board member of the Lucky Chance Mine in California, and during his tenure, its unlucky stock price fell from $1.62 per share to a nickel, and then to two cents. The mine became flooded with water and with ambiguity over who would own any gold that might have been found. Elsewhere, Jeb, who had been the Secretary of Commerce for the State of Florida and was the husband of a Hispanic wife, got involved in Dade County politics. He had worked as a lobbyist for an organization that turned out to be corrupt and went belly-up. Then Neal got into financial trouble in Denver.

Mostly, the First Lady candidate watchers kept their eyes on Barbara herself, an idea which Barbara did not care for: "I have no yearning to be First Lady. Besides, a woman doesn't run for the position of First Lady—that [idea] sort of offends me." Nevertheless, with the example of Nancy Reagan's strong-handed First Ladyship in the daily press, everyone was pondering Barbara's style, wondering what her approach would be. On the one hand, Barbara Bush was no Nancy Reagan. Barbara had constantly to answer pointless questions from the media about whether she and Nancy were personally at war with one another, and how Barbara as First Lady would differ from Nancy. Barbara met the questions with her consistent good humor: "As you know, [Nancy and I] have a lot in common. She adores her husband; I adore mine. She fights drugs; I fight illiteracy. She wears a size three . . . so's my leg."

But Barbara made clear that she did not relate to George in the direct way that Nancy worked on Ronnie: "I don't have to talk to his staff," she said: "I'll tell George." She sat in on planning meetings, needlepoint in hand, and yawned her way through a session on the economy, but perked up with interest when they talked about day-care: "I sat and did my needlepoint and listened . . . But I sat in on as much as I possibly could because it's like going to college. It's fascinating, and I would love to do that any day of the year." Barbara, said George, was "all fired up" to move into the White House.

On the other hand, Barbara resisted the Rosalyn

Carter image of the politically-involved First Lady.

> You'll never see me in a Cabinet meeting. . . . If I think something is wrong, I tell him privately upstairs, and I am very careful to have facts, though, because he's not one who loves rumors. But very rarely do I disagree with him. We've been married so long, and we've really grown up together. We've had the same experiences, we've met the same people; he's just better briefed than I am.

Barbara's description of how her relationship with George worked seemed borne out as the campaign progressed. She urged him early in the campaign to attack Robert Dole's "straddler" position on tax increases. George listened and modified, with success. Towards the end when the campaign got stuck in mudslinging, Barbara reasoned against George's use of "negative ads" and his harsh attacks on Democrat candidate Michael Dukakis. George listened and modified, with success. She told George that his response on the "women and children issues" and homelessness during the Presidential debate was inadequate. "She really talked hard at him," an aide was quoted as saying, "and rode him until he got it right." George started promising to become "the education President." Sheila Tate, a Bush spokesperson, said: "Every time he says 'Head Start,' that's Bar."

As they traveled about during the campaign, staying in one hotel after another, Barbara proposed a novel idea to go along with the information about the homeless that she was feeding George: "When we stay in a hotel, we are given five bars of soap. George and I share one, and I send the other four to the shelters so each woman can have her own soap." George made fun of Barbara's soap crusade, at first; but she encouraged the campaign entourage to follow suit. The

Hyatt hotel administration responded to her initiative, and started "Operation Soap," supplying the homeless with leftover hotel toiletries that otherwise would go to waste. As on other issues, George had listened and modified.

A President and First Lady who treated one another as equals and adults, who spoke forthrightly and listened attentively to one another—it seemed a novel and refreshing idea. A local Democrat at a Kitty Dukakis campaign stop said: "Of the four who are running—George and Mike and Kitty and Barbara—I'd vote for Barbara Bush." Someone else said: "The best thing about George Bush is Barbara." But Barbara would never have agreed with that. Her vote was solidly for her man: "George is the strongest, best-qualified, most decent and kindly man running for President. . . . Am I prejudiced about George? You bet I am!"

When Barbara woke up in the White House to begin her new career as First Lady, she was living with George in their 29th home in 17 cities over 44 years of marriage and moving—8 years in the Vice Presidential mansion had been the longest time that the Bushes ever lived in one place.

"I think we grew together," says Barbara. "I think that when you have a child die and you survive, and you've been through a war and you survive, and you build a business and you survive, you either grow apart or together. We always turned to each other."

Shortly before they moved into the White House, Mr. and Mrs. Bush were interviewed together, and George began to complain about all the heavy packing boxes that Barbara had been making him lug around for a week. Barbara put a stop to that—she reminded the interviewer that George had been fishing in Florida throughout the entire week: "So much for the packing story!"

BEHIND EVERY SUCCESSFUL PRESIDENT

The President and First Lady-elect got trapped in a stalled elevator with two Secret Service agents and Christopher Buckley, son of the classic conservative, William F. Buckley snitched: ". . . the Bushes started pinching each other's bottoms. He pinched her, then she leaned over and did the same, saying 'Hi-ya, fella!'"

Barbara's humor extended to include Denis Thatcher, roughly her English counterpart, the husband of British Prime Minister Margaret Thatcher. When the Bushes paid a transatlantic call, Denis Thatcher, displaying old-world charm, kissed Barbara's hand. Some of the reporters missed the photo op, so it was agreed to stage an instant replay. With the cameras rolling, Barbara grasped the moment and grabbed Mr. Thatcher's hand, bent over and kissed it.

The new First Lady was planning a "noisier and jollier" White House—George was a Country Music fan, and the big First Family loved barbecue get-togethers and horseshoe pitching matches. With ten grandkids frequenting the establishment, it could hardly be otherwise. She remodeled Nancy Reagan's beauty parlor room in the Mansion into a playroom for the new generation, and redecorated the living quarters with "a warm and comfortable look," but without the help of an expensive interior decorator.

After she had been First Lady for a while, Barbara said: "It's much more fun than I thought it would be." And the First Lady of Literacy has kept up her own reading (mysteries and best-sellers), time allowing, though she laughed at the myth that had grown up around her that she read a book a day. The aerobic First Jogger also continued her T'ai Chi and tennis for the sake of fun and good health. "I'll play [tennis]," she says, "with friends while they can still play . . . I'll garden while I can still bend over." One Washington neighbor remembered Barbara from congressional days: when the neighbors went on vacation, Barbara would mow their grass, if she thought the next-door yard was looking a little long and shabby.

The grandchildren called her "Ganny," but they might as well have called her "Killer." George P., Jeb's boy, challenged Ganny to a tennis duel when he was ten years old, bucking his way up the family ladder of sporting rank. Jeb described the match: young George "jumped to a five-nothing lead, then couldn't close. She came back and won. There were tears and rackets thrown, and my mother had to preside over this, mark it down as a learning experience. It shows that she's the kind of competitor who didn't let him win. She went for the jugular there."

Not even a bout with Graves' disease, a hyperthyroid disorder that caused her to lose 18 pounds, slowed her down. She also began in high visibility with a flurry of project-intensive activity, boasting especially one notable success: First Dog Mildred Kerr, a.k.a. Millie, an English Springer spaniel, on account of whose lying-in the First Lady "evicted" the President from the Executive bedchamber for a couple of nights, delivered a litter of White House pups, to the front-page delight of the dog-loving First Lady. George groused good-naturedly that Barbara had been better at disciplining the kids than she was with the dog. (Less good-naturedly, a critic who cared little for Bush politics caviled in a classic bit of damned-if-she-does, damned-if-she-doesn't First Lady pettifoggery that Mr. Kerr-Bush's midwife ought to have adopted some grand-dogs from the pound, and set an environmentally responsible example by having the bitch fixed.)

Barbara talked about First Ladies of the past: "The ones I respect the most are the ones who did their own thing," especially Betty Ford. She mentioned Pat Nixon's

BEHIND EVERY SUCCESSFUL PRESIDENT

dignity and Bess Truman's naturalness. "I get needled for liking [Democrat] Bess Truman; but she was a 'What you see is what you get' sort of person." And so was Barbara Bush: "Trying to be anything else would only be a waste of time." But she had trouble identifying with Eleanor Roosevelt, whose energy she admired: "She just irritated my mother!" Sidestepping Party loyalty, Barbara called Lady Bird Johnson her favorite: "She was all that Texas style, and there's just something so graceful about her."

Within her first three months in office, Barbara had already achieved her first organizational goal: she announced the formation of the Barbara Bush Foundation for Family Literacy, a privately funded effort in pre-school programs and non-public schools to teach children and parents at the same time. Barbara yielded day-to-day governance of her foundation to its first executive director, Benita Somerfield, of the Simon & Schuster publishing company.

Barbara focused public attention on her cluster of interdependent concerns—illiteracy, homeless mothers and children, and the on-going battle against drugs and drug-related diseases—by paying well-publicized visits to spots where a First Lady's touch could work its magic. She took Valentines to the aged at the Washington Home for Incurables. Donning her apron, she made sandwiches and ladled soup at Martha's Table, a non-profit mobile kitchen. She sang "We Shall Overcome" at a Black History Month school assembly. "I don't feel my job is to do the Senator's job, or the President's job," Barbara made her concept of her role as First Volunteer clear. "I feel my job is to encourage the corporate and private sector to help, whether it's individuals or agencies or Rotary Clubs or Lions Clubs."

Barbara herself was most affected by her visits to

hospitals where AIDS patients and babies contaminated by their parents' habits were being cared for. She held hands with the AIDS afflicted and hugged them, giving some of that "warm and comfortable" grandmotherly affection to people in dire need of it, and demonstrating to everyone else that AIDS victims are not contagious pariahs. After a visit to Harlem Hospital, Barbara came away, she said, "angry" and "positively militant about what to do with drug users and dealers...I was so angry at the end of the day."

A standard First-Lady issue developed in Barbara's first one hundred days: the political effect on the Presidency of her relationship with George. Barbara's answer to the question, like her public image, left one with a puzzle. On the one hand, she proclaimed: "I'm not a wave-maker." Adding: "One thing I learned in married life: you don't really advise." And stating: "I don't fool around in George Bush's office, and he doesn't fool around with my household."

On the other hand, she fooled around with a handful of issues and made plenty of waves right at the start of the Administration. No one doubted that Barbara was all wool and a yard wide; nonetheless, she was as wily as she was foxy: "Washington is not the real world," she proclaimed, "It's a media world." The savvy new First Lady had taken adroit control of her press even before she had entered Office, and continued pulling the strings of the press far more effectively than almost all her predecessors had done. For starters, she hired Anna Maria Perez to be her Press Secretary, the highest rank yet achieved on the East Wing staff by an American of African descent—and with an Hispanic name, to boot. Then, Barbara began to make her influence felt on other, assorted issues that mattered to her.

Abortion: "I can't get into that. I can tell you what George thinks. But I won't tell you what I think." This not entirely artful dodge meant that Barbara was more pro-choice than George was.

The ERA: "I support the Equal Rights Amendment, but that is not a major item with me." George, too, had once supported the ERA, before he came under the political sway of the Reagan Administration. But as the ERA had become a dead issue, the Bushes agreed to approach equal rights issues in other ways. As the First Lady-elect commented: "I'm not against it or for it. I'm not talking about it."

Gun control: Barbara, who said that she was afraid of guns, and was afraid that were she to own one she might shoot the wrong person," also said she thought that semi-automatic assault weapons were already outlawed. Informed that they were not, and asked if she thought they ought to be, she replied: "Should be, absolutely." George, at the time, was not of the same opinion as Barbara; a sportsman familiar with firearms, he initially did not favor their Federal control.

The homeless in America: On this issue, George Bush acknowledged that he and Barbara had "got into a big argument. She had been telling me I had to do more, and I think she's right."

Says Barbara, finally:

> George Bush and I don't agree on all political points, but there's enough mutual respect to know that the other has weighed all possibilities before coming down on any one side. Years back we sort of argued, but no more. Now I say, "I don't like such and such," and he explains his position. Then I say, "I still don't like it, but okay." We have a good arrangement: I tell him what I think, and he tells me what he thinks, and then we are united . . . We kid each other about our difference.

Anne Frances "Nancy" Robbins Davis Reagan

Leading Lady

𝓕IVE HOURS after the gunshot, the operation was over. Nancy went to Ronnie in the recovery room. She grabbed his arm and, holding on tight, managed to squeeze out through her tears: "Darling, I love you!" She bent over to kiss his forehead, steeling herself at the sight of her stricken hero, ghastly grey, tubes sprouting from his throat, his veins, and his side.

He grasped for a clipboard and scrawled: "I can't breathe." Nancy held his hand tighter; a machine was breathing for him. In the next bed, she saw "a terrible sight" —Jim Brady, his forehead agape. Jim's agony ricocheted through Nancy's head: how could he live with a bullet hole in his brain? And if he should live, how could he ever be well again?

Back at the White House, Nancy let go, at last, and cried it out. Months would pass before she could make any but olique references to "the thing that happened to Ronnie." Nancy's buddy, Frank Sinatra, flew in from the Coast to be with her, and helped her make it through the

Anne Frances "Nancy" Robbins Davis Reagan

trying days. But Ronnie Reagan's Leading Lady was a trouper, an old hand who knew, no matter what the shock or threat, that "the show must go on." The President's wife therefore took the matter firmly in hand and began to direct the Executive production on behalf of her beloved co-star.

As Nancy saw it, her first job now that Ronnie was wounded, as it had been in every other situation, was to take care of Ronnie. She saw to the preparation of his favorite foods—macaroni and cheese, meatloaf—even having some meatball soup flown in from California, when Ronnie lost his appetite. She joked with him, she romanced him, she kept things light. Nancy knew that she had to boost Ronnie's spirits if his recovery were to take hold.

Nancy did more than oversee the President's menu: she scrutinized his medical treatment, organized his on-going Executive activity, and controlled access to the head of state. She watched every move the doctors made.

Nancy had learned from her demanding stepfather not to let doctors weasel out of answering pointed questions. Later on, Ronnie's doctors gossiped respectfully about the First Lady, using phrases like "pretty savvy," "put us on the spot," and "tough lady." They also described her as funny, warm, and grateful, "kind of huggy, kissy, actually."

Nancy set in order the hospital's Presidential suite: a his-and-her command headquarters. Secretary of State Alexander Haig had committed his schoolboy howler by claiming to be "in command at the White House." Who was really in command was—neither Haig nor, as the Constitution would have it, the Vice President, but—Nancy. She limited the number of doctors and advisors; she redesigned Ronnie's diplomatic schedule; when the PR photo was released, Nancy made certain that the nurse in charge of the tubes draining Ronnie's chest was cropped out of the picture.

BEHIND EVERY SUCCESSFUL PRESIDENT

The assassination attempt had taken place on March 30, 1981, a scant 70 days into the Reagan Administration.

"Nancy" was a nickname that Anne Frances's mother gave her; another of Nancy's little-girl names was "Lucky." She did not always feel lucky.

Nancy's birth-father, Ken Robbins, took off before Nancy's first appearance; and Nancy's mother, Edith Luckett (friends called her "Deedee") was an itinerant actress. Deedee carried Nancy around with her from theater to theater, a backstage baby with a travel trunk for a cradle. But when Nancy—born Anne Frances Robbins on July 6, 1921—got too big for the trunk, Deedee planted the two-year-old with kinfolk in Bethesda, Maryland, just outside Washington.

Life for Nancy was pleasant with the Galbraith family, although sometimes lonely in the absence of Mommy. Nancy remembered those five years both ways, keeping "wonderful memories" of her young childhood, and, yet, because she missed her mommy, lamenting "all those wonderful years that I never had." Isolated with scarlet fever or alone in her room with double pneumonia, a little girl with a traveling mother just naturally had to feel sorry for herself: "If I had a child and she got sick, I'd be with her."

Otherwise, life with Aunt Virginia was a happy time. Saturday nights were made memorable when Uncle Audley shared round a family-sized piece of block chocolate from the cellar. Cousin Charlotte—an almost grown girl of five—was always willing to play with Nancy, taking her everywhere she went. Charlotte was good at "Kick the Can" and was not afraid of dogs. Nancy played with the other children as she chose; there was one little boy who could almost always lure her outside, willing as he was to pull her about in a little red wagon. Roller skates, hopscotch, wildflower-picking in the vacant lot and the fabrication of daisy chains filled up the young girlhood of Nancy Robbins prettily. On one Fourth-of-July occasion, Nancy and Charlotte decorated Ginger, their wirehaired terrier, in bunting and marched him in the parade.

The two girls attended Sidwell Friends, a prestigious Quaker school, at the end of a daily four-mile streetcar adventure. There the children of Washington's powerful were treated to a privileged education and, at Christmas time, to a child's fantasy at the estate of Edward and Evalyn Walsh McLean (Edward was one of Warren Harding's poker-playing cronies, and Evalyn was Flossie Harding's best friend in Washington). Once when Grace Coolidge was living in the White House, Nancy got to roll Easter eggs on the White House lawn.

Deedee's glamorous profession made her seem both elusive and alluring. Whenever she visited in Bethesda, she always brought a box of better chocolates. When she played in New York, Aunt Virginia would take Nancy up to see the performance. During one scene, Mommy the actress died on stage, and real-life Nancy in the audience would not be comforted. She wailed so loudly, Deedee was required to rise from the dead and wave to Nancy so that the performance could continue. Deedee bought Nancy a blond mop of Mary Pickford curls, and Nancy wore it everywhere. When she grew up, thought Nancy, she would be an actress on the stage, like Mommy, or maybe in the movies.

When Nancy was seven, Deedee remarried and set another pattern that Nancy would follow later: Deedee gave up her acting career to become the wife of a famous man. Loyal Davis was a doctor, professor, author, and

BEHIND EVERY SUCCESSFUL PRESIDENT

founder. Nancy, hesitant at first, became happy about the marriage when Mommy told her that now they would be living together in Chicago. It was hard at first to call her stepfather anything but "Dr. Loyal." He was a "rock hard disciplinarian," surgically neat and orderly, a perfectionist who instilled in Nancy his hard-work definition of happiness: "the pursuit of excellence in all aspects of one's life." He loved Nancy and adored her mother, and Nancy loved him and would always claim him only as her true father. Nancy described him as one of those people who "make you stretch to reach your fullest capabilities. . . . He always demanded the best of you and made you want to give the best you had." More than that, he was generous with Nancy both with his own time and affection, and he provided everything for her that his wealth and position could purchase. Even better, to young Nancy's mind, Dr. Loyal let her watch him perform brain surgery, and took her with him on hospital calls. Best of all, to cure her skinniness, the medical paragon prescribed a strict regimen of black-cow sodas (ice cream and root beer), himself expertly preparing and administering the medication. A dad like that is hard not to love.

Nancy visited her birth-father a few times, not always with a happy result. Once when Nancy defended her mother against an unfair remark that Robbins had made, he locked Nancy in the bathroom. Robbins quickly realized his mistake, let the girl out, and apologized; but it was too late. Nancy would never forgive him and would afterwards "feel trapped" in small rooms and behind locked doors. The ineffectual Ken Robbins had been swept aside in Nancy's affections by the attractive and powerful Dr. Loyal. Her attachment to him shaped one of her dominant characteristics: Nancy's ability to choose, acquire, and keep the man she loved.

One evening, little Nancy knocked on the door of a retired judge, neighbor to the Davises.

"Judge," said his serious-minded caller, "I've come to see you on business."

"What is it, Nancy?"

"I'd like to know how to adopt Dr. Davis," she explained.

"That's a little difficult," mused the jurist, "but I think it can be arranged."

After Nancy's legal interview concluded, the judge called Davis and reported the visit. Doctor Davis was pleased; he had always wanted to adopt Nancy, but had hesitated to bring the subject up.

When Nancy turned fourteen and had the legal right, she persisted in the attempt to adopt Dr. Loyal. At Davis's suggestion, Nancy boarded a train for New Jersey with her own adoption papers in hand to visit with Robbins and gain his acquiescence to her becoming a Davis. Robbins still loved Nancy, and hid from her how unhappy it made him to have to give her up. (In the coming years, their relationship would remain formally amicable by being kept distant.) On her return to Chicago, Nancy told the other girls at school that they could call her "Nancy Davis," now.

Later on, as wife of the Governor of California dictating her official biography, when someone quoted *Who's Who* to Nancy, reminding her that she had been adopted, Nancy responded with a wave of her hand and a preference for emotional, rather than historical, reality: "I don't care what the book says! He is my father. In my mind, he is my father. I have no father except Loyal Davis." Nancy had known what she wanted, and she had gone and got it; both her name and her identity were realities partly of her

BEHIND EVERY SUCCESSFUL PRESIDENT

own fashioning.

Life in Chicago was tops, and included for Nancy acquaintance both with the cream of the Chicago social crowd and with Deedee's show-biz friends, among them actress Colleen Moore (whose fabled "Fairy Castle" doll house became a prized display at Chicago's Museum of Science and Industry), comedienne ZaSu Pitts, agent Myron Selznick, and actor Reginald Denny; Walter Huston was "Uncle Walter" to Nancy. The ever-popular Deedee was also a woman of good causes, who conveyed to her daughter the social skills and *noblesse oblige* that go with celebrity. Along with schoolwork, boyfriends, and good grooming, Nancy gave entertainments at the Martha Washington School for Crippled Children, worked with the Service Club follies, and raised funds to buy guide dogs.

Loyal and Deedee sent Nancy to Chicago's exclusive Girls Latin School, where she thrived under the discipline of manners. Nancy was relieved of her primness by being best-buddies with her mom, who let her sit at the studio during Deedee's NBC soap-opera broadcasts. Deedee, Nancy, and a girlfriend sneaked giggling to the kitchen, tiptoeing past the slumbering Dr. Loyal, for Nancy's first taste of champagne. Nancy made the Chicago papers when her parents indulged her in an Easter trip to Bermuda; and she squeaked through the Depression as Dr. Loyal's daughter Lucky, rightly so-called, wearing nice clothes, going to summer camp, vacationing with friends, glowing at her coming out along with that year's Chicago crop of other debutantes. Indulged but not spoiled, Nancy seemed more mature and a little ahead of everyone else in her set.

Already Nancy's professional dream was beginning to come true: she starred prophetically in the title role of the high school senior play, *The First Lady*, by George S.

Kaufman. Nancy learned her own part and everyone else's too; and when the others muffed their lines, Nancy prompted or improvised. The Girls Latin yearbook for 1939 shows Nancy in a grey sweater with a string of pearls; the caption reads as if written to be a permanent legend under any photograph of Nancy Davis Reagan: "Nancy's social perfection is a constant source of amazement. She is invariably becomingly and suitably dressed. She can talk, and even better , listen intelligently, to anyone from her little kindergarten partner of the Halloween party, to the grandmother of one of her friends."

In afteryears, Nancy's mother said: "She was very beautiful—but she was a lady, you see. Nancy was a lady, always—always. . . . People thanked me for my daughter's dignity onstage." And, she was a lady with a heart: Deedee told about the time that teenaged Nancy slaughtered her bank piggy in order to give Nellie, the laundry girl, cab fare home, when Nellie became ill on the job. She was about to take the streetcar, but Nancy said that Nellie was too ill for that: "So you take this money and you go home and if you're all right tomorrow, that's fine. And if you're not, my mother and I will do the laundry."

At Smith College, Nancy the would-be star majored in theater. Her group, the Banderlogs, wrote and staged *Ladies on the Loose*, a musical review full of college humor and innocent sophistication. Nancy was a hit; but the performance took place on December 5, 1941. Two days later, after the Japanese attack on Pearl Harbor, risqué ditties about shaking one's hips and maracas had lost their kick. Then, about a week later, the tragic times seemed to single Nancy out: Frank Birney was killed.

Frank had been a Princeton lad who had won Nancy's heart in a single afternoon. The whole Princeton Triangle

BEHIND EVERY SUCCESSFUL PRESIDENT

Club, along with the standard Chicago crowd, had been invited to Nancy's coming out; but, almost everyone arrived late. Brought up to be punctual, Nancy felt in that moment as though the whole world were standing her up. In her virginal white silk and silver lace, she was a damsel dazzling in her distress. Frank, an early arrival passing through the reception line, observed Nancy's unhappiness; so, he went to the end of the line, affected a different name and accent, and came through again—and again, and again—each time as somebody else. Funny Frank made Nancy laugh and put her at ease until the rest of the party arrived. But now, Frank was dead—killed on the train tracks at Princeton mysteriously. Had it been an accident or suicide? Frank had been depressed, worried about his grades, worried about the war, worried about the world. Nancy knew that she was not responsible for Frank's death; and yet, when he was killed, he had been on his way to see her. Fate had taken away a man whom Nancy might have chosen for her partner.

Graduated from Smith, Nancy was engaged for a while to Lieutenant Jim White, a college boyfriend now more handsome than ever in his Navy whites. On the home front, Nancy, a salesperson at Marshall Field's in Chicago, did battle with a shoplifter. When she confronted the woman who had heisted a piece of jewelry, the shoplifter snatched at the top of Nancy's button-down dress and ripped it down the front. The attack by the woman had been an excessive measure; the store rewarded her for her toughness, and she felt proud. About as soon as the engagement with Jim had been buttoned down, it, too, ripped apart. Nancy realized that she was not yet ready for marriage—she was still thinking about an acting career.

Nancy got her first, three-line part in family-friend

ZaSu Pitts's play, *Ramshackle Inn*. Nancy won no awards for that performance, but it did take her to beautiful Broadway and life among the Manhattan theater elite. The struggling starlet may have been hungry for roles but she was hardly starving; even so, during dates at the Stork Club, Nancy pinched the occasional dinner roll for a morning-after breakfast. Sherman Billingsley, head Stork, treated his shoplifter with greater aplomb than Nancy had treated hers—he sent a note and a package of butter over to her table: "I thought you might enjoy some butter with my rolls." But Nancy was not a hungry artist in some Greenwich Village garret; she lived at the Plaza, the Barbizon, and an East Side apartment; and she dated—among others—Clark Gable.

Spencer Tracy, another of Deedee's friends, had given Nancy's New York phone number to Clark. It was no big romance, but "the King" found out what many a glamour guy would realize: that Nancy Davis was a really nice girl, a great date, and an unusually good listener. He liked her because she liked going to baseball games with him. She said that the secret of his charm was that "he made whoever he was with feel important.... When he was with you, he was with you and only you, and never looked over your shoulder to see who else was in the room." Some of Nancy's dates said the same about her.

A less glamorous guy, John Tracy—Spencer Tracy's son, a polio victim, almost deaf and partially sighted—found out that Nancy was more than just a good date. Nancy showed John the town—museums, restaurants, Broadway shows—and she let him sleep on her couch. When a certain Hollywood climber, who had dated John in California only so that she could get to Spencer, stood John up in New York, Nancy gave the sweety a chewing-out over

BEHIND EVERY SUCCESSFUL PRESIDENT

the phone. Nancy herself took John out to dinner and dancing that evening. When John's week in New York was over and he was leaving for the airport, Nancy tried to help him with his bags. "Oh, no," said Johnny, "You're my princess and I'm your slave." Nancy kissed him and puddled up as John waved good-bye.

Nancy worked as a hat model, and got bit parts in other shows—*Lute Song* (with Mary Martin), *Cordelia* and *The Late Christopher Bean* (with ZaSu, again). Nancy's first big break came after a blind date with Benny Thau, a VP at MGM on a trip to New York. "Why don't you come out and make a screen test?" asked Benny. Nancy called Deedee; Deedee called Spencer Tracy; Spence called director George Cukor; Benny Thau set up the test, and big, good-looking Howard Keel played opposite her. George Folsey—one of the best—aimed the camera. Nancy said that the screen test was "the most terrifying experience I've ever had." MGM signed her in 1949 with a standard seven-year contract, $250 per week to start, and put her to work in her first B-picture.

Never to be a sex kitten nor a superstar, Nancy filled in the blanks of her MGM studio biography as follows:

Birth: "1923" (the standard Hollywood deduction allowed a fudge factor of two years).

What you would do if you could not work in pictures: "Lord knows!"

Your greatest ambition: "Sure to have successful marriage."

(This girl was looking for a husband, not an Oscar. Nancy would say later that she had become an actress in the first place only because she had not yet found the man she wanted to marry.)

Your philosophy of life: "Do unto others as you would

have them do unto you—you get back what you give."

Your phobias: ". . . superficiality, vulgarity, esp. in women, untidiness of mind and person—and cigars!"

Nancy added a P.S.: "My most treasured possessions are two baby pictures of my mother and father—never am without them, and a locket of my great grandmother's with a baby picture of my mother inside. Why? Because I'm a sentimentalist, I guess."

Nancy got parts (a total of eleven films from 1949 to 1956), but never great roles; and, almost always, was typecast as the girl-next-door, loving wife, pregnant mother. In one film, Nancy got John Hodiak, "a very serious young man" who had "run out of laughs" after several takes, to laughing on cue when she whispered "belly button" in his ear. It was the funniest thing she could think of, she said. Nancy "basked in [Johnny's] gratitude for days." Her friends agreed that Nancy could be a very funny lady on the spur of the moment.

Nancy landed her biggest role in Dore Schary's *The Next Voice You Hear;* but that flick bombed. By that time, however, Nancy had started dating Ronnie Reagan: "I had seen him in films and, frankly, I had liked what I had seen."

In 1949, Nancy showed a friend at MGM a list she had made up of Hollywood's most eligible males—lawyers as well as actors, directors, producers, and agents. Ronald Reagan's name headed the list: chisel-featured, six-gun slinging, football-kicking screen hero with Mid-Western good looks, destined for B-movie immortality as co-star to a chimpanzee in *Bedtime for Bonzo*.

Nancy organized her first meeting with Ronnie by cueing producer Dore Schary and his wife Miriam to arrange a dinner party to which Nancy and the object of her conspiracy were both invited. They became acquaintances, but not lovers—Ronnie was preoccupied elsewhere with matters of the heart. But then, an unforeseen happenstance availed Nancy the entrée she was seeking. Four people were using the name "Nancy Davis" in Hollywood, and one of them had signed some radical petitions and was on Communist-front propaganda mailing lists. Whoever the fellow-traveler was, she was certainly not identical with the lucky girl from the home of the arch-conservative Chicago physician. Nancy had never been particularly interested in politics at all, much less the left-wing kind. Clever Nancy saw her opening: she would approach Ronnie—who happened to be a union-organizing Democrat and president of the Screen Actors Guild (SAG)—through his love of politics. She pressed Mervyn LeRoy of MGM to get Ronnie to give her a call.

Waiting for the phone to ring, Nancy checked it a couple of times to make certain that it was not out of order. At last, he called. Apologizing for the last-minute invitation, he suggested that it would have to be a short dinner engagement, as he had an early call the next morning. (Ronnie was fibbing to protect himself against a possible dud date.) Agreeing that it was awfully short notice, Nancy said she could just manage it, as she, too, had an early call the next morning. (Nancy's coy acceptance was as artful as Ronnie's invitation.)

Ronnie showed up supporting himself on canes—he had crunched his leg in a Sunday night charity ball game, and, as a result, had lost his role in the movie *Fugitive from Terror*. Adding insult to injury, the divorce action brought against him by his first wife, actress Jane Wyman, had become final on July 18, 1949, while he was lying in the hospital. Ronnie had a lot to get off his chest the night he took Nancy to dinner at LaRue's on the Sunset Strip, and then to Ciro's for Sophie Tucker's show. They sat through Sophie's first and second performances, and left the nightclub at 3:10 in the morning—so much for early calls!

Ronnie was a talker, a philosopher, and a raconteur; he had a small ranch and raised horses; he knew everybody in show business; he ranged from serious political discourse to his ton of funny stories to tell. He was an old-fashioned boy and as sentimental as Nancy was. She turned her great, wide eyes on him and absorbed everything Ronnie had to say: "I loved listening to him," Nancy said later. "And still do!" After that, it was every night for a week, and then regular dating for about two years. "I don't know if it was love at first sight," said Nancy, "but it was something close to it." Nancy had found the man she wanted; so, she waited, played along, and did things Ronnie's way. Three years later, she finally eased him to the altar.

After Ronnie married Nancy, Jane's relationship through the years with her ex, their children, the ex's new wife remained distant at best, and often troubled. Michael said that Jane "always spoke badly of Nancy, whom she considered 'that other woman.'" Divorced Mom, Jane did what so many parents do in a tug-o'-war over the kids: she pulled hard. According to neighborhood gossip, competitive Jane wanted hers and Ronnie's kids to be better than Nancy's and Ronnie's kids, so that Ronnie's second set would compare unfavorably with his first. Gifts from Ronnie and Nancy to the kids were viewed as competition —when Ronnie gave Mike a horse, Jane resented that the best she could do was supply the saddle and bridle, since the horse was a bigger, better present. The kids in the middle, who loved both Mom and Nancy, learned better than to make any positive remarks about Nancy to Jane, as they produced "cold, almost hostile" responses in the former

BEHIND EVERY SUCCESSFUL PRESIDENT

Mrs. Reagan.

In the other household, remembered Michael, "Nancy didn't like Mom any better. . . . Nancy was livid with Mom because my teeth had been let go for so long." He had almost a dozen cavities. "She also took me shopping for new clothes, something Mom rarely had time for."

Jane and Ron and Nancy tiptoed through one of the rare occasions of all three being in the same place at the same time in 1964 at Maureen's second wedding. Michael's wedding in 1975 likewise proved to be a narrow passage. A wedding picture was about to be taken including the father and *mother* of the groom. "Uh oh!" thought Michael. If Dad and Nancy got up, Jane would be upset; if Jane got up to stand beside Dad, Nancy would be upset. "You could have heard a pin drop. Nancy was looking at Dad, who continued staring straight ahead. . . . After what seemed like an eternity, Mom stood up, looked directly at Nancy, and said, 'Nancy, don't worry about a thing. Ron and I have had our pictures taken together before. If you'd like to join us, fine. Now Ron, come on! The photographer's waiting. Let's get our pictures taken.'" It turned into a *full* family portrait.

Apolitical Jane kept her opinions to herself as her ex rose to Presidential power. She was not to become First Lady, but, she said, she had "no regrets. . . . Oh no, the White House is not for me!" Her typical response to questions about Ronnie was bristly—sometimes she would turn on her heel and stalk away from an interviewer who broke the rules and asked about the divorce. Jane felt that her marriage to Dutch Reagan, a third of a century before he became President, had nothing to do with her life in the 1980s. Her typical comments for the press fell a bit pat: she spoke of "perfectly wonderful memories of him," and of

Anne Frances "Nancy" Robbins Davis Reagan

their being and always remaining good friends. Following the assassination attempt, which Jane called "a very dramatic thing," she said, somewhat more heartily: "I think he's doing a marvelous job, I really do. We're very good friends and I just adore him." Jane did enjoy dispelling one rumor about Ronnie, no doubt to his great pleasure: "Ron dye his hair? Oh, no! The Reagans have marvelous hair. Ron's the image of his father, who didn't have more than about three gray hairs when he died. I don't think Ron has a gray hair in his head and never will have more than two or three. I wish I could say the same."

During the Presidential years, Jane's name remained an unspoken word at the White House. Only the Democrats had found use for it: a 1984 campaign slogan ran: "Do what Wyman did—dump Reagan." A button blazed: "Jane Wyman was right." After Maureen began to make it big as a Republican, campaigning for her father, working on the Republican National Committee and at the U.N., she became better buddies with Nancy, even calling her "Mom," the term of endearment previously reserved for Jane. One day, Maureen called Michael, and said: "Washington [meaning Nancy and Ronnie] and I would appreciate it if you never mentioned your mother again in interviews. Jane Wyman is not and never will be a member of the First Family. *We* would like for you to cease and desist from mentioning her name."

Michael retorted: "My mother is also your mother!" and hung up. After that, said Michael, Maureen ceased to be the "devoted aunt" to Michael's children.

Nancy realized that she would have to execute her logistics carefully. Jane's breakage of Ronnie's heart in 1949 had left him ravenous for, but wary of, the ladies. Eminently eligible Dutch Reagan, back in the market, was dating lots of girlfriends besides Nancy Davis—among them actresses Virginia Mayo, Ruth Roman, Doris Lilly, Penny Edwards, and Adele Jergens; model Betty Underwood; and singer Monica Lewis—all the while still carrying his torch for Jane. So, Nancy took up Ronnie's interests—horses and ranches (although she cared little for either), his children and his politics. Where Jane had darkened, Nancy shined: she got active with SAG. She ran for Board membership in 1950, and lost; she ran again in 1951, and won. She kept on loyally seconding Ronnie's motions at SAG for about ten years: politics was the way to this man's heart.

One day, at a boring meeting of the Motion Picture Industry Council, Ronnie suddenly passed a note to his buddy Bill Holden: "To hell with this, how would you like to be my best man when I marry Nancy?"

"It's about time!" Holden answered.

On March 4, 1952, at the Little Brown Church in the (San Fernando) Valley, Nancy was in a daze: her persistence was paying off, her dream was coming true, but she was out of touch with the ceremony. Bill and Ardis Holden stood up as best man and matron of honor. (Maureen, age 11, and Michael, age 7, had not been invited.)

Holden leaned over and said: "Let me be the first to kiss the bride."

Nancy exclaimed: "You're jumping the gun!"

"I am not." Bill kissed the surprised Mrs. Ronald Reagan.

On the morning after Nancy's wedding night, her bridegroom suggested that they give the flowers to an elderly lady they'd seen at the inn—that was the kind of whimsical thing Nancy loved about Ronnie. During a honeymoon visit in Phoenix, Ronnie got on famously with

Anne Frances "Nancy" Robbins Davis Reagan

Nancy's parents. In the time to come, he would traditionally send Deedee flowers on Nancy's birthday, thanking his mother-in-law for having made him the happiest man in the world. Ronnie, who already had a lot of Republican friends in Hollywood, was impressed by the thoughtfully conservative Dr. Loyal. Later on, Dr. Loyal would be a major early financial backer of Ronnie's career in conservative politics. Deedee would remain a favorite with the Republican crowd till she died of old age—she knew more dirty jokes than anybody else, and could outcuss Barry Goldwater. Ronnie's honeymoon was, in political principle, one of several important turning points in the remaking of Mr. Democrat Reagan.

On the return drive, they ran into a desert sandstorm that ripped open the canvas top of their convertible. While Ronnie kept driving, Nancy knelt on the seat beside him holding the halves of the flapping canvas top together, lest it be torn away completely. Ronnie Reagan began to realize that he had married himself one tough lady.

The Reagans were not a typically glamorous, high-living couple. They knew Hollywood to be death on marriages, and they were determined to make a go of theirs. They did, however, eat out most of the time: "I always said I wanted to be a wife and a mother," said Nancy, "I never said I wanted to be a cook." Patti Reagan was born by Caesarean section seven and a half months after her father and mother were married, and Ron Jr. ("Skipper") was born in 1956. As part-time Mom of Maureen and Michael and with two of her own, Nancy now was what she said she had always wanted to be: she had traded her career in the movies for a husband to love and children to mother. Ronnie now had what he wanted, too: his own, permanent leading lady. Nancy Davis' last movie was *Hellcats of the*

BEHIND EVERY SUCCESSFUL PRESIDENT

Navy (1956), a World War II submarine staple; she starred opposite Ronald Reagan, playing his fiancée. Where the script called for our heroine to say good-bye to her sailor-man, three times they had to stop the camera, while Nancy dried the puddles. It was just too sad for Nancy to have to send Ronnie off to war, even if it was only a movie.

Ronnie did better on TV than he had done in the movies. While he hosted, and sometimes starred in, *General Electric Theater* and *Death Valley Days*, Nancy decorated her avant-garde all-electrical indoor-outdoor dreamhouse built around its swimming pool in Pacific Palisades. Everything matched, and there were lots of bright flowery colors and soft pastels, lots of antiques, lots of glass, lots of red. G.E., Ronnie's bosses, supplied every electrical gadget available, while the grateful recipients tried to figure out how to pay the electricity bill: eight separate circuit boxes and a wall-sized switchboard were needed to keep it all blazing.

Nancy wrote flippantly to a friend in 1962 about the prospect of Ronnie's getting elected to high office: "It boggles the mind but maybe it'll get me out of the carpool." Truth was, politics exhilarated Nancy as much as it did Ronnie; speaking for them both, he said: "Sometime after I'd become governor, and we were sitting in the living room, all of a sudden it came to both of us that what we were doing made everything else we'd ever done seem dull as dishwater—that was the expression [Nancy] used."

Ronnie became the chief executive of California at one minute after midnight on January 1, 1967, and left office in 1974. California had become Nancy's abalone. The First Lady of the Golden State started off by redecorating the Governor's drab office. Opening the blinds to the surrounding panorama, she let the sun shine in. She hung the works of California artists—designing for her leading man a proper stage set from which he could command the attention not only of California but also of the nation.

Another early First-Lady act involved Nancy in her first political brouhaha: she rejected the Gothic nightmare of the Governor's Mansion in Sacramento as no appropriate place to raise her upper-middle-class children. The neighborhood consisted of two gas stations, a motel, and a Legion hall. The grand old Victorian looked like a movie set from one of Ronnie's Wild West flicks—damp, drafty, unheatable, with seven unsafe fireplaces prohibited from use by law, and without fire escapes. When Nancy asked the fire marshal how Skipper was supposed to escape the building in case of fire, the answer came back that she should teach him how to break out a window with a piece of furniture. Over the protests of the Governor's aides, the Reagans moved to a nice house in the suburbs.

Something else Nancy disliked about the capital city: "No one in Sacramento can do hair!" And as to shopping, even at I. Magnin's, "Here everything is scaled down for these Valley farm women." "Thank heavens," snooted his Excellency's Ladyship, "we can escape to Beverly Hills on the weekends."

Nancy's starring role as the Governor's wife became her vehicle of influence, and she handled it brilliantly. The Reagans, merely millionaires, were the economically poorest, but politically chic-est, members of a very sociable set of Southern California multi-millionaires. Nancy relieved Sacramento boredom with lunch and gossip in Beverly Hills, shopping sprees along Rodeo Drive, and hobnobbing with her well-heeled friends, "the Group" (as the media dubbed them). Chief among the Nancy boosters were Betsy Bloomingdale (wife of Alfred, the founder of Diners Club—

BEHIND EVERY SUCCESSFUL PRESIDENT

he would later become the focus of a raunchy sex scandal), Lee Annenberg (publishing), Marion Jorgensen (steel), Mary Jane Wick (nursing homes, movie production), and Jean Smith (law). Jerry Zipkin, professional partygoer (inherited apartment houses, art collection) was the male member of Nancy's Group. Nancy relied on this genial fop for impeccability in matters of taste, sensing in Jerry a faint image of the same selfless devotion that Nancy accorded Ronnie. Nancy could count on Jerry for a critique of her latest outfit or party plans without the complication of some self-seeking hidden agenda on Jerry's part.

On one occasion, when someone advised her against marital hero-worship, especially in public, Nancy replied: "But he *is* my hero!" She called him "Daddy," and he called her "Mommy." Reagan campaign aides, from the California gubernatorial bout on, learned quickly to put themselves on "the Mommy watch" when making plans for Ronnie.

The main thing for Daddy and Mommy was just to be together—at the Ranch floating on the pond in their canoe, the *TruLuv*, his sentimental silver-wedding-anniversary gift to her. Whether in the Governor's Mansion or, later, upstairs at the White House, a perfect evening for Ronnie and Nancy was being alone together in their pajamas, eating dinner from silver TV trays, watching the news or a favorite show on the tube. So inseparable were Nancy and Ronnie, they would be apart for as long as a week for the first time only after thirty-five years of marriage, when he had become President of the United States, and First Lady Nancy traveled alone to England to attend the royal wedding of the Prince of Wales and Lady Di.

Mother bear protecting a cub, Nancy tolerated neither attack on, nor apparent disloyalty to, Ronnie, and she stalked the ones she mistrusted. The long list of those who would fall before Mommy Nancy's pre-Presidential wrath began with campaign aide Lyn Nofziger. His misdemeanors, besides not leveling with Ronnie, included untidiness in dress and speech—Nancy thought him profane and uncouth; he wore a Mickey Mouse tie and left his top shirt button unbuttoned—hardly the image of good form that a graduate of Chicago Girls' Latin could approve. She reportedly gave him the silent treatment for five weeks before he was finally fired. In similar behind-the-scenes machinations, Nancy orchestrated exits and entrances of assorted other aides and advisors.

Her influence on the candidate was equally direct. More than once, Nancy's calming hand on Ronnie's arm abated his fiery Irish temper. Occasionally, she cued him, bailed him out of the embarrassing pickles into which his rambling style, liberal treatment of facts, and hardness of hearing got him. Nancy called these moments of her strategic intervention "facilitating a situation." In 1979, when a reporter cornered Ronnie with some questions about pot smoking, which to have answered would have implied the candidate's personal acquaintance with the weed, Nancy facilitated with a stage whisper, "You wouldn't know."

"I wouldn't know," repeated the candidate.

Nancy facilitated campaign spirit, too, by keeping things light. As the Reagan plane would take off, Nancy would roll an orange down the aisle, to the glee of the press corps and staff. Like an airline hostess, she made her way down the aisle with a box of chocolates. When some of the media people wondered if it might offend the potential First Lady to turn down her bonbons, and word of it got to Nancy, she did the chocolate bit next time with a sign stuck to the candy box: "Take one—or else."

BEHIND EVERY SUCCESSFUL PRESIDENT

Nancy's first year on the job as First Lady was her hardest. She got off to a rocky start with the press when, afflicted with stage fright, she performed shyly at her first First Lady press conference. After a mutually non-cooperative interview session, Nancy rolled a promo-film about the Foster Grandparents Program, and then ducked out under cover of the darkened room. The media corps cried foul.

Nancy took the slashing media knives personally. Trapped in the Executive Mansion, she could go out neither shopping nor socializing; so, she spent the first six months escaping into gossip sessions on the phone with members of the Group, and accepting gifts of expensive dresses (most of which she would have to give back) and jewels (which she would keep). Nancy's growing staff now numbered 17, and she had a half-million-dollar budget, but she still lacked a First-Lady project worthy of her Office. She kept up her "Us *vs.* Them" hostile standoff with the media, telling the press as little as possible, time and again stonewalling on issues that she wanted to control. Typical of her reactive attitude, Nancy called it "mean" when the evening news showed diagrams of the female mammary and detailed her operation for breast cancer.

Even with national sympathy over the assassination attempt, Nancy's first year as First Lady was a lonely one. Elaine Crispen, Nancy's press secretary, said that Nancy had been "really frightened—more than any of us know," by the event of March 30th. Then, when her hard start was followed by Ronnie's cancer surgery and the death of Nancy's beloved father Loyal Davis in 1982, things seemed to be getting worse, not better.

The East Coast media crowd, liberals for the most part, reacted negatively to "The Group"—Nancy's high-rolling Rodeo Drive clatch who descended on D.C. like a Santa Ana wind. These "millionaires on parade" were too rich, too famous, too snobbish, and said to be an "embarrassing, crazy fagotage." The allegations about the First Lady were many and uncomplimentary: she was a holdover from the '50s; she had "piano legs;" she wore too much red. They called her "Queen-bee Nancy," chuckled "Gucci, Gucci, coo!" and quipped that her favorite junk food was caviar.

"I believe very strongly that the White House is a special place, and should have the best of everything," proclaimed the First Lady. "I think people want it that way." She hired the best and bought the costliest to tidy up the threadbare dwelling, spending her entire $50,000 Congressional allowance on design consultation alone. (The Carters had not exhausted their $50,000 on the whole House.) Then, she lavished upwards of a million privately donated, tax-deductible dollars to make of the White House a glowing showcase of exquisite Americana. Quoting Nancy from the "Collector's Edition" of *Architectural Digest* (December 1981): "This house belongs to all Americans, and I want it to be something of which they can be proud."

When, however, "Queen Nancy" spent $240,000 on the most extensive, most expensive set of china in White House history, some of her critics went window-shopping for a guillotine.

Nor were Nancy's children particularly contributive to her image as the ideal National Mom. The four noisy younger Reagans took their turns in the headlines of the grocery-store check-out-counter tabloids, and America wondered what kind of fashionable trash had moved into 1600 Pennsylvania Avenue.

Maureen, a liberated California girl, made her opportunistic assault on a career in Republican politics so roughshod and right-wing that even Daddy and Mommy kept their distance. Later, Maureen and Nancy became pajama-party girlfriends, establishing personal detente on a common political premise: loyalty to Ronald Reagan. Maureen's book, *First Father, First Daughter* (1989), was the friendliest airing of the family laundry. She described Nancy, National Mom, armed with home remedies and chicken soup:

"What are you?" Maureen asked, "a Jewish mother?"

"That's exactly what I am!" answered Nancy.

Michael's effusive, tell-all autobiography, *Michael Reagan: On the Outside Looking In* (1988), was a venting of his feelings about having been a battleground between the famous people who were his adoptive parents. Under suspicion for theft in 1984, and getting the cold shoulder at the White House, Michael—stated an East Wing press release—was "estranged" from his Presidential parents. A family summit was held, reconciliation achieved, Nancy retracted her statement of estrangement, and the First Grandfolk could no longer be charged with ignoring Ashley, their not-quite-two-year-old granddaughter whom they had never met. According to Michael, then age 40, it was the first time Nancy had ever apologized to him for anything, and the first time his father had ever told him: "I love you."

Michael revealed that as a child he had been sexually molested. His description of how his father and two mothers received the news succinctly characterizes the three personalities:

Jane Wyman was at first dubious about Michael's writing a book at all, and said she didn't have time to talk: "When are you going to stop living off your father's name? I can't believe you have anything to say at this time in your life that's worth reading." When Michael persisted in telling her about the molestation, Jane asked: "What do they think about that in Washington?" When Michael replied that Dad and Nancy were supportive, Jane sarcastically retorted: "Well, that shows how good their judgment is!" The phone conversation ended when Jane said she'd be in touch, and hung up. Shortly thereafter, she canceled Mother's Day with Michael and his family, and she and he did not speak again.

When Michael told the First Parents, Nancy took charge of the conversation, as she did for Ronnie in other cases of personnel management. Michael was wondering if Nancy would react to his revelation as she had done to his bad grades as a teenager: then, she had pounced on him—"You're not living up to the Reagan name or image, and unless you start shaping up, it would be best for you to change your name and leave the house."

This time, out at the corral at the Ranch, things went more smoothly. "Dad gazed into the distance. He has always deferred to the women in his life, and this occasion was no exception."

"Now, Michael," said Nancy—her eyes "pinning" Michael's—"will you please give your father and me some idea about what's in the book you are writing. What's in it that we are not supposed to know?"

Michael began his sad account. Motherly Nancy was moved, put her arms around her stepson, and began to rub the back of his neck, as she had done when he was a child. Michael could not raise his downcast eyes to his father.

"Tell us," Nancy said softly.

"I was molested by a camp counsellor," Michael blurted out.

"What?" was Ronnie's registered shock.

"He was molested, honey," said Nancy.

"By who [sic]?" asked Ronnie.

"By a counsellor at day camp," Nancy repeated patiently.

"Who was the guy?" the Chief Executive demanded to know. "I'll find him and kick his butt."

"Let Mike get it out of his system, honey," Nancy told Ronnie firmly.

A few weeks later, Nancy paid a visit to Michael's home—her first in a long time—bringing a picture for Michael of his dad and Grandmother Nelle Reagan.

Nancy's daughter, Patti Davis—the name change was a sure sign of declared independence from parental Reaganism—was the rebellious one whose very lifestyle seemed calculated to embarrass her celebrity parents. Self-consciously unconventional Patti rebeled not only against her father's name but also against his politics, lined up with anti-war protestors, became a groupie with the Eagles Rock group, and "lived with" her mate rather than marrying.

The mutual exile of Patti Davis and her parents increased and became permanent during the Presidency.

Overprotected Ron, Jr., (wisecracking Brian in Patti's novel) also in real life went his autonomous way, kicking over the traces of school discipline, resisting to the uppermost Mom's and the dean's best efforts to get him to cut his fashionably long hair—not even the powerful Nancy Reagan could triumph in the Hair Wars! A Yalie dropout, adult Skipper became a professional dancer—giving pause to his parents and the press: if young Ron was a ballet dancer, was he also gay? Eventually, Ron Reagan, the Great Communicator, Jr., not bashful about using his marketable name to land jobs on TV, in news journalism, and in the medium of glossy print, got a job writing for *Playboy* and married a good-looking girl. The First Parents breathed a sigh of relief about the name-bearer's sexuality. Nancy's one child who did not write a book about his parents, Ron also defended Mom when she needed it most.

As the swallows return to Capistrano, so, after a while, did most of Nancy's social moths return to California. There was no getting rid of the children, of course; and Nancy kept in touch with the Group over the phone; but one California buddy she continued seeing was Frank Sinatra. Nancy admitted that she had always had a crush on "Francis Albert," as she and Ronnie called him. For a while after the assassination attempt, "Ol' Blue Eyes" became a monthly visitor at the White House, ranking his own Secret Service code name: "Napoleon." One of the few times Nancy kicked over the traces of etiquette restraint was in order to go on a date with Francis Albert. After a dinner in honor of Prince Charles, she skipped out with Sinatra before the program and the protocol were concluded, leaving some Congressional Wives a bit huffy at (and jealous of) the First Lady for having "broken rank."

Nancy's change of image started with Ronnie's reassurance that she was, after all, a trouper, an actress good enough to hide it when the critics left her bleeding inside. If Ronnie could be the "Great Communicator," so could Nancy. Her first job was to turn the fickle media from enemies into friends; and for that, she drew upon her showbiz ability to be a funny lady and "banderlog" the fickle media from enemies into friends. That happened on a March night in 1982, at the annual white-tie tribute to the media elite, the Gridiron Dinner.

During the entertainment, a performing reporter roasted Nancy with a parody of the ditty "Secondhand

Rose," making reference to the controversial White House china, Nancy's opulent wardrobe, Ronnie's calling her "Mommy," Rodeo Drive, and Ronnie's raw deal to the welfare programs. As the song ended, Nancy jumped up from her seat at the head of the table and rushed from the room. Some reporters were already scribbling their headlines: "First Lady can't take it!" Ronnie thought she'd gone to the Ladies' Room.

Presently, an utterly outré apparition of low couture traipsed on stage: white feather boa, aqua skirt with floral pattern and safety-pin touches, red blouse, red picture hat with pink feathers and a black bow; accessorized with yellow Wellies and a belly-length double strand of big beads. It was Nancy! The audience, at a roar, was on its feet in ovation. The President, in stitches, had been taken totally off guard. Holding up a plate painted to look like the infamous Presidential crockery, her First Ladyship sang a reprise of "Second-Hand Clothes":

> . . . *Even my new trench coat with fur collar*
> *Ronnie bought for ten cents on the dollar.*
> *Second-hand gowns*
> *And old hand-me-downs,*
> *The china is the only thing that's new.* . . .

"Brava!" they all shouted. Nancy sang a second chorus, and broke the plate for a smashing finale. The Presidential star of stage, screen, and campaign trail had reminded the news crowd that she and they were, after all, in the same business: show biz. Washington, in its own way as much a Tinsel Town as Hollywood, gave the Lady rave reviews. On the great stage of government, where image is portrayed as substance, the press reported the media event as news. Thereafter, although Nancy's critics would not

Anne Frances "Nancy" Robbins Davis Reagan

cease to attack, they now acknowledged that their prey was plucky. Commenting on her Presidential comeback, Nancy said: "People love it when you laugh at yourself."

A "deliberate sitting down" did take place; a White House meeting, "Project Nancy's Image," of only the most trusted was called. Ronnie, also skilled at "banderlog," wore to the meeting a pair of gag shades equipped with windshield wipers in case of severe puddling up—Ronnie said that sentimental Nancy puddled up when she sent the laundry out! She had joshed him over the rough spots in the past; now he was doing the same for her. Tensions relaxed, and Nancy went ahead with the project to find a "project."

Nancy had always been a moralist; and under the pressure of Office, she emerged as a national moral force against drug abuse. She started off as wobbly as her half-formed, early opinions read: "We have to get marijuana out of the movies." Advisors resisted her drive: an anti-drug campaign seemed too negative, and was therefore a political downer. Moreover, Nancy started out uninformed; her speeches were repetitious; and all she did was sit and hold hands with drugged-out kids, all puddled up, saying things like: "I'm so proud of you and I love you, too."

The "Just Say No" motto had popped up out of the conversational exchange of the First Lady with one of her youthful interlocutors.

"What should I say if someone offers me drugs, if someone wants to give them to me?"

"Just say NO!" Nancy answered, "That's all you have to do. Just say no and walk away." Young people spontaneously started forming Just-Say-No Clubs shortly after the media reported the incident.

Nancy's images as banderlogger and moralist ultimately proved less interesting than her wheeling and

BEHIND EVERY SUCCESSFUL PRESIDENT

dealing in behind-the-scenes politics. The extent of Nancy Reagan's gloved Executive power was the most widely discussed substantive issue during her second term.

In 1985, when the President underwent major surgery for colon cancer—and, for the first time in history, the Twenty-fifth Amendment was invoked, Vice President George Bush becoming Temporary President for about eight hours on July 13th—Nancy held up unflinchingly, relying for emotional support on her stepbrother Richard Davis. Even more than she had done following the assassination attempt, she became a powerbroker of "the ultimate access" in American government. She took command of Ronnie and the situation, laying down the law to Chief of Staff Don Regan, describing herself as a "manager" of Ronnie's time and energy, a "sort of a stand-in" for the President. On the blistering hot and wiltingly humid Washington day of the surgery, she made a speech in the President's place at a gathering of the diplomatic corps, at a 100th-birthday celebration for the Boston Pops on the White House lawn. That afternoon, she greeted three hundred international diplomats, insisting that America was open for "business as usual." The foreigners commented that the President's wife had demonstrated reassuringly that the American government was not weakened by the President's ill health.

With Nancy standing beside him after the surgery, Ronnie broadcast a sentimental message over his weekly radio show telling all America how it was between him and Nancy, and incidentally telling all America how the First Ladyship works:

> There's something I want to say, and I wanted to say it with Nancy at my side, as she is right now, as she always has been. First Ladies aren't elected, and they

don't receive a salary. They have mostly been private persons forced to live public lives, and in my book they've all been heroes. Abigail Adams helped invent America. Dolley Madison helped protect it. Eleanor Roosevelt was FDR's eyes and ears. Nancy Reagan is my everything.

Nancy puddled up.

Two weeks after Ronnie's first cancer surgery, when an unrelated skin cancer had to be removed from his nose, Nancy did more than puddle up. In a delayed reaction, she became as irrational in her bodyblock of the media from this news as she had proved solid during the earlier, much more serious operation. She forbade Press Secretary Larry Speakes to be up-front about the President's condition, further eroding trust in White House truthfulness, already under suspicion on account of the Iran-Contra connection coverup.

Just because Nancy could weep did not mean that she was weak. Where Ronnie was concerned, Nancy was always strong. She cared little about most political issues *per se*, and was unconcerned whether Ronnie toed the chalkmark of right-wing Republicanism; in fact, she urged him to reduce military spending, not to push the Strategic Defense Initiative "Star-Wars" defense shield at the expense of the poor, and she favored a diplomatic solution in Nicaragua.

Her main areas of expertise continued to be personnel relations internal to the Reagan power elite, and Ronnie's (and her own) public impression and image in the history books. For example, she counseled Ronnie not to take part in a wreath-laying at the Bitburg cemetery in Germany, where some S.S. officers were buried. Had the President heeded his wife, he would have saved himself considerable embarrassment with the American Jewish community.

BEHIND EVERY SUCCESSFUL PRESIDENT

Nancy's way with Ronnie was to elicit from him his own best instincts, and keep the beat with her own flawless sense of timing, almost always working indirectly: "Does the President sometimes say no to me? Sure. Does his 'no' always end it? Not always. I'll wait a little while; then I'll come back at him again."

Particularly significant in view of the Reagan-Gorbachev rapprochement, Nancy was credited (although she denied it) with considerable effect in "coming back at him again" on the issue of USA-USSR relations. Nancy sided with the moderates against the belligerent Right and helped turn around Ronnie's cold-war rhetoric against "an evil empire." Nancy did admit to helping change Ronnie's movie image as a gun-slinging cowboy ready for a shoot-out with the Ruskies at the Star Wars Corral. But she made her moves more according to instinct than intellect—Nancy never pored over briefing papers from the State Department, as some of her predecessors had done.

Mike Deaver—Nancy's ally, as Deaver said, in "protecting Ronnie, whether he wanted it or not"—spent hours on the phone with her, sometimes several times a day, planning the President's schedule, going over the details to Nancy's perfectionist satisfaction. Deaver summarized Nancy's style of influence and the areas of her involvement: She knows you cannot barge in and tell him he has to fire Dick Allen or James Watt or Don Regan; that someone he likes has lost his effectiveness or has ill served him. She will wage a quiet campaign, planting a thought, recruiting others of us to push it along, making a case: "Foreign policy will be hurt." . . . "Our allies will be let down." . . . "Nancy wins most of the time. When she does, it is not by wearing him down but by usually being on the right side of an issue . . . I have never, not in the years I have known them, seen

Anne Frances "Nancy" Robbins Davis Reagan

the Reagans engage in a no-holds-barred argument."

Nancy's preoccupation with personnel management may have been of paramount importance to the Reagan Administration; and, if anything, Mommy needed to have been even more on guard. The Reagan Presidency—characterized by Ronnie's hands-off managerial style—was riddled with scandal that never quite seemed to stick on the "Teflon President." From the Iran-scam/Contra guns-for-hostages machinations (some of it with Latin-American drug lords), to influence peddling, to sex scandals, to the HUD rip-off that came to light only after Ronnie and Nancy had left Washington, more people from the Reagan clique—including the First Lady's own chief advisor, Mike Deaver—were indicted for sundry abominations than in any other Administrations, including Nixon's Watergate and Harding's Teapot Dome. Nancy's marksmanship as political nemesis, starting with political aides in California, and culminating in D.C. with Chief of Staff Donald Regan, filled her trophy case with the heads and hides of aides and advisors, and a Cabinet member or two: among them, James Watt, political buffoon and Secretary of the Interior; Richard Allen and William Clark, national security advisors; David Stockman, the Judas of Reaganomics. All these, and others, she "got," but she never "got" Secretary of State George Shultz, no matter how much he grumbled.

After he was ousted, Regan revealed "the most closely guarded domestic secret of the Reagan White House" and a main source of his aggravation with the First Lady: Nancy was into astrology. Both Ronnie and Nancy had consulted Carroll Righter, astrologer to the stars, regarding the conduct of their screen careers in the early '50s—a Hollywood thing to do. When Ronnie became Governor of California, astral influences increased: the unusual Reagan gubernatorial inauguration, which took place shortly after midnight, was said to have been scheduled according to planetary propitiousness. For a while, Jean Dixon was Nancy's wisewoman from the West Coast; and Joyce Jillson, another celebrity seer, claimed momentary conjunction with the Reagans, although this was denied by the White House.

After 1981, all other luminaries were eclipsed by Joan Quigley (a.k.a. Angel Star, author of books on astrology, columnist for *Seventeen* on astrology for teenagers), who was known according to Nancy's informal East Wing code as "My Friend." The "Friend," a satellite of Nancy's posh California set, was seen at the White House only once, for a state dinner in 1985. While in office, Don Regan seems never to have known the "Friend's" name.

Nancy and her Friend talked over the phone, mostly on weekends when Ronnie and she were taking it easy out at Camp David—although on one occasion, Nancy in the White House was talking on two phones at once, in one ear a direct line to the stars via her Quigley satellite, and on the line in the other ear, someone in frustration trying to arrange the President's schedule. "I advise them when to be careful," said the seeress, "I don't make decisions for them."

The final words inevitably belonged to Ronnie and Nancy. When Ronnie was asked whether his wife was now running the government, the Chief quick-shot one of his from-the-hip answers (while dashing to a helicopter or somewhere), shouting: "That is fiction, and I think it is despicable fiction; and a lot of people ought to be ashamed of themselves!" Then, realizing that he had overreacted, Nancy's champion cooled down the rest of his run-on response somewhat: "You've touched a nerve there, but the idea that she's involved in governmental decisions and so forth, and all of this, and being a kind of a 'Dragon Lady,' there is nothing to that." (Howard Baker, the new Chief of Staff, had in good humor, though he meant it, called Nancy a "Dragon Lady.")

Towards the close of Nancy's First Ladyship, a challenge new in the annals of international First Ladying presented itself in the person of Raisa Maksimovna Titorenko, wife of the Russian head of state, Mikhail Gorbachev. Raisa was a First Lady as tough in her own way as Nancy was in hers, and enjoyed a marriage with her own Chief Executive as vital in its Russian way as Nancy's "truluv" affair with Ronnie was romantically American. Raisa and Mikhail read Dostoyevsky's novels together, listened to classical music, and attended the ballet. The pattern seemed familiar enough to First Lady watchers—sounding a little like Eleanor Roosevelt, Raisa said of herself and her husband: "We have a division of labor. He's working and I'm looking around. Then I'll tell him about everything I see." In Russia, they called her "the Czarina." Raisa, too, had started an alcohol-abuse campaign as PR-impressive (and, in fact, as unsuccessful) in the USSR as Nancy's equivalent work against drugs in the USA.

While Ronnie and Gorby jousted for the limelight over nuclear disarmament and "Star Wars," Raisa and Nancy parried ad lib on TV over the Russian tourist's pointed questions about American history and art. It was a live performance for which Method acting had not prepared Nancy, involving a kind of dramatic substance for which glitzy Hollywood gives no Oscar.

Nancy's and Raisa's public comments about each other were pure propriety; but, Nancy had taken a dislike to Raisa almost from the start. Off camera, Nancy chafed: "Who does that dame think she is!" They competed in the clotheshorse race. They maneuvered at long distance. They got physical up close, jostling one another for center stage before the cameras. Nancy judged Raisa to be "pedantic and inflexible," and "a dogmatic Marxist."

Nancy had handled Russian males well enough. Once in the private quarters at the White House, when Andrei Gromyko, the Soviet foreign minister, intruding upon the small talk, put this question to the First Lady: "Does your husband believe in peace or war?"

Nancy stopped sipping her Perrier and answered forthrightly: "Peace."

The Russian, having expected polite evasion, sipped some more fruit juice, and returned: "Are you sure?"

More small talk, more sipping, more tinkling of glasses and conversation, and Gromyko came at the subject again: "You whisper *peace* in his ear, then, every night?"

Nancy smiled her big-eyed smile, this time with an impish nod: "I will," she promised, "I'll also whisper it in *your* ear!"

Nancy and Ronnie vacated the White House in evident good health, young for their years. Though they won no medals for attendance at Sunday School while in Office, part of their Presidential legacy was a chapel to be built at Camp David. They retired to a nice house in "old Bel Air," a high-rent western L.A. suburb, and to their California ranch, where First Dog could be at home on the range and Ronnie could be a cowboy again. The house, like many of Nancy's best dresses, belonged to someone else: some members of "the Group"—Betsy Bloomingdale, Marion Jorgensen—and a few others of the Reagans' California crowd had bought the property dirt cheap for $2.5 million, in an area where neighboring properties were selling for $14 million and up. During the Reagan Administration, the rich

Anne Frances "Nancy" Robbins Davis Reagan

had gotten richer, but not that rich; so, Ronnie and Nancy leased their new house (for an unspecified amount) and settled among the stars—within walking distance of mailboxes sporting familiar Hollywood names more famous in lights than in history books.

Late in Ronnie's second term, some loyal Republicans were feeling disappointed that there was not time enough to repeal the Twenty-second Amendment of the Constitution before the next election. So, a few people put bumper stickers on their cars: "NANCY IN '88." At one point, the First Lady's ratings in the polls had been higher even than the President's usual highs. Demure Nancy, of course, was not for electing. But her exercise of Office had re-taught America the lesson of the historic First Ladyship: that women have ruled, and a woman can rule, in America. It was a little like one of the lines in Nancy's 1939 Chicago Girls Latin school play, *First Lady*: "They ought to elect the First Lady, and then let her husband be President."

Eleanor Rosalynn Smith Carter

First Lady with the Cabinet

$\mathcal{R}$OSALYNN Carter—born Eleanor Rosalynn Smith on August 18, 1927—the peanut processor's wife from Georgia, was the first First Lady consciously to think of her office as a function of the American Presidency. Rosalynn entered the White House with not merely a First Lady's "project" on her mind but helping herself to a full-scale Presidential agenda on her plate. The first First Lady in the 20th century to attend her husband's Cabinet meetings, she was also the first to explore on purpose the full political and social implications of her office as precisely that: an office of public trust and incumbent responsibility.

A crushing defeat at the polls in 1980 held the Carter Presidency to a single term, leaving Rosalynn licking her wounds. Once she had regrouped, the First Lady they called the "steel magnolia blossom" published a bristling reaffirmation of her and Jimmy's policies and ideals in *First Lady from Plains*. Rosalynn's forthright autobiographical statement is the first political treatise by a President's wife. It appropriately includes a chapter titled "The Office of the First Lady" and concludes with as strong a statement of political readiness as any made by an American woman of the 20th century:

> With [Jimmy's] philosophy of fiscal conservatism and compassion, I believe our country would be well on the way to curing some of the ills that are now threatening to tear our society apart and divide us even more than ever before into the haves and have-nots. . . . One thing I know: things would be different if we were back in the White House. I would be out there campaigning right now if Jimmy would run again. I miss the world of politics. Nothing is more thrilling than the urgency of a campaign—the planning, the strategy sessions, getting out among people you'd never otherwise meet—and the tremendous energy it takes that makes a victory ever so sweet and a loss so devastating. I'd like people to know that we were right, that what Jimmy Carter was doing was best for our country, and that people made a mistake by not voting for him. But when all is said and done, for me, our loss at the polls is the biggest single reason I'd like to be back in the White House. I don't like to lose.

Words as tough as these would have been impossible for the Rosalynn of only a few years back, the mumbling woman who lost her lunch by the side of the road before giving her first scheduled political address on Jimmy Carter's behalf. But years of hard schooling in the hustings had disciplined her. She could greet public occasions as a willing campaigner, capable not only of making speeches but also of going nose-to-nose with Latin American dictators, holding dying Cambodian refugee babies in her arms, and standing against the meanest opposition to her resolute social activism on behalf of the mentally ill, the old, the sick, and the homeless.

Rosalynn started out, she says, "naive enough to think that politics were straight, and that country officials and political figures really had the best interests of the people at heart." When Rosalynn remembers how they had to fight the dirty politics of local demagogues, always afraid that the Carter peanut warehouse would be burned down in retaliation, she admits that she was not very courageous, at first. But, with Jimmy's help, Rosalynn perdured, uncracked in the teeth of racial bigotry in small-town Georgia and unseduced by the honeyed rationalizations of local church folk. The Carter family stood up for what is right during the stormy civil-rights days when Kennedy and King were killed.

The day John Kennedy was shot, Rosalynn remembered, she was at the beauty parlor; and when Jimmy phoned her with the news, she ran back to the warehouse office to be with him and listen to the radio, her hair half up in rollers, half down. When the children got home from school that night, the news only got worse. Chip Carter told his parents that when the announcement had been made in his class, his teacher had blurted out: "Good!" and the students had applauded. The outraged fourteen-year-old had picked up a chair and thrown it at the teacher. Chip had to explain to his folks why he would be spending the next few days in the principal's office.

The whole Carter family was becoming politicized in a way that made them feel like outsiders in their own hometown. A vote for Lyndon Johnson was a vote for integration, and the Carters were for Johnson. But farmers out at the Carter warehouse and kids at Chip's school were issuing threats. "If one [meaning a black person] tries to go to our school," said one of Chip's classmates, "I'll stand behind a bush with a baseball bat and knock him in the head." Chip would go off to school, defiantly wearing his LBJ button pinned to his shirt pocket, and then come home in the afternoon so his mamma could sew his torn shirt pocket back on. He pasted an "I'm a Democrat" sticker on his notebook. That afternoon when Chip failed to come home, Rosalynn found her boy crying in his schoolroom. Somebody had pulled his chair out from under him, he sobbed, and had dumped him on the floor. Chip had run outside into the tall weeds, taken off his button, and ripped the sticker off his notebook.

"I'm not going to be a Democrat anymore," he told her.

"But," wrote Rosalynn, "the next morning he put his pin back on and left for school with a brand-new Democratic sticker on his notebook."

Something Chip's mother had said—or did not say—had made political and moral good sense to a fourteen-year-old, enabling him to go back in there and stand up for what he knew was right. His sister Amy had not been born yet; but when she arrived, she would be a Democrat, too.

Things were no better at church. The deacons forced a vote favoring keeping blacks in their place. Rosalynn told Jimmy she hoped they could avoid controversy, this time; but Jimmy insisted on going to the meeting. A business meeting that would normally have attracted about fifty souls had packed the churchhouse with more than two hundred. Jimmy was the only one to speak against the resolution; he and Rosalynn, Chip and his brother Jeff, Jimmy's mother (Ms. Lillian Carter), and an elderly gentleman who may have been hard-of-hearing or slow of understanding were the only ones to vote for letting black people come to church. Some fifty votes were cast in favor of the deacons' anti-black proposal, and the majority remained silent.

By the time the Carters got home, the phone was ringing. Person after person called to say that they had agreed with the Carters' lonely stand, but were afraid to say so in public. Rosalynn, who admits she would have been willing not to take a stand, was learning some hard lessons, first from brave Chip, then from the timid church people: being the only one tough enough to vote against a whole community of beloved friends and otherwise respected neighbors is not easy. Moreover, Rosalynn was finding out that even good people only sometimes follow a brave leader, when the cause, however true, is unpopular. (Her boys, Rosalynn says, never forgave the church for voting to keep the black folk out.)

The tensile strength of that magnolia's steel was further tempered with tobacco juice. Rosalynn remembered the day vividly during Jimmy's first gubernatorial campaign against one of the good ol' boys way out on the right wing: "I handed a brochure to a man standing in the doorway of a shoe shop in Washington, Georgia, and asked him to vote for my husband. He was chewing tobacco, and it was drooling down his beard of several days' growth. 'I'm for Bo Callaway, lady,' he said. Then he spat on me."

Throughout the educating of Rosalynn, her mentors had been the best: unwitting instructors in a finishing school for Presidential ladies. When Ms. Lillian Carter—Rosalynn's mother-in-law—campaigned for Johnson and racial integration, she would just smile sweeter and work harder after she found her car smeared with soap and her radio antenna tied in bows. Ms. Lillian had been a country nurse who had sat by the bedside of half the county. A "gray panther" original, when she was forced into retirement from the Post Office, Ms. Lillian—at age sixty-eight—overcame her depressing sense of rejection by joining the Peace Corps. Ms. Lillian went to India, where she wrestled against disease and poverty, lost forty-four pounds, honed the keen edge of her spirit to greater brightness, and gave Rosalynn a prime example of a Presidential woman to live up to.

Before Ms. Lillian, there had been Rosalynn's daddy, Wilburn Edgar Smith—a man in whose upright moral opinions Rosalynn heard the demanding voice of God calling her to self-discipline, achievement, and excellence. Wilburn Smith's family was of the Baptist persuasion; but he didn't let it make a fool of him. He would kiss his wife right in front of the children and he kept a bottle of whiskey in the house—for medicinal purposes and eggnog at Christmas—even if it did take the family fourteen years to use up that one bottle. When her daddy died at forty-four of leukemia, young Rosalynn struggled mightily to discern the invisible hand of God at work, just as later, in 1980, she would question how a God of righteousness could allow a compassionate Presidency to be succeeded by a—to her way of thinking—much less caring Administration.

A rural Southern girl with little education, Rosalynn viewed Jimmy's fledgling career in Admiral Hyman Rickover's hatchling nuclear Navy as her one-way ticket to civilization. She got busy having babies, filling up her educational vacancies, and settling in to the comfortable, if unchallenging, role of a Navy wife. She read women's magazines, listened to radio soaps, and experimented with household tips and new recipes; she bought a sewing machine; she started listening to classical music; she learned to hula in Hawaii and committed Shakespeare to memory in Virginia; they read the "Great Books" together, they also managed to save an enviable twenty-five percent of Jimmy's monthly salary.

Rosalynn and Jimmy in the '50s were a Norman Rockwell portrait of a conventional couple, middle-class and committed to togetherness. But then, when Jimmy's daddy died, Jimmy had a born-again experience with his love of Georgia, small-town life, and the good things his father had stood for. Gathered round Mr. Earl Carter's deathbed, the neighbors told Jimmy about how his daddy had lent them money so they could buy seed and fertilizer, and how he had helped support a widow in town for years, and how he had bought new outfits for poor kids so they could look nice on graduation night. Jimmy thought about Mr. Earl's service on the school board and the hospital authority, his membership in the Lions Club and the State Legislature, and he knew he had to see it continue. So, Jimmy resigned from the Navy and dragged Rosalynn, pouting and yelling, crying and arguing, all the way back from New England. He would enter politics.

Back home in Plains, Rosalynn got right to work making herself aloof and miserable. She turned down invitations to avoid boredom with bridge or while away the day over sociable but pointless cups of kitchen coffee. But, soon, wifely duties and motherhood got stacked up alongside running the peanut warehouse and corn mill, and before long, she was in charge of the office and keeping the books. The stack of duties only got deeper when Jimmy—following in his daddy's footsteps—involved himself in local service organizations, the school board, and then ran for the Georgia State Legislature. That was when the Carter political partnership experienced its first persecution for democracy's sake: "Coons and Carters go together," sneered the racist sign stuck up on their office door in the night by the opposition. Rosalynn was finding Plains less and less boring.

> I liked being a political wife. . . . Some [Senate wives] felt burdened with all the responsibilities while their husbands were away. I stayed at home and took care of the children, but I never felt burdened. I had an important task. I had to keep the business running while Jimmy was gone. I liked the feeling that I was contributing to our life and making it possible for him to pursue a political career. I was more a political partner than a political wife, and I never felt put upon. During the next four years . . . I only had to call him home once, when one of our old brick warehouses collapsed, dumping several hundred tons of peanuts into the street!

As Jimmy's political career got going, so did Rosalynn's. One shake after another, Rosalynn shook hands across Georgia. Always running their campaigns on a shoestring, she drove borrowed cars and slept in friends' homes instead of hotels. After one loss at the polls, they decided to go big-time; they bought an automatic typewriter to help keep track of the names, addresses, and descriptions of political supporters. Everybody they met now got a personalized letter. She kept a clippings file for Jimmy, articles on every important subject, so his speeches could be well-informed. And, she kept working on her own speechmaking. Rosalynn may have started out a shy girl from a small town; but, as she said, she found the strength to "do the things that had to be done."

As Rosalynn campaigned, she met the people—poor people, people in trouble with the law, sick people, and a group of people who particularly unsettled her: people afflicted in their minds. It set Rosalynn to thinking, when the mother of a mentally retarded child asked her what Jimmy would do to help, if he got elected governor. One night, when the time came to meet the candidate, Rosalynn herself got in line. Before he noticed it was his wife, Jimmy was smiling his famous smile, shaking hands and being asked: "I want to know what you are going to do about mental health when you are governor." Jimmy kept smiling and answered: "We're going to have the best mental health system in the country, and I'm going to put you in charge of it."

Like most politicians, Jimmy kept only half his campaign promise. When the newly-elected Governor Carter set up his Commission to Improve Services to the Mentally and Emotionally Handicapped, he did not put Rosalynn in charge, professionally unqualified as she was for the job. She did, however, attend all the meetings of the Commission and went to work helping mentally handicapped people help themselves.

At first, it just did not occur to anyone to associate the name of Jimmy Carter with the Presidency. When Jimmy had told Ms. Lillian that he wanted to become the President, she had asked: "President of what?" On the trail, Rosalynn turned the oft-repeated campaign insult "Jimmy who?" into a slogan with deft answers. Theirs was a grassroots, homegrown, accessible Presidency, with a "y'all come" guest policy of open doors at the White House.

Rosalynn championed the never-ratified Equal Rights Amendment to guarantee women equal justice before the law, Rosalynn emphasizing the "equal pay for equal work" part of it. In symbolic and substantial ways, the Carter Administration fomented a statistical gender revolution in U.S. government. A Presidential Advisory Committee for Women was established and, for the first time, women stood in the Presidential honor guard. Women were appointed as general counsels and inspectors general. Hitherto, only three women had ever been Cabinet members; now there were three more. Three of the five Cabinet undersecretaries and eighty percent of the assistant secretaries were Carter appointees. Previously, only five women had presided as Federal judges; the Carters swelled that number to forty-six. The previous all-time total of female ambassadors had been twenty-five; the Carters appointed sixteen more. It was "always understood" between Jimmy and Rosalynn that he would appoint a female Justice to the Supreme Court, were a vacancy to occur during their Administration.

Government of, by, and for the masses was reflected also in a democracy of aesthetics at White House get-togethers. From Country and Western, jazz, rock n' roll, and the *1812 Overture* to Zukerman and Sills, Price and Perlman; from feminist plays to a fêting of American poets, the Carters celebrated the full spectrum of artistic taste. Although Jimmy felt uncomfortable with too much musical "hailing to the Chief," Southern hospitality and Southern dignity combined informally to keep receptions appropriately stately without being staid. "Welcome to your house!" Rosalynn liked to greet her guests. Theirs was a Mom-and-Pop Presidency.

> In the White House my relationship with Jimmy was the same as it had always been. We discussed business and strategy when we were working together in the warehouse, or campaigning, and when he was serving as governor, the way most husbands and wives do when they take an interest in each other's work. I often acted as a sounding board for him. While explaining a particular issue to me, he

could think it through himself; and I and the rest of the family often argued with him more strenuously than his advisors or staff did. To us he was the same participant in our nightly dinner table discussions that he had always been.

Jimmy saw it that way, too, calling Rosalynn his "political partner," with whom he invariably discussed policy issues, and (in a reference to the Roosevelts and a reminder of Rosalynn's first name) "his Eleanor." She was like a second Vice President, doing what the President would do, taking independent action subject to the President's concurrence. Sometimes, Rosalynn put in appearances for Jimmy, standing in for him, for example, at one reception for the Hispanic community and another for the Italian-American community, when Jimmy was holed up for nearly two weeks with Israel's Begin and Egypt's Sadat during the Camp David summit. Other times, she was like a ground wire, keeping the President from becoming isolated, and a trunk line from the people, able to get beyond the Presidential entourage to hear actual individuals' specific concerns and then report back to him. "A President . . . can become very isolated if he's not careful," she said. "Maybe something I reported to him would have an impact as he struggled with a problem; maybe not. If I disagreed with him about something, I told him. For the most part, however, Jimmy and I agreed on issues."

But they did not agree on everything. Rosalynn disapproved of capital punishment and she was more liberal than Jimmy was on abortion; but mostly what they disagreed about was political timing. Whereas Jimmy was more a statesman than a politician, Rosalynn, no less a statesman, was more of a politician. An idealist, Jimmy would not postpone politically unstrategic decisions: He curried disfavor when he refused to delay until a second term his renegotiation of the Panama Canal treaty; he made himself glaringly unpopular just before election time by cutting budgets that affected Democrat constituents, imposing a grain embargo just before the Iowa primaries, and boycotting the 1980 Moscow Olympics. On these occasions, fabled domestic bliss in the Carter household gave way, as Rosalynn's better head for politics turned Presidential bed chamber into a buttonholing caucus room:

> My pleas always fell on deaf ears. "If securing a second term was more important to me than doing what needs to be done, then I'd wait," he would snap at me. But I didn't always give up. . . . His standard answer when I talked about political expediency was a seemingly pompous: "I'll never do anything to hurt my country." But he meant it, and I meant it too when I appealed to him, loudly sometimes when I was very concerned: "The thing you can do to hurt your country most is not get re-elected." I believed it then. I believe it now.

Jimmy got blamed for the OPEC oil embargo and long lines at the filling-station pump and got laughed at by the unthinking for his energy conservation measures. (Even Rosalynn, wrapped in sweaters and arguing through chattering teeth, couldn't persuade Jimmy to up the White House thermostat from 65° to 68°.) Jimmy's Presidency ended anticlimactically on the day after his successor's inauguration when the former President flew to Europe to welcome home the hostages from Iran. During the 444-day Iranian hostage situation, Jimmy had appeared indecisive, when, in fact, his careful negotiations did eventually resolve the unprecedented dilemma without involving America in a war with Muslim fanatics—though too late to help him at the polls. One must wonder, however, had politically astute Rosalynn been the Chief Executive and Jimmy, the idealistic Presidential spouse, whether the Carter Administration might have been a two-term Presidency.

Rosalynn's involvement with the President's Commission on Mental Health was the primary concern of her First Ladyship, continuing the work she had found so gratifying as First Lady of Georgia.

The media steamed Rosalynn, however, when they informed her mental health was not a "sexy" issue. The press initially gave more lines of print to the Carters' Baptist-bred, cost-cutting decision not to serve hard liquor at the White House than to their equally religiously inspired and costly plans to minister to the mentally and emotionally damaged. Rosalynn soon found out that all her political know-how was required to keep her high concern from being "dismissed as a First Lady's 'pet project.'"

Both the press and the public were looking to criticize: The media hardly knew what to do with the details of the First Couple's budget-wise notions in the White House: for example, when the Carters removed the superfluity of 325 television sets and 220 FM radios from the Mansion, the media found it more amusing than telling. Too much had been made of Jimmy's born-again Evangelical experience and his artless admission in a *Playboy* interview that he "lusts in his heart." A couple married this cozily, this devoted to the piety of doing good rather than doing well, and without any whisper of immorality about them, was perceived as too simple to be taken seriously by Washington's sophisticates.

Even Liberal Democrat Ted Kennedy, who might have been expected to be a staunch supporter of the Carters' social reforms, became sharply critical. "President Carter is making the poor eat cat food," said the man from Massachusetts with the magic name; and then, at a Senate subcommittee hearing, Teddy scuffled with Rosalynn the lobbyist over how much Federal money to spend on public health.

In addition, Rosalynn was a genuine threat to residual male chauvinism. The first shock wave unsettled those who think of the First Lady's primary responsibility as the White House hostess when Rosalynn, at Jimmy's invitation, attended her first Cabinet meeting on February 28, 1978. Although Rosalynn sat among the other non-Cabinet participants (secretaries, aides, observers) and never took vocal part in the discussions, she did take notes. During her "working lunches" with the President on Tuesdays, she was, no doubt, (so the rumor ran) telling Jimmy what to think.

Paranoia among the male-dominants mounted when Jimmy sent Rosalynn as his special envoy and official representative to six Latin American nations to urge the cause of "human rights," the dominant theme of the Carter Presidency. State Department officials, Congressmen, European diplomats all deplored sending a woman into the males' den of Latin-American macho politics. Rosalynn, who had first exercised her political muscle as a Southern lady among the genteelly condescending, had no hesitation employing her female advantage among traditional, male public figures. She practiced her Spanish and looked forward to the test of her authority as Presidential surrogate:

> Every one of the leaders wanted to talk to the President of the United States. And who is closer to the President, who better has his ear, than his wife? Moreover, as Jimmy noted when he announced my

trip, I had long been his "partner." . . . I was not only prepared but eager to discuss the issues and report what I had learned directly to the President. I was *determined* to be taken seriously . . . [In addition,] being a woman in Latin America was more an asset than a liability. I could get away with a lot of things another representative of our government could never do . . . I could say the unexpected.

Enjoying dinner and the evening with Alfredo Poveda, one of the military dictators of Ecuador, she rendered the Admiral defenseless with her peach-blossom laughter and said: "See what you could do for your people if you just didn't spend all your money on so many weapons? You could educate them all, as Costa Rica does. Then you would be a real hero!" Rosalynn says, "I wasn't really teasing, and he knew it."

While in Ecuador, a critical U.S. reporter pressed her: "You have neither been elected by the American people nor confirmed by the Senate to discuss foreign policy with foreign heads of state. Do you consider this trip an appropriate exercise of your position?"

Peach blossoms turned again to steel magnolia and Rosalynn snapped at him: "I am the person closest to the President of the United States, and if I can explain his policies and let the people of Latin America know of his great interest and friendship, I intend to do so!"

The trip was a success. Latin machismo was charmed by Rosalynn's genuine interest in the people and instructed in democracy by her skill at diplomacy. After she won over one chap in a military uniform by calling him "my favorite dictator," Rosalynn then argued human rights with him for several hours into the night, as she might have contended with Jimmy. Later, when this same man, Morales Bermúdez, was popularly elected president of Peru, Rosalynn, as promised, returned for his inauguration to celebrate the reestablishment of democracy in that country. Among them all, Rosalynn had distinguished herself an able representative of her own and Jimmy's perennial concern for *derechos humanos*.

Rosalynn's notes on the meeting between Sadat of Egypt and Begin of Israel, when Jimmy achieved his greatest symbolic achievement as an agent of reconciliation, are the best, and only detailed, record of that historic summit. "Begin and Sadat shared the Nobel Peace Prize that year," says Rosalynn, "but it was Jimmy who made it possible."

When she left the White House, her tenure having coincided with a time when "the role [had] changed dramatically along with the expanded opportunities of other women in America," Rosalynn Carter could congratulate herself on having reached the highest mark of political involvement of any to have held her office. As Mamie Eisenhower commented to Rosalynn: "I stayed busy all the time and loved being in the White House, but I was never expected to do all the things you have to do."

Elizabeth "Betty" Ann Bloomer Warren Ford

A Shining Example of Recovery

ETTY FORD—born Elizabeth Anne Bloomer on April 8, 1918—became First Lady by accident: two accidents. The first accident was Spiro Agnew, the second was Richard Nixon. In 1973, when Agnew, known to be the Worst Veep in History pleaded "nolo contendere" on bribery charges, Betty's husband, Jerry, got promoted into the Vice-Presidential vacancy after being Minority Leader in the House. (The Congressman from Grand Rapids didn't consider it much of a promotion —now he had to preside over the Senate.) Then, eight months later, when the President he'd been working for didn't want to have to plead anything in reference to Watergate, and resigned, Jerry got bumped upstairs again. Betty called it "the saddest day of my life . . . the day my husband took the oath of office as President of the United States."

The majority of Presidential wives have claimed they never wanted the job, didn't run for it, and had no way of training to perform in the role that got dumped on them. In

Elizabeth "Betty" Ann Bloomer Warren Ford

Betty's case, the claim seems to be true—she had no campaign through which to hype herself up to First Ladyship and fantasize herself pouring tea into White House China cups with a pattern of her own choosing. She didn't even have time to pick a "pet project"—Betty's best project would come only after she left office.

"If I had known what was coming," says Betty, "I think I probably would have sat right down and cried." Still, Betty Bloomer, never known for her modesty—not, at least, in public—lost no time in becoming the best stand-up comic ever known to lie down in the same bed with a President. "There was a good deal of whooping and hollering right at the beginning because I'd said Jerry and I were *not* going to have separate bedrooms at the White House." On this, and a few other points, Betty states mildly, "at least . . . my reputation for candor was established."

She came out in favor of the Supreme Court's liberal ruling on abortion: "It was time to bring abortion out of the backwoods and put it in the hospitals where it belonged."

She opined that "all citizens—and that includes females—should give two years of service to their country." Republicans everywhere clutched: being a hawk's one thing; drafting our darling daughters is something else! What kind of a rad fem was this Betty Bloomer Ford?

When living life as a politician's wife had clouded her gray matter, Betty didn't mind talking right out loud in public about having gotten some psychiatric care: "I got a standing ovation. Because so many people think it's shameful to confess that they can't make it alone, that it's an admission of something terribly wrong with them. There was nothing terribly wrong with me. I just wasn't the Bionic Woman."

She admitted that maybe her kids might have smoked

some grass (which, they said, they hadn't). She talked up front about what her response might be if her daughter Susan were to have an affair with an older man (which Susan hadn't, yet). She theorized that premarital sex might lower the divorce rate. Now, both Republicans and Democrats were clutching.

In the White House, Betty took down from the dining room walls Jackie's antique wallpaper—that decorative historic document showing scenes from the Revolutionary War and bought at a cost only a Kennedy could afford. "I couldn't stand to look at soldiers fainting and dying while I was eating my soup." ("Pat Nixon hadn't liked it either," observed Betty, making the whack at the Kennedy wallpaper a solid Republican move.)

Jerry added to his wife's luster (and did himself damage at the polls) when he let it slip that Betty and he had talked over the issue of Nixon's pardon, saying that she had had "a great deal of influence."

Maybe worst of all, Betty came out in favor of women and the ERA—no Republican move, that! And, what's more, she claimed to be seducing the President all the while. As she said: "As wife of the Vice President, I was already involved with the Equal Rights Amendment, and when Jerry became President, I kept pushing, trying to influence him. I used everything, including pillow talk at the end of the day, when I figured he was most tired and vulnerable. I championed the idea of women in high places."

In case anyone had missed the point, Betty started flying a First Lady's flag that somebody made for her, a rampant pair of red and white calico bloomers (symbolic of both her maiden name and of Panty Power), bearing the legends "Don't tread on me" and "ERA."

What was a dutiful Republican matron, mother of

Elizabeth "Betty" Ann Bloomer Warren Ford

three sons and a daughter, and from the state of conservative Michigan doing on the wrong side of all these issues? Betty's rags were glad, and her twice-a-week hairdos made her look Republican. All her campaign buttons said that she was a Republican. But she talked like a Democrat and behaved even more unlike a Republican. Betty Ford was a donkey in elephant's clothing: she even hinted at it herself, owning up that she had often been "tempted to split" her ticket.

In the past, she had behaved like a good Republican wife by default, keeping mum on hot political topics, remaining casual about her husband's campaigns—except when she could have some fun. Betty had got her first clue about what being married to a politician would be like when Jerry, coming in from a campaign, showed up late for their wedding rehearsal dinner. Forgivingly, Betty had gone on to perform her campaign headquarters duty anyway, stuffing envelopes full of propaganda and licking her obligatory stamps. Being a fashion model and a dancer, Betty got all the other models and dancers out working for Jerry—not a bad approach to politics. And, although Betty felt unprepared to be a political wife, she didn't worry: "I didn't think he was going to win."

Then, after Jerry won his House seat, and every two years kept on winning automatically, Betty was off the campaign hook. So, Betty did her bit as a Congressional wife, some of it pretty neat stuff: she co-produced an educational TV series on American government, folded bandages for the Red Cross, and stuck up for abused kids. But a lot of it was fairly ho-hum—cultural programs, helping Jerry on the weekends in his office with the filing, visiting hospitals, playing bridge, giving book reviews, drinking lots of tea and martinis—the usual.

BEHIND EVERY SUCCESSFUL PRESIDENT

Probably the most enlightening thing Betty did was hang out up on the Hill, sitting in the galleries of Congress, listening, figuring out how things worked. The main thing she learned there is that "in politics, you need a hard shell." Probably the most pleasantly surprising thing she discovered was that some cave dwellers (long-term, insider Washingtonians) are genuinely useful and enjoyable people.

Item: Early on, when Betty was ominously pregnant, she attended a White House tea party on a rainy winter's day and, as she was going through the receiving line, said: "Oh, Mrs. Truman, it's so nice of you to have us." To which Bess replied: "Heavens, it's you who are nice to come out in such terrible weather." Betty says: "With that, she went straight to my heart. I had not thought any First Lady—and she was my first experience with a First Lady—could stay so humble."

Item: At one of the first Washington parties the Fords attended, Lady Bird Johnson called her husband the Senator over and said, "Lyndon, I want you to meet this young couple, they've just come to Congress." Betty says: "Lady Bird was that kind of really friendly, outgoing woman; she made a special effort to include us."

Trumans, Johnsons—it may all have been a conspiracy to convert those good Grand Rapids Republicans to the other side of the House; and in Betty's case, it may have succeeded, secretly. LBJ, after years of working with Jerry on all the creative compromising that makes the government go, said: "Jerry, you're a great man, but you belong to the wrong party."

Then, when Jerry began to be a big Republican, Betty took it on herself to shake up the Republican wives.

I thought the Democratic wives were more effective.

Elizabeth "Betty" Ann Bloomer Warren Ford

"If anybody asks you to do anything, say yes," I advised my peers. "Get off your duffs. It's always the Democratic wives who model in the fashion shows for Multiple Sclerosis or the Heart Fund." I coerced a lot of women who'd never done any modeling in their lives into chasing up and down runways for charity, and they go.

There were other telltale signs of creeping Democratism: Betty was the only other nationally famous white person besides Jimmy Carter who went to the funeral when Mrs. Martin Luther King, Sr., was assassinated. Betty and Jerry did away with the unofficial court chaplaincy in the White House, commenting: "There aren't going to be any more private services in the East Room for a select few." They marched right up to Immanuel-on-the-Hill, like any good Episcopalians—where everyone could see them. Jerry didn't want the White House called a Mansion anymore (preferring "Residence" instead), he tried to outlaw the playing of "Hail to the Chief" every time he turned around, and he compared golf scores with the butler. When First Lady Betty left the White House, she went around shaking hands with the nurses, the groundskeepers, and the flower arranger, saying: "Presidents come and go, but you people are the White House." To be sure, other Republican First Ladies also shook hands with the help; but the evidence mounts up—Betty, at least, if not Jerry also, may have been a closet Democrat! Which might explain why Jimmy and Rosalynn beat them by such a narrow margin in 1977: you couldn't tell the difference, except by the accents.

Betty made a great First Lady, partly because she was so unprepared. The first night she slept (in the same bedroom) with the President-designate, she wasn't talking pillows: "That night I lay in the dark and stared at the ceiling. 'My God,' I thought, 'what a job I have to do.'" But she went along. Betty discovered within herself her own natural untapped "resources with which to respond to a series of challenges. You never know what you can do until you have to do it." Being First lady is not entirely unlike being a mother, having a handicap, living your daily life in the Circus Maximus, and taking on the Old Boys Club in defense of your embattled womanhood. Betty already knew how to do all that, and now she proceeded to do it on stage at the White House.

Herself a devoted mother, Betty kept on tending to children—retarded children, crippled children, children of soldiers lost or missing in action, abused children. Herself having to put up with a permanently pinched nerve and creeping arthritis, Betty raised sizeable sums for the cancer and arthritis foundations.

Remembering her own dancing days, Betty became patroness of the arts. One of her proudest moments was when Jerry presented Martha Graham, first lady of modern American dance, with the Presidential Medal of Freedom.

Jerry, hanging on to his Republican ways, had not wanted to single out Ms. Graham for special honor; he'd wanted to mix her in with a few males. But Betty pillow-talked him into it: "I kept after him until Martha got her dinner and her medal. You know, if you bring up a subject long enough with a man, why finally he gets so tired of it he agrees to anything. There might be a woman on the Supreme Court now if I'd just brought it up more often."

Betty said, "I've worked hard on my husband" on feminist issues; and she viewed his record with pleasure. Jerry was the first President to start appointing women in significant numbers to important government posts. In 1975, he signed an Executive Order establishing a National Commission on the Observance of International Women's

Elizabeth "Betty" Ann Bloomer Warren Ford

Year—a symbolic document without legal force; but, says Betty, "it meant [that] a President of the United States was standing up for women and the ERA, and against 'legal inequities between sexes.'" On that occasion when Jerry welcomed Betty to speak any "words of wisdom or encouragement," she congratulated Mr. President, saying: "I am glad to see that you have come a long, long way."

On a more sobering occasion, Betty distinguished herself by mastering a situation in the commanding way we expect of our Presidents. In 1976, at a fund-raiser for the Jewish National Fund, Maurice Sage, the Fund's president, collapsed on the dais with a heart attack. Everybody was becoming hysterical, not knowing what to do. Betty didn't know what to do, either.

> But I truly believed that if I could get up there and pray, and get all those people to pray with me, we might somehow save Dr. Sage's life. I moved to the microphone and asked the people to bow their heads, and I asked God's blessing on Rabbi Sage. It was a simple prayer, along the lines of, "We know You can take care of him, we know You can bring him back to us, we know You are our leader and our strength." After that, I asked everyone to pray silently, each in his own way.

As long as everyone prayed, the man stayed alive; once they got him to the hospital, he died. Afterwards, Betty got a lot of credit for doing the right thing at the right time; but, she countered, explaining what it means to be a Presidential person: "I don't think [the] praise is warranted. What I did was instinctive, not an act of will. . . . For some people in a public situation (as opposed to private life, where you're a real person), an inner strength takes over, and you don't know where it comes from, and you can't take credit for it."

Betty had an Episcopalian personality—she's that type of classy dame with the heady ability to be secular and devout at once, to imbibe humor and piety in equal amounts, to mix gin and Jesus. This sophisticated style, which can seem shallow in brassy women and stuffy in smug men, is essentially a cover-up, either for a pervasive mystical faith they are embarrassed to admit, or for an equally embarrassing lack of faith.

The result, with Betty, was her bottle came uncorked, and so did Betty; it led to her much publicized, gratifyingly successful rounds with the psychiatrists.

Next, Betty was diagnosed as having cancer. She had been First Lady for about six weeks when Betty entered the National Naval Medical Center in Bethesda, Maryland, and had a mastectomy. Like her psychiatry, Betty's radical surgery was also a success. Betty lost a breast, but the doctors had not taken out Betty's womanhood or her candor or her wit. The nationwide response of pity and love was expected; but Betty's characteristically outspoken style of First Ladyship provided leadership for American women. Betty found that she had become Ms. American Everywoman, overcoming the initial horror of breast cancer enough to go in for an examination, have the dreaded operation, endure the painful recovery, and discover the durability of her love-affair with her husband. Women, especially, wrote to Betty, telling how she had encouraged them; some sent money, others sent recipes for cancer cures, from asparagus to rhubarb leaves. "Men wrote too," she said. "Men married to women who'd had mastectomies tried to buck me up by telling me that they still loved their wives. They did buck me up. I was touched, and overwhelmed."

Clinics suddenly were overflowing with women getting that checkup they'd been afraid to go in for, and Betty suddenly realized the impact that the First Ladyship can have: "Lying in the hospital, thinking of all those women going for cancer checkups because of me, I'd come to recognize more clearly the power of the woman in the White House. Not *my* power, but the power of the position, a power which could be used to help."

Although she was unable to admit it while she was still in the White House, Betty had become an alcoholic and a drug addict. That painful pinch, the arthritis, and the pressures of office sent Betty to her doctors and the friendly neighborhood pharmacy to fill the prescription for legal chemical dependency—Valium. And Betty, awash in Washington—the boozingest small town in America—washed down her pills with the finest vintages, the best years, and the highest proof. While Betty wasn't watching, the fuel she was consuming was making the First Lady an embarrassment to herself, to her family, and, on a couple of occasions, to the Republic.

Once, when Betty was in Moscow set to narrate *The Nutcracker Suite*, her pills and potation earned her a breath analysis from the critics rather than a review. They sniped alliteratively about her "sloe-eyed, sleepy-tongued" performance. Betty was shutting her eyes, not seeing herself as others saw her, not acknowledging that grog had gotten the better of God. Her brassy personality was covering up systematic abuses of controlled substances.

Betty's abusive personality had become a tangle of emotional Gordian knots—not only the drinking and the drugs, but also the feelings and misconceptions that go with that slowly suicidal behavior, left her willing but unable to stop what she was doing. She described herself in retrospect as full of "honest self-deception" and ordinary self-pity, full of rage and resentment at life's existential injustices, full of fears about appearing stupid and playing the fool, full of false pride to cover up self-doubt and low self-esteem. At the same time, Betty said she wanted to be admired, less scared, and more likable. "I covered my own feelings of inadequacy by trying to appear very sure of myself."

Their mom, said Betty's kids, was smiling and open on the surface, yet oversensitive and self-centered underneath, having no real interest in other people's needs. Betty, said Betty, was an "egocentric baby" who in her weakness had to "control everyone" else and had to be "forced to focus on other people." In Betty's celebrated case, there was the double stinger of a celebrity hang-up: "I considered myself a very special person who had been married to a President of the United States, and I didn't think I should have to discuss my personal problems with just anybody." Betty had become that insufferable kind of person who has to be coddled into hearing the unpleasant truth about herself.

Instead of trying to untie the Gordian knot, Alexander the Great took out his sword and sliced through it. So also did Jerry and his kids—they cut through the noose of Betty's chemical and emotional tangles: they staged an "intervention." Betty's family dragged her kicking and crying to the water of health, and then held her head under until she would drink or strangle. Betty called the pommeling she took an "avalanche of love."

Intervention is a group happening, a direct and painful confrontation of the addicted person by the people she loves the most, and who love her the most, backed up by some expert support people. They forced her with stubborn love to admit to herself that she was an alcoholic and addicted. Then, once Betty saw her own unlovely reflection in the eyes of her beloveds, she might begin to make use of the expertise available from the medical, psychiatric, and counseling professionals. The Ford children instigated the procedure, and Jerry—hard as it was—took equal part in the only right move they could make. In the end, Jerry's ongoing love for Betty—the love of the ex-Congressman, who had often been too busy, and the love of the President, who had often been preoccupied—was available now, if she would allow. Their son, Steve Ford, told the ever-after ending to this Presidential love story that is happier than some have been:

> Dad . . . was not one to backtrack and pick up people that couldn't keep marching. He kept going, she stumbled, and the wonderful thing is that he finally came back and got her. He slowed down enough to reeducate himself, to find out what was the problem. Mom helped herself a lot, but if Dad hadn't turned around and come back and got her— Everybody's got a little piece in this thing, but to me, theirs is a wonderful love story.

After the intervention, and after her tears were dried and her sobbing had subsided, Betty had come to her more sober self. Reflecting on her high times, the tinkling crystal, tippler's wit, and the bubbles, Betty wrote: "It's romantic as long as you can handle it—for years I could and did—but it's misery when you become addicted."

Then, the woman who is famous for her candor surprised no one by concluding: "If I was going to go all the way as far as my treatment was concerned, it was better to do it publicly rather than to try and hide behind a silk sheet."

The candid Betty Ford had been effective as First Lady at least in part because of her narcissism—Narcissus was the

Greek beauty who fell in love with his own reflection in the water. The psychological quirk that doesn't mind showing itself off is useful in teachers, leaders, and dancers (and Betty was all three), because it makes them need to show off for the enjoyment of the audience, the guiding of the followers, and the enlightenment of learners.

When the "avalanche of love" fell on Betty, she was no longer the First Lady, but she was still a Presidential woman and a female Narcissus. Consistent with everything else she had done since becoming celebrated, her drying out and sobering up and getting straight had to take place in public. As she had led the nation before to ponder knotty moral problems and to face breast cancer, now Betty became a medical and moral *cause célèbre* that gave courage to women (and men) hooked on prescription drugs and alcohol. Woman to woman, Betty was saying to the less courageous of her species: "Coward, take my coward's hand."

The institutionally smashing result of Betty's candid ability to be as honest with herself as she was with everybody else is the Betty Ford Center in Long Beach, California—a lovingly stubborn and expert bunch in whose company other addicts and alcoholics can do what Betty did.

Jerry and Betty—still sounding like clandestine Democrats—insisted that the monuments to their Presidential selves be a "monument to the average man." Jerry's museum in Grand Rapids houses his Boy Scout uniform and his football memorabilia, and makes the statement: "This can happen to anyone"—meaning that any boy or girl in America can run for a touchdown and grow up to be the President. Betty's monument in Long Beach is a place of healing not just "for the rich and famous. It had to be for everybody, or it would not work."

"Unless you send us your truck drivers," Betty stipulated, "we don't want your executives."

Rehearsing for health meant that Betty had to learn to give in to what others want, while remaining OK about not getting her own way. Sometimes, this meant acting like a Party-loyal Republican and silencing her thudding feminist heart. Betty had already packed her white dress for the ERA march at the 1980 Republican National Convention in Detroit; she wanted to be a part of it. Just because she was out of the White House did not mean that she had ceased being a Presidential woman:

> I had eaten enough creamed chicken and sat through enough speeches to have earned a presidential pardon. At one time during my husband's administration I made the smart-aleck remark that a First Lady ought to be paid, she had a full-time job, and I'm not sure I wasn't right. When your husband is serving, you're an extension of him, you can't always express what you feel, and I'd never been good at keeping my mouth shut if I had a strong opinion. In the White House, I had embraced the Equal Rights Amendment, I had said I'd been to a psychiatrist, many of my public statements might have mortified a lesser man than Jerry.

But then, Jerry—a Republican, after all—asked her, as a favor to him and for the sake of the Party, not to march. For Betty, it then became no longer a political issue but a psychological question! Did she always have to have things her own way, or would she, for once, do it "their" way? "I can't tell you how many Republicans came to try to talk me out of it," she said. "They said it wouldn't reflect well on the party if I marched. I was mad at the party anyway. The

BEHIND EVERY SUCCESSFUL PRESIDENT

Republicans had been first to support ERA, and now they were dropping the ERA plank from their platform."

That was a hard decision for strong-willed, self-directed Betty, but remembering how well she had performed in the First Ladyship helped her balance the contrary values: "So I didn't march. I stood there in the window of our hotel suite, and watched the parade go by, a dutiful wife and a disappointed feminist in one quivering package. Other days, there were other wonders outside that window."

Flip Wilson, the black comic, calls Betty "First Momma." A momma in the black community is a mother, often of physical proportions to match her largeness of soul, who can tell other people what to do and get away with it. Betty may not have marched for the ERA that time, but the Republicans did not muzzle her permanently; now, Momma that she is, Betty, through her writing and at "Betty Ford" is telling people what to do about their alcoholism and other addictions. She's working on Jerry's chemical dependency on ice cream and nicotine, having herself overcome, among her other habits, the need for a twice-a-week hairdo fix. But she's still an Episcopalian and not entirely dogmatic; while she counsels with you, particularly as opinions vary on the causes and cures of alcoholism, Betty faithfully reports all the partial answers, and guides you down the *via media* to health.

Betty has a message, now; and to represent her fairly means to repeat her message. Betty is in favor of intervention, a kind of "love bombing" that leads you not to membership in some religious group, but back to your senses. It's not the total solution, but for Betty it was the right place to start for the honestly self-deceiving addict.

Doctors are part of the answer, says Betty, speaking

Elizabeth "Betty" Ann Bloomer Warren Ford

especially woman-to-woman, just as they have been part of the problem. The medical profession, quick on the draw with their prescription pads and largely untrained in coping with chemical dependency, "couldn't fix your car, either."

> Too many psychiatrists and other physicians contribute to addiction and help maintain addicts in their habits. Because while they don't dispense [beverage] alcohol [Betty discusses elsewhere in her book the high alcohol content in some medicines.] they do write prescriptions. Mostly for women. And women, more than men, become dependent on their doctors and on the drugs they prescribe. A woman thinks her doctor can help her emotionally as well as physically. And we love those prescriptions! We've spent a long time waiting for the appointment, we've got dressed and gone to the office, we're going to have a hefty bill to pay, and we don't want to go home without that little white piece of paper covered in hen tracks; it's the return on our investment of time and money.

An addict's family can help, but often doesn't. They are as involved in denial of the sickness as the alcoholic is and actually contribute to the social disease of alcoholism by covering up and refusing to face facts. Betty came to realize that her father and her brother before her, and her first husband had all been alcoholics. The tendency to become alcoholic was in both her genes and her social conditioning.

The old moralism about will power overcoming the sinfulness of booze and dope is one of the worst non-helps of all, Betty says; and yet, once Betty's will was free again to choose against chemical dependency, she learned (as First Lady Nancy Reagan became famous for preaching) to "just say no." Now, Betty just says "no" to pills and the bubbly:

BEHIND EVERY SUCCESSFUL PRESIDENT

"You say no, thank you, to spinach if you don't like it; you say no, thank you, to strawberries if they make you break out; what's wrong with saying no, thank you, to a glass of wine?"

The life of sobriety is the successful exercise of the freed will, one day at a time.

Alcoholism, say some of the expert advisors at "Betty Ford," is a certifiable disease, primary and chronic, "a psychological lesion—we think the site is in the brain," that makes some people drink themselves to dying, "and it's genetically transmissible," or at least "determined by environmental factors in genetically susceptible persons." It's like "a snake who lies back in a dark corner of the mind and who, every now and then, maybe every three or four years, will open one eye to see if the alcoholic is still on guard."

That metaphor makes substance abuse sound like the Primal Snake in Eve's Garden, and suggests that religion might be one among the many ways to help drive out the demons of chemical dependence. On that subject, Betty is both a believer and an agnostic. When the preachers lean too heavily on the uses of willpower, she says, and mistakenly call the illness of alcoholism a sin, or recommend just praying more and going to church rather than to a rehab center, Betty becomes a doubter. As she candidly (as ever) points out, plenty of people have made it back to sobriety not in church, but in Alcoholics Anonymous; not calling on God by name, but by appealing to that generic "Higher Power" that the AA creed teaches.

At the same time, Episcopal Betty no longer hides her faith behind talk of "accidents" and "fate." Now, she just goes ahead and says "God." "We have to trust," she says, in order to get free from the notion that we can control our own lives, and get out from under a preoccupation with oneself and "what I have done wrong." Alcoholism is "a disease, not a sin. Today we believe the sin is in not doing something about it." Chemical dependency—from alcohol and nicotine to prescription drugs and street dope—is a demon that comes out not only with prayer and abstinence, but also with help from expert support people and the reorientation towards living life to its non-addictive fullest without chemical crutches.

Betty is pondering what the "real problem" is with people in America. Is it that "Americans drink more alcohol than milk?" Is it the human inability to make a New Year's resolution to find happiness this year? Is it at bottom a soul sickness—a loss of God and family and self, stability and freedom? Is it, for women, their special rage, their greater toxicity, their special hurt, especially in view of how men have treated them?

For Betty, the answer was all of the above. "Accidents" or "fate" or "God" got the ball rolling through the loving "intervention" of her family; but then, Betty herself, always with all the help she could use, had to sort through the contradictions of all the right and wrong questions and all the right and wrong answers on her own. Because of Jerry and the kids and the friends and her expert professionals and the response of America itself to Betty and her cause—because of all this "sweetness in my life," Betty is wary of taking too much credit to herself. She is resisting that "most insidious of temptations . . . the temptation to sainthood." It's a help, of course, that not many Episcopalians get made into saints, anymore. Nevertheless, First Momma emerges as a miracle-worker among women and a sign of wonder among men. The Betty Ford Center is her pilgrimage site where healings happen regularly. Cancer couldn't kill her,

BEHIND EVERY SUCCESSFUL PRESIDENT

Washington didn't do her in, and she handled the serpent of drink without dying. The final proof of sainthood is the saint's resistance to the temptation of appearing to be holier than she is. But as it does now appear that Betty has a shot at dying sober rather than stinking drunk, she may have to settle for odor of sanctity.

Thelma Catherine "Pat" Ryan Nixon

*T*HE DEPRESSION. Poverty. Truck-farming in Southern California. Mom died of cancer; Dad, of tuberculosis. Three orphans holding their family together. Grit, pluck, and hard work. Up by the bootstraps.

Thelma Catherine "Pat" Ryan—born on March 16, 1912—was a self-made woman. Somber colors of struggle shade the background, and—as with many people who barely made it through the Depression—lingering at the edges a lifelong resentment of those who "had it easy." Years later, long after Pat Ryan had become Pat Nixon, she would —for a single unguarded moment—let everyone else glimpse the churning mind of a person driven by work-engines and Depression fears: "I never had time to think about things like [childhood's dreams and hopes] who I wanted to be, or who I admired—or to have ideas. I never had time to dream about being anyone else. I had to work. I haven't just sat back and thought of myself or my ideas or what I wanted to do. . . . I've kept working."

Thelma Catherine "Pat" Ryan Nixon

But Pat kept all of this out of the foreground. The young bright Pat Ryan at the center of the picture stands out. Pat's mother Kate, of sturdy German extraction, died when Pat was thirteen, and her Irish father, Will Ryan, died four years later. Pat learned early on to live on her own and be happy, even when loved ones disappointed her, let her down.

Will had not succeeded as a whaler or a surveyor, a man bitten by the gold bug, a truckfarmer fighting low prices and dry wells near Santa Ana; neither did he succeed particularly well as a husband, his mercurial personality fluctuating between romantic bigheartedness and the abusive effects of too much Irish whiskey. But he did succeed in convincing his daughter that she was "St. Patrick's Babe in the morning"—a child born on the eve of the Irish patron's day—so that, after her father's death, Thelma chose to become Pat.

Pat Ryan's mother left her with a memory of hot and tasty cinnamon rolls, delicious-smelling as they baked, and the interior strength to endure anything; from her father, Pat got the makings of a new identity, and a private joy in living, regardless of what the rest of the world was doing.

Tom, Bill, and Pat Ryan held it together, Pat doing the cooking, washing the clothes, and keeping the accounts. At the bottom of a page in her ledger for August 1930 to January 1931, Pat summarized the facts of their economic existence: "Total deposits: None made since a year ago January." Pat scrubbed the floors at the local bank and did bookkeeping in the afternoons; they rented the truck farm to a Japanese strawberry grower, and Bill went to work as an electrician. Scraping and saving, Pat managed to go to Fullerton Junior College for a year and, while there, the especially pretty freshman starred in the school play.

BEHIND EVERY SUCCESSFUL PRESIDENT

When an elderly couple needed a driver, Pat got the job. She drove their Packard across the primitive highways of the early '30s to Connecticut—a one-way ticket out of Artesia (now Cerritos), California. In New York, Pat found work with her Aunt Kate, a nun who ran the X-ray lab and pharmacy at Seton, a hospital for terminal tuberculosis patients staffed by the Sisters of Charity. When her good looks won Pat a movie contest, she returned to California; Pat had decided neither to become a nun nor to marry the charming Irish chief of the medical staff at Seton. "I felt I had not lived yet."

In 1934, Pat entered the University of Southern California and proceeded to work her way through college. Brainy and industrious, she improved her secretarial skills, earned a teaching certificate, and worked as a research assistant in educational psychology. At the same time, growing self-confidence made her good looks marketable— Pat was getting bit parts in Hollywood and dazzling fashionable shoppers as a model at Bullock's Wilshire. But Pat made a choice: Movie-making struck her as boring and Hollywood meant that other people would control her; Pat wanted to be free. She became a schoolteacher at Whittier Union High School—the prettiest, the youngest, the liveliest of all the teachers in the conservative Quaker town. Pat relished close contact with her students, insisted on hard work from them, and delighted them with her bounding energy by sponsoring the Pep Committee.

At the urging of Whittier High's assistant superintendent, Pat tried out at the community theater for a role in the Woollcott and Kaufman melodrama, *The Dark Tower*. She got one of the leads, a "tall, dark, sullen beauty of 20, wearing a dress of great chic and an air of permanent resentment." Another member of the cast, Dick Nixon, played the smaller part of Barry Jones, a "faintly collegiate, eager, blushing youth of twenty-four."

Pat tells it this way: Dick fell in love with her on the night of the tryouts and told her, that very night, that he was going to marry her. The promising young lawyer uncontradictably and with the sure-footed self-assurance of a mountain goat climbing the Rockies reasoned his case with her for the next two years. She had other beaux, but the terms Dick offered seemed so romantic, so persuasive, so intensely tuned to her receptivity that "Miss Pat" finally stopped toying with him. For example, one night when she had barely eluded him by bolting the door and pretending not to be at home, he took their walk without her and then wrote:

> I took *the* walk tonight and it was swell because you were there all the time. Why?—because a star fell right in front of me, the wind blowing thru the tops of the palms making that strangely restless rustling, a train whistle sounded just as I got to the bridge. The Dipper was turned upside down right over where your house should be and was pouring down on you all the good things I've wished, looking up at it in the past. And because there was no moon, the sky was full of stars—every one filled with good wishes for you. Yes—I know I'm crazy and this is old stuff and that I don't take hints, but you see, Miss Pat, I like you!

There was no reason to doubt him, and Dick's offer to pour down on Pat all good things was the rainwater of affection her heart was thirsty for, after all those years of Santa Ana winds. And she had a lot to offer him: she had a "stubborn Irish" personality and years of inbred toughness; she had been a tomboy who wore jeans when girls didn't

BEHIND EVERY SUCCESSFUL PRESIDENT

wear jeans, and she had been a starlet, a model, and a heartthrob. She'd known how to "hook" her brother's bike or car when she needed wheels, and in New York she had sneaked out of the hospital where she worked to go on all-for-fun sledding expeditions with the patients. Now, she was eager to turn all that vitality towards building a happy family with Dick: "A woman must first and foremost be a homemaker."

During the War, both Pat and Dick worked for the Office of Price Administration in D.C., until Dick got bored and applied for active duty in the Navy. For a while, they carried on their newlywed love affair through the mails while Dick was in the South Pacific. After the war, Dick answered a newspaper ad placed by a Whittier Committee of 100 for "any young man . . . preferably a veteran, fair education, no political strings" to become the Republican candidate "picked" to unhorse the local liberal Congressman, Jerry Voorhis. Pregnant with their first child, Pat went along with Dick's excitement at his new career, and the "Pat and Dick team" was born. Some women (some men, too) give themselves up and go along. They begin to live their life through the other person's until they suffer what feels like a personality loss, the loss of the "irreducible me." Fresh, bright, open Pat Ryan began to get lost as she became reserved, tense Pat Nixon, the candidate's wife.

All the old hard-earned talents and persistence found a new use. Accomplished bookkeeper and stenographer, she became Dick's entire full-time campaign staff—the baby in one corner, stacks of the *Congressional Quarterly* in another, pounding a borrowed typewriter. She pounded the pavement, too, handing out campaign literature, and took in contributions "almost dollar by dollar." In 1946, a politically active wife-of-the-candidate was a novelty; so

Thelma Catherine "Pat" Ryan Nixon

the two together worked the constituency with special effectiveness. At Republican-sponsored coffee "klatches," the candidate would appear for half an hour, make a brief speech and answer questions, and then leave his wife to socialize with the ladies and win votes.

Pat got over her naive trust of politicians quickly. A man walked into their headquarters and requested one hundred of the four-page, illustrated pamphlets that introduced the candidate to the voters. Pat herself had bought those brochures dearly; she had paid for them by selling her third of the family farm at Artesia to her brother Tom—Pat's entire inheritance. But Pat intuited something about the man, and finally got the slippery Democrat to admit his Party loyalties. She refused to give him the pamphlets. That same week, Nixon headquarters was broken into and the remainder of their political pamphlets was stolen. That was only the first such experience to sour Pat Nixon on the scurvy side of politics. Years later, in the Watergate summer of '72, when President Nixon's men paid a return visit to the Democratic National Committee, Pat would remember the earlier break-in, which had gone unnoticed in the press, and comment acidly: "I wonder why it is played up so much. No one cared when it happened to us in '46!"

World War II had been a great equalizer for ordinary American women; thus, the "Pat and Dick team" had a fresh appeal for voters. That was at the public level; privately, a new reality had intruded on Pat's life that she could never cope with. She had wanted freedom, not to be controlled by others; now her husband's career, the opinions of his entourage, and the demands of his constituents all came before what Pat might want; and Dick's own arbitrary leadership also intruded upon their

BEHIND EVERY SUCCESSFUL PRESIDENT

marriage and denied Pat the private world she had wanted.

Politics, as far as Dick Nixon was concerned, was a dirty, hard-hitting, man's game. He listened to the game-plans laid out by his battle-wary professional advisors rather than to the wishes of his wife. The same persistence in him that had earlier won her romantic heart, now turned to climbing the political mountain. It would take Dick Nixon to the top; he assumed, correctly, that Pat would come along, too. But as she struggled beside him, Pat had to abide with what she did not like, always choosing to do rather than die.

Pat continued to be Dick's staunchest backer, his "Girl Friday"—homemaker, secretary, receptionist, business manager, and prettiest campaigner. In 1952, when Eisenhower left Nixon, his V-P candidate, dangling, Pat had to be Dick's defender and consolation, as well. The "Checkers speech"—an unprecedented nationwide, televised chat with the voting public—was forced on Nixon to clear up charges about the sources and uses of his political expense fund. (Checkers was a dog the Nixons had been given by a supporter, a political gift they refused to give up.) Before, during, and after the telecast, Pat stood by her man.

Overwhelmed by despair just as the cameras were aimed at him, Dick heard his voice break and felt he could not go on. "Of course you can," Pat told him matter-of-factly. She took his hand, and they walked on stage together. During the broadcast, while Dick explained himself, Pat sat perfectly still, absorbed and interested in what her husband was saying, unflinching. Taking a dig at the Democrats and the scandal of a $9,000 fur coat recently given to a White House secretary, Dick referred to his wife sitting on the couch behind him: "Pat doesn't have a mink coat. But she does have a respectable Republican cloth coat." It was the nation's first approving look at "perfect Pat."

Although the camera panned on her only a few times, Pat's projection of utter loyalty lent credibility to the words being spoken. When it was over, Dick's off-timing had not allowed him to conclude his address as planned; he groaned to her that his talk had been a failure. Pat countered emphatically and buoyantly "Dick, I thought it was great." They had both played their parts to perfection.

During the address, Dick had referred to Pat as a "wonderful stenographer." In later speeches he would make more extensive use of her (and his daughters), as the pitch to women voters became an increasingly important move in the political game: "Whatever you think of me," he would say, "I'm sure you'll agree that Pat will make an excellent First Lady."

Earlier campaigns had hurt Pat, but 1952 permanently wounded her. A few years before, in the mudslinging with Helen Gahagan Douglas, Dick had called his opponent a "Pink Lady"—fighting words in days when to be suspected of being a pinko, a Commie, or a dupe was like having political TB. Mrs. Douglas reciprocated with equal amounts of Red-baiting and by calling Nixon "tricky Dick" —a label that would stick. Pat habitually took the slurs personally. But, when Eisenhower did not immediately embrace Dick over the Checkers speech, Pat's Irish temper was set to boiling: "What more does that man want!" Four years later, when Ike again proved to be a less reliable political partner than he had been a general, repeating his lack of performance by being slow to intercept a "Dump Nixon" movement within the GOP, Pat was again angered and humiliated. Her privacy had been violated, their personal finances had been exposed before the nation under the glaring lights of a television studio, their integrity had been questioned, and Dick's running mate was less politically loyal to him than his life's mate. Moreover, the other Party was as culpable, if not more so, than the Republicans.

Whatever was left of Pat's illusions about politics was swept away entirely with their marginal defeat in 1960 by the Kennedy/Johnson ticket. Pat was convinced that the election had been stolen by fast dealing in Johnson's Texas and the conniving Democrats' machine under Chicago's Mayor Daley. Politics is crooked, and Pat was delighted through and through to be out of it, as she hoped, forever.

Once again, in 1960, Pat had taken the defeat personally, and she dished out her hot resentment with a classic serving of cold shoulder. During that one brief unshining moment when Pat and Jackie Kennedy were sitting on a couch together waiting for JFK's Inauguration, Pat snubbed Jackie by turning and talking to someone else. (Later on, when the Nixons were in the White House, Pat's resentment of the Kennedys—people who had "had it easy" —would still itch: Pat had the White House usher remove Jackie's memorial plaque to Jack from the Lincoln bedroom.) Then Pat, defeated, went back to gardening and entertaining friends in the cherished privacy of her home; she was a relaxed, warm, and happy person again.

Political life, Pat had learned from the start, imposes unpleasant constraints. Pat had not chosen the limits to her freedom, the curbs on her energetic spontaneity. Nor did she expect chilliness in her relationship with Dick—he seemed casually to accept it as the affordable price to be paid for fame and power. The intrusion of politics between herself and Dick was, perhaps, the worst disappointment of all. Pat had learned not from Dick himself but by watching

Thelma Catherine "Pat" Ryan Nixon

TV in the mid-1950s that her husband had accepted the nomination to run for the Vice Presidency. So unhappy was she with her unchosen lot, Pat required and received from Dick a written promise that he would not run again; but, as with other pledges, it was forgotten.

The turmoil of politics kept Pat, placid on the outside, churning within. The close wins and losses, which seemed to be the rule for their campaigns, tied her stomach in knots and made her vomit. Pat turned in upon herself and Dick turned out and away from her. Essentially a private person, Pat refused to make speeches, hated giving interviews, kept no diaries for posterity, and would have preferred being a gardener to being a First Lady. When Dick decided to make his political comeback in 1968, he did so—as their daughters Tricia and Julie knew, and as Julie wrote in her diary at the time—against Pat's wishes, though with her stoic resignation. Friendly, sunny, outgoing, approachable Pat Ryan, after two decades of being Dick's political wife, became uptight, frosty, noncommunicative Pat Nixon. After they had reached the White House, close associates worried that the consummate politician was too distant a husband. He never talked about her to others, unless he was making political mileage; he would ignore her in public and leave her unattended in situations requiring his attentions. If he loved her, he did not let it show. White House help gossiped that they had overheard Pat charge Dick: "You have ruined my life."

One of the most painful demonstrations of the distance between them took place in public view before a televised performance of the Grand Ol' Opry. It was the eve of St. Patrick's Day, 1974, and the President and Mrs. Nixon paid a visit to the Opry. The Blue Grass band rendered "Hail to the Chief" with a hillbilly beat, and Roy Acuff called on the

BEHIND EVERY SUCCESSFUL PRESIDENT

audience to sing "Happy Birthday" to Mrs. Nixon—if the President would accompany them on the piano. Pat, seated, smiled and waved her acceptance of the roaring tribute; then, she stood and walked across the stage, her arms outstretched to Dick for a birthday hug. Dick, preoccupied with political presence, turned away from his wife, engaged Cousin Roy in an infamous bit of banter about a yo-yo that happened to be handy. Pat dropped her arms to her sides and went back to her seat, embarrassed, and watched Dick play with his yo-yo. It was incongruous compared to her support of him during the Checkers' speech.

Whatever was true of the married couple in private, in public Pat never wavered as Dick's number-one supporter and traditional spouse: "A man has a right to make his own decision about his career and a woman should support that decision."

From the first campaign in California to the resignation after Watergate, Pat willingly chose to go along with Dick in the conventional role of supportive wife, being submissive to him in every way. Then, to protect herself and her submerged feelings, Pat Ryan, the pretty but tough starlet from Artesia, became perfect Pat Nixon, the model candidate's wife. Not a hair out of place, always meticulously attired, the visible ideal of conservative housewifeliness and motherhood. Some said she looked like a wind-up plastic doll, a robot, too mechanically perfect, that her "greatest fault is faultlessness." Some of her comments sounded as unreal as she sometimes looked: "We've never quarreled. Dick and I are too much alike. We don't ever differ in our opinions."

Thelma Catherine "Pat" Ryan Nixon

And only in the later days did she herself tamper with the pluperfect image. Pat finally got tired of the attention she had attracted to herself. Once, she declined to be photographed in a domestic setting, saying: "I think we've had enough of this kitchen thing, don't you?"

Dick dedicated his book *Six Crises* (1962) with good literal intentions but with a tin ear to the music of language. "To Pat," he wrote. "She also ran." An "also ran" is a horse that comes in second or worse. Pat Nixon, however, paid a high price to achieve her husband's political success for him. Where she had control, he did not fail.

Henry Kissinger, Nixon's Secretary of State, in a passage even more purple with male chauvinism and with similar good intentions praised Pat as "a silent patriot" and "a loyal and uninterfering female in [the] man's world of politics, speaking only when spoken to, and not sullying the cigar smoke with her personal opinions." Kissinger was referring to Pat's self-imposed policy: "I never discuss politics."

As wife of the Vice President for eight years, Pat accompanied Dick on six major goodwill tours around the world. Even Eisenhower, who thought that women in public should behave like Mamie, acknowledged Pat's usefulness and told Dick to be sure to "take Pat." Nixon conceded that his wife's presence on these trips was as important as his own.

In Venezuela and under threat of assassination, Pat and Dick coolly confronted anti-American revolutionary mob action—tear gas and spit, baseball bats and rocks bashing in the windows of their limousines. Pat ignored the onslaught and stopped to hug a child who had given her some flowers. She leaned across a barricade to shake hands with a young woman who had just cursed and spit at her.

BEHIND EVERY SUCCESSFUL PRESIDENT

The girl turned away in shame, her eyes full of tears. Spittle and tobacco falling from balconies above them were like rain from a clear sky, streaking Pat's new red dress with brown. When the driver of Pat's limousine started the engine again, he had to use the windshield wipers to be able to see through the saliva. Safely away from the near-lynch scene and out of Venezuela, the Nixon party arrived in Puerto Rico, and Pat heard music issuing from their hotel. Harsh reality now out of mind, Pat was ready to enjoy the pleasant reality of a new situation. "Let's go dancing!" suggested Pat to the shaken entourage.

Dick had resolved to reinvent the Vice Presidency as something useful, which, with Pat's help, he did. Later, as First Lady, sometimes on solo missions, Pat's capacity to charm world leaders—her "personal diplomacy," she called it—continued to be a notable strength of the Nixon Presidency. Whether as political campaigner or official representative of the United States government, Pat Nixon on the road both fulfilled the image of herself that she had flawlessly projected and accomplished the purposes of statecraft.

The Republican National Committee/Women's Division responded to Pat's singular political talent during the unsuccessful 1960 campaign by proclaiming "Pat Week." They sent Pat around to contact as many precinct workers and dwellers in neighborhoods as she could greet, dispensed "Pat for First Lady" buttons, and heralded her advance with this news release: "When you elect a President, you are also electing a First Lady whose job is more than glamour. The First Lady has a working assignment. She represents America to all the world. Pat Nixon is part of the experienced Nixon team. She's uniquely qualified for the position of First Lady."

Thelma Catherine "Pat" Ryan Nixon

Pat, however, felt uncomfortable with this mass marketing of a style that she felt was individual to herself and personal. Although she went along with the week's work—inveterate campaigner that she was—Pat was embarrassed. The nation was electing a President, she reasoned, not a First Lady. Nevertheless, after Dick had won the Presidency, Pat—unintentionally—changed the office of the First Lady as substantially as Dick had revised the Vice Presidency. A "new Pat" expanded into the new role, and the old spunky, independent Pat Ryan surfaced again. The lady who had said she would never wear pants in public, because her husband disapproved of them, appeared in a national magazine wearing pants. On abortion, First Lady Pat—contrary to President Dick's expressed opinion—said: "I think abortion should be a personal decision." On women as political candidates, the Pat Nixon who "did not discuss politics" said: "I would campaign for women candidates, even if they were not Republicans. I've always believed in supporting the person, not the Party."

In Vietnam, she was the first First Lady ever to visit a combat zone. In Panama, she was the first U.S. dignitary ever to visit a leper colony. In Peru, she flew precariously into an Andean earthquake devastation area to spearhead relief efforts. In America, she confronted bellicose peace demonstrators during the Vietnam era. Pat picked up what looked like a piece of confetti thrown during a demonstration and read the message written on it for her: "If this were napalm, you'd be dead."

Pat braved it all with utter cool, and wherever she went, Pat hugged the children, visited the hospitals and orphanages, and reached out one-on-one to as many people as she could touch. The alleged wax doll was immensely popular and totally and tirelessly accessible to tens of thousands, one human being at a time. "I think she is put together with iron and courage, not skin and bones," said one close associate.

Not everyone saw Pat in a positive way. Dick's own hard-nosed, male-chauvinistic Presidential advisors—particularly H. R. Haldeman and John Ehrlichman, who kept their eyes more on the popularity polls than on the people behind statistics—failed to recognize Pat's unique contribution to the Nixon Administration and did what they could to undercut her, estrange the First Lady's staff from White House power, and generally keep her "quiet and out of sight." Haldeman called her "Thelma" behind her back. When Pat returned from a particularly significant solo expedition to Africa, however, Charles Colson belatedly "discovered" her effectiveness, and wrote in a memo to the President:

> As you know we have tried for three years to project "color" about you, to portray the human side of the President. . . . Mrs. Nixon has now broken through where we have failed. She has come across as a warm, charming, graceful, concerned, articulate, and most importantly, a very human person. People, men and women—identify with her—and in return with you.

One of Republican Pat's special talents was the pure democracy of her entertainment policy at the White House. She invited the public to tea by the tens of thousands at an average rate of 26,000 per year. She invited 225 elderly from the District's nursing homes to Thanksgiving dinner at the White House. Pat hostessed the largest dinner ever given at the White House, and the Executive Mansion entire, from the public rooms downstairs to the living quarters upstairs, made welcome more than 600 Vietnam POWs and their families. Irving Berlin led everyone in singing "God Bless America." The Nixons retired between midnight and one a.m.—Dick was agonizing over whether or not to resign as a result of the Watergate affair—but the dancing went on till dawn. Not since the days of Andrew Jackson had the White House doors and its rugs and furniture been thrown open to so many.

Pat's foreign travels particularly favored the hundreds of American Foreign Service wives; but she also welcomed women of the Appalachian Fireside Crafts group, who brought Mrs. Nixon a cherry-tree quilt. The impoverished, timid hill people were so awestruck at meeting the First Lady, many of them were weeping. Without a word, Pat went gently from woman to woman, giving each a big hug, easing their tension. The tears began to flow, instead, from the eyes of Pat's staff.

Pat's staff commented on her way with people. Penny Adams, who was with her for four and one-half years, said that Pat was "a great equalizer," who "showed interest in everyone she met and found something special in each. We all want to be loved and that's what she looked for." People never felt she was two-faced, waiting for the cameras to turn on, and then turning it off when off-camera. She was always Pat Nixon, always herself. First Ladies have been expected to develop a "project," and Pat was criticized for lacking one. Pat announced before the election that she would foster adult education and job training. Then, a brief trip to the West Coast in 1969 after the Inauguration was headlined as showing her interest in volunteerism—a Republican virtue intended to take the place of more Social Democratic government efforts. After that, she tried fostering a "Right to Read" program; and later she talked

BEHIND EVERY SUCCESSFUL PRESIDENT

about moving into the "environment field." When that proved as fruitless as all the rest, she proposed a new, even more amorphous project, to "improve the quality of life." Pat Nixon was no more a champion of public causes and pet projects than she was a TV star or leader of the masses. First Ladyship for Pat Nixon was not a planned, programmed exercise of public office, but the expression of one woman's natural ability at reaching toward individual people. But rarely did Pat pour her sea of personal feelings into the dry words of a statement that might almost sound like a policy: "Get involved," she said. "Instead of complaining, go to work. People should participate in local political groups. Each community has some kind of organization in which it is possible to become active. Work for a candidate whom you believe to be qualified—they are the ones who can take a problem to the top."

When Coral Schmidt was leaving the First Lady's staff, she wrote a farewell letter to Pat, reflecting on the lack of a "project" and commenting on two of Pat's policies: her refusal to allow any of her guests to be rushed through a receiving line with a perfunctory touch of the fingertips, and her exhausting policy of answering every letter as personally, specifically, and helpfully as she could, signing each reply in her own hand.

Sometimes Pat's "personal diplomacy" gave the Secret Service guards fits; sometimes the results were funny, and inevitably humane. During the first Legacy of Parks trip (the Nixon Administration turned 50,000 acres of Federal land over to the States to become parks), Pat presided at a ceremony on the border between Mexico and California at Border Field. She could see the hundreds of Mexicans standing just feet away on their side of the border behind a barbed-wire fence. During her speech, she paused, ordered the fence separating Mexico and the United States cut, then continued, stating that no fence was needed to "separate the people of two such friendly nations." Over the protests of her guards, Pat and her entourage moved easily among the Mexicans at the conclusion of the ceremony, clasping hands, signing autographs, hugging kids.

Once, when some of the many disabled "poster" children were visiting the White House, one little boy challenged Pat, stating that this was not her house. When she asked him why he thought that, he swallowed his terror and replied: "Because I don't see your washing machine." Pat put the official proceedings on hold, took him by the hand and up the elevator to the third floor, down the red-carpeted hall to the laundry room and showed him her washing machine, proving to him that it really was her house. He came back happy; his parents told Pat it was the first time he had ever gone anywhere with a stranger.

After the Nixons' return from China—and the opening of relations between the United States and the Peoples' Republic of China, arguably the most significant achievement of the Nixon Administration—an editorial writer for *Chicago Today* (February 24, 1972) correctly formulated the importance of Pat's contribution to foreign policy and world peace:

> We are starting to wonder whether future historians . . . won't take the view that the President talked business and politics with Chinese leaders while his wife did the important work. Mrs. Nixon's presence in Peking and her unfailingly warm, gracious conduct are accomplishing something that official discussions, important as they are, cannot do. She is establishing direct and friendly conduct with the Chinese people on a normal human level; the level where children and

BEHIND EVERY SUCCESSFUL PRESIDENT

families and food and service and health are the most important things. As, indeed, they are.

Pat's personal touch was not always in the realm of invisible human relations, however. It was Pat's idea to illuminate the White House at night, like the other public buildings of Washington, an improvement she ordered on the sly as a surprise for Dick. More significantly, Pat continued, without fanfare, the restoration of the White House begun by Jackie Kennedy. Pat added more than five hundred period pieces to the collection. At the beginning of Nixon's Administration, approximately one-third of the Mansion's furnishings were authentic and historic; at the end, about two-thirds were, including Gilbert Stuart's portrait of Dolly Madison, which Pat hung in Dolly's sitting room, redecorated in Dolly red. But when time came to show the nation her accomplishments, daughter Tricia, not private Pat, became the TV personality for the night and conducted the televised tour of the Mansion.

Pat tried unsuccessfully on one substantial issue in particular to advise Dick Presidentially: appointment of a female Justice to the Supreme Court. In an uncharacteristic moment of candor with the media, Pat commented: "Don't you worry; I'm talking it up. . . . If we can't get a woman on the Supreme Court this time, there'll be a next time." Dick took a halfhearted look, but he and Attorney General John Mitchell could find no female nominee who had both enough judicial experience and was conservative enough to suit them. As Dick's controversial male picks, Powell and Rehnquist, wrestled the Senate for approval, dinner upstairs at the White House became a little tense. Pat urged her reasons, again, for a woman nominee. Dick—as Julie remembered—"with exaggerated weariness finally cut off the conversation: 'We tried to do the best we could, Pat.'"

Thelma Catherine "Pat" Ryan Nixon

The Watergate debacle tried Pat's Presidential mettle but also availed her the opportunity to make perfectly clear what she meant by a wife's standing by her husband. As the pressures mounted and Dick became more distant, Pat kept giving him the companionship and attention he appeared not to need and to which he seemed callously indifferent. And when it was over, she would have the resilience to get her family packed and out of the White House in two days; and after that, she would keep pouring out the affection and encouragement that kept Dick from sinking irretrievably into depression.

Pat had not liked Dick's band of Watergate advisors from the outset and had said so; she saw what the nation was seeing—more and more power vested in a handful of men surrounding the President and his loss of direct involvement in matters for which he was held responsible. As the scandal exploded, Pat, like Dick, blamed the prying press. Pat had always taken political slurs to heart, and she had never sought an open relationship with the hardcore press corps. Even more, she was offended at the hypocrisy of the Democrats—posturing as though they had never pulled the same shenanigans in the nasty game of politics.

Pat started keeping a clippings file on the history of bugging. She filled it with tidbits about LBJ and Bobby Kennedy, articles with headlines like this: "The peacetime Kennedy Administration had tapped more wires than the wartime Nixon Administration," and comments like John Roosevelt's about Franklin: "Hell, my father just about invented bugging. He had them spread all over, and thought nothing of it."

Dick, as usual, did not consult Pat about what to do. If he had, she would have offered him (according to Julie) the politically sound—if ethically questionable—advice of burning all the tapes while they were still his private diary and before they became public property.

Pat kept steady, her loyalty to Dick never wavering in her conviction that Watergate was a political witch-hunt rather than a matter of principle, and keeping herself busy with her own responsibilities while finding relaxation in quiet walks. The last family photograph in the White House before Dick's resignation shows a six-way hug and everybody seems to be laughing: "Our hearts were breaking and there we are smiling."

After the White House, the Nixons retired to San Clemente, their home on the California beach where Dick had proposed to Pat. Relieved to have regained her privacy, Pat resolved never again to grant an interview; she turned down almost every social invitation for years, turning instead to gardening (and reading) to let her soul heal.

Fifteen members of Dick's staff went to prison over Watergate; now, Dick watched the sea off San Clemente. Pat, the recluse, wrote to Julie about "two broken people here." Despairing, Pat let her feelings out a little: "Dick, I don't know how you keep going." He replied. "I just get up in the morning to confound my enemies."

After President Ford's summary pardon "for all offenses against the United States that he, Richard Nixon, has committed or may have committed . . ."—Dick called it "the saddest, most humiliating day of my life"—blood clots in his legs began to move towards his vital organs and Dick nearly died. As ever, Pat toughed it out beside him. And then, her turn for devastating illness came.

Revolutionary sticks and stones had not broken Pat's bones in Venezuela, but names had always hurt her. Dick was never impeached in Congress, but Pat was found guilty by the media of being, among other things, a lush. After the pressures of Watergate and after, the Nixons' marital numbness, new humiliation piled on Dick when the New York State Bar disbarred him, and Pat's years of having suppressed it all with too tight a clamp on herself—caused Pat's blood pressure to blow the top off. She had a stroke that left her partially paralyzed.

Pat made it back to health enough to be able to enjoy her grandchildren and her gardening. While she was in the hospital, she received an outburst of loving support from the nation—and thousands of messages and dozens of floral bouquets arrived daily for a week, more than a quarter-million get-well wishes in all. This rich resource, Presidential Pat viewed as a window of opportunity for continued "personal diplomacy." Each day, in spite of the stroke and her fatigue, she administrated the redistribution of flowers among the hospital's other patients.

Claudia Alta "Lady Bird" Taylor Johnson

Lady Bird, the Self-Improved

"IT ALL began so beautifully. After a drizzle in the morning, the sun came out bright and clear. We were driving into Dallas. In the lead car were President and Mrs. Kennedy, John and Nellie Connally, a Secret Service car full of men, and then our car with Lyndon and me and Senator Ralph Yarborough. . . ."

"Beautiful" was a big word in Lady Bird Johnson's vocabulary. It was the right word against which to contrast the rest of an ugly day, November 22, 1963. Lady Bird—born Claudia Alta Taylor on December 22, 1912—the diarist of the White House, went on to describe the assassination of President Kennedy and the events that moved her husband Lyndon into the Presidency and herself into the First Ladyship: ". . . a sharp, loud report. It sounded like a shot. . . . Have they shot the President? No, it can't be!"

In the hospital hallway, she put her arms around Jackie Kennedy, her own feelings too much a tumult to speak words of comfort to the younger woman. She hugged Nellie

Claudia Alta "Lady Bird" Taylor Johnson

Connally, too—the Governor was going to be all right.

At the Dallas airport awaiting takeoff, she wrote: "There, in the very narrow confines of the plane—with Jackie standing by Lyndon, her hair falling in her face but very composed, with me beside him, Judge [Sarah] Hughes in front of him, and a cluster of Secret Service people, staff, and Congressmen we had known for a long time around him—Lyndon took the oath of office."

During the flight to Washington, everyone was silent, "each sitting with his own thoughts." On the day of the funeral, Lady Bird told Nellie Connally: "I feel like I am suddenly on stage for a part I never rehearsed."

Minnie Lee Patillo Taylor's baby was a girl; but she wanted to name it after her brother Claude, so they called her Claudia. Then, when Miz. Alice Tittle, the lady who worked for Minnie and would be the child's sometimes mammy, looked at that baby, she exclaimed: "Lord, the child's as pretty as a ladybird!" Everybody loves ladybirds, those little red and black polka-dotted friendly bugs that gardeners welcome among their roses to ride herd on the aphids. Beauty is what Lady Bird would finally be all about; and meanwhile the nickname would stick: somebody carved it in big square letters across the back of the little girl's wooden highchair—LADYBIRD.

Minnie Taylor, an aristocratic descendant of early Spanish settlers, loved all things beautiful. Every winter, she traveled up to Chicago for the opera season, and she owned a collection of classical music on phonograph records. She also had her own library of beautifully bound books—Greek and Roman myths, poetry of all kinds, *Ben-Hur*, German legends—all of which she read to her daughter.

Lady Bird remembered: "Siegfried was the first person I was in love with."

Minnie was not one of those Southern Gothic ghosts flitting about her big old house inside a Faulkner novel. She had broken with tradition first of all by marrying "down"— Minnie had loved a redneck. Then, she sent her two boys back East to New York boarding schools. What was more, she came out in favor of women's suffrage, she rolled up her sleeves and went to work on behalf of the poor people of color around Karnack, and—maybe worst of all—she became a vegetarian and refused to eat meat: bumper stickers a generation later would proclaim that "Texans eat beef every day." Minnie Lee Patillo Taylor was somebody special. Then, when Lady Bird was only five years old, Minnie took a bad fall and died.

"T. J. Taylor—Dealer in Everything"—that is what the sign said outside Lady Bird's daddy's general store and cotton gin at Karnack in deep East Texas. The T. J. stood for Thomas Jefferson. He "never talked about anything but making money," said Lady Bird; and some said he was ruthless in its pursuit. He was tall, fat, loudmouthed, and hardworking. He stayed in the store or at the gin at night till nobody else wanted to do any more business, and then he went home to his bookkeeping. He loaned money at usurious rates to the black folk, and then foreclosed on them when they failed to pay. Over a lifetime, T. J. pieced together for himself and his heirs a plantation in excess of 18,000 acres. People called him "Mister Boss," and he lived in a white antebellum mansion called "Brick House." It had classic Greek columns across the front, and had got its name because it was the only brick house for miles around; it was also the first to have electricity and indoor plumbing. T. J., a likely character for a Faulkner novel, was the fulfillment

Claudia Alta "Lady Bird" Taylor Johnson

of the saying that Confederate money had been worth saving after all.

When T. J.'s wife died, he sent his daughter to live part of the time with her Aunt Effie in Alabama. Effie was a gentle soul in poor health, but a lady in love with life; and she, as Lady Bird said, would "read to me as long as her eyes held out. And then later on, I read to her." Aunt Effie taught Lady Bird to love nature: "She opened my spirit to beauty." However, Bird regretted that Aunt Effie did not teach her how to dress or dance or choose one's friends or get along with boys. Indirectly, Aunt Effie did teach Lady Bird to be strong: "I saw how inhibiting it was to her life to be so weak and full of illnesses, and so I set my sights on being more like my father, who was one of the most physically strong people I have ever known."

Bird grew up in a world of books, her own imagination, and the primal beauty of East Texas' Big Thicket. She tolerated playmates, rather than seeking them—Bird preferred boating alone along the mossy bayous of Lake Caddo, looking at the wildflowers, "When the first [daffodil] bloomed, I'd have a little ceremony, all by myself, and name it the queen." Half a century later, she would still be thinking about the Spanish moss that hangs down the trees, and remember watching alligators slither along muddy banks.

A thoughtful girl, and more than a little bit shy, Lady Bird did not appear at first to be smarter than other girls, but in Marshall High School—which she entered at age 13 and graduated from at 15—she proved that she was smarter than most. When it seemed that shy Bird was going to be either valedictorian or salutatorian, she prayed either for low grades or smallpox, so she would not have to make a commencement speech. Lady Bird's prayer was answered:

BEHIND EVERY SUCCESSFUL PRESIDENT

she came in third.

Claudia was growing up into a fine-looking woman, but she was never a belle; she thought her beak was too hooked. At high-school dances, she was a wallflower, and she was not accepted into the "in" clique: "I was still in socks when all the other girls were wearing stockings." A handsome fellow on the football team started paying attention to her, but Lady Bird would leave the room when she saw him coming. Otherwise, like Aunt Effie, she was friendly and good-natured and cultured; and, like T. J., she excelled at stick-to-it-iveness.

In Austin, as a coed at the University of Texas, Bird still was not much of a looker. T. J. had given her an unlimited charge account at Neiman-Marcus in Dallas while she was attending St. Mary's Episcopal Girls' School, and now she had her own permanently stocked checking account in Austin; but Bird was not much of a dresser, either. She preferred not to spend money foolishly. She dated little, but was popular with the other girls—having her own Buick to drive around, and plenty of gas money during the Depression. The couple of Longhorns she did date remembered Claudia as determined, ambitious, and able-minded. Behind that bashful exterior was a desire to excel, the capacity to get her own way (in a ladylike manner, of course), and the patience to find a man strong enough to be her equal.

Lady Bird decided to improve herself, and took aim at her backwardness. She became a reporter for the *Daily Texan* so she would have to learn to speak up. She took shorthand and typing—"the tools that can get you inside the door." She studied hard, and graduated "with honors," taking her first degree in Primary Education, and her second in Journalism. She thought that "with a little skill and a

Claudia Alta "Lady Bird" Taylor Johnson

great deal of industry," she could "take over the business—or else marry the boss." As it turned out, Bird did both.

Lyndon Johnson asked Lady Bird to go out with him the first time while he was on his way to pick up some other girl for a date. She turned him down, and that was Day One.

It was August 1934, and they were in the Capitol building in Austin, where Bird had dropped by to visit her best friend Eugenia ("Gene") Boehringer. Gene had tried earlier to get Bird and Lyndon together, suggesting that Bird call on the go-getter of a secretary to Congressman Richard Kleburg when she went for a visit to Washington; but Bird was too shy for anything like that. On this day, LBJ happened to be visiting in Gene's office; so, when Lady Bird chanced to walk in, Gene took another shot: "Oh, Lady Bird, here he is at last. Now I'm going to make sure you-all get together!"

Lady Bird was impressed: he was "terribly, terribly interesting" and "very good-looking, with lots of black wavy hair, and the most outspoken, straightforward, determined manner I had ever encountered. . . . I knew I had met something remarkable, but I didn't quite know what."

On the morning of Day Two, right at breakfast time, Bird just happened to be walking past the Hotel Driskill coffee shop, which just happened to be where and when Lyndon had said he would be, and he just happened to see her through the window, and she just happened to see him. He jumped up and started waving and hollering: "He just flagged me down. So I went in." Later on, Bird said she had had a "queer sort of moth-in-the-flame feeling" about her "remarkable man."

After breakfast, he took her for a lickety-split ride in

his Ford roadster. A mile a minute, he questioned her about herself; "he really wanted to find out all about me." Then, he careened from true confessions about himself to answering questions that had not been asked, car speeding, tongue tied in the middle and loose at both ends, overwhelming Lady Bird with information about his ambitions, his work for Congressman Kleberg, his salary, his family, his insurance policy, "all sorts of things." She thought him "extraordinarily direct."

On Day Three: he asked her to marry him. "I thought it was some kind of joke," she said, or "sheer lunacy."

On Day Four, he drove her down to San Marcos to meet his parents: a good meeting.

In the days that followed, Lyndon—still driving and talking to beat 60 the whole way—drove Bird to South Texas to meet the Klebergs, the cattle barons of the King Ranch and Lyndon's political bosses: another good meeting. When the time came for Lyndon to drive back to Washington, Bird rode with him as far as Karnack. The strong man who had raised a strong daughter, ol' man T. J. Taylor, sized Lyndon up. The younger man was taller than the older man, tallness being a matter of some importance to a Texan. After supper, T. J. told Bird: "Daughter, you've been bringing home a lot of boys up till now. This time, you've brought a man."

Even so, cautious Lady Bird still did not say yes—but she did kiss him good-bye. From D.C., Lyndon kept the heat up under his pressure-cooker courtship, promising anything, everything, to persuade her: "Every interesting place I see," he wrote, "I make a mental reservation [sic!] and tell myself that I shall take you there when you are mine." He got his friends to help him spell his letters correctly, telling them: "You know, Bird's got a journalism degree." He sent her his picture: "For Bird, a lovely girl with ideals, principles, intelligence, and refinement, from her sincere admirer, Lyndon." He phoned her nearly every day.

She wrote him back cozy letters, "thinking about getting engaged," talking about being "together" and reading books to him: "All good things are better shared, aren't they?"—She wasn't quite up to the speed that Lyndon had in mind to go.

Lady Bird got out her *Book of Common Prayer* and read the wedding ceremony. It reads like a contract, she noticed, and that set her to thinking: "My gosh . . . what if I had married one of those boys? That would have been disaster." When Bird did finally make up her mind to enter into contractual relations with Lyndon, it was a conscious "decision," that no matter how much she, or he, might change, she would go "forward with hope" and "promise to love" him "forever."

In late October, Lyndon was back in Texas. First stop: Karnack. He put it on the line: "Let's go out and get married, Bird, not next year . . . but about two weeks from now, a month from now, or right away!"

One of Bird's friends had counseled her to wait six months, and Bird wanted to talk things over first with Aunt Effie. So, while Lyndon barreled off down towards Kleburg country, Lady Bird made a pilgrimage to Alabama. Aunt Effie was more than cautious; she was ready to shift into reverse. But when Lady Bird got back to Karnack, T. J. blew away all of Effie's bothers: "If you wait until Aunt Effie is ready, you will never marry anyone . . . Some of the best deals are made in a hurry."

Bird was still stalling—wanted to talk it over with Gene; but Lyndon was not having any of that: "We either get married now or we never will. And if you say goodbye

BEHIND EVERY SUCCESSFUL PRESIDENT

to me, it just proves to me that you just don't love me enough to dare to."

She dared to, but cautiously. Bird allowed as how she had always dreamed of getting married in St. Mark's Episcopal Church in San Antonio. Taking that for a "yes," Lyndon let out a "Texas yip," and they were on their way to San Antonio. Bird said later that she did not "really say firmly 'yes' until that morning; Lyndon said he was still twisting her arm as they walked up the church steps on the afternoon of November 17th, 1934—three months after their first meeting. Without family or flowers, almost without a ring, they were wed. Inside the church, Lady Bird asked: "You did bring a wedding ring, didn't you?"

"I forgot!" cried Lyndon. A friend was dispatched and came back with a trayful of rings from Sears-and-Roebuck. Lady Bird picked one out, understood that it was to be a temporary ring for use in the ceremony only. It set Lyndon back $2.98.

The priest sighed his benediction, as the new Mr. and Mrs. Johnson roared off towards a honeymoon in Mexico: "I hope that marriage lasts!" (Thirty-six years later, when Lyndon asked Lady Bird why she had never upgraded her $2.98 ring, she replied: "I wanted to wait and see if the marriage would last.") Next morning, Bird telephoned Gene to say: "Lyndon and I committed matrimony last night."

The honeymoon ended, however, and the marriage started before they got across the border. Stopping in McAllen to see some friends, Lyndon noticed that Bird had snagged her nylons. "You've got to change your stockings, Bird," he said. "You've got a run." His saying that embarrassed Lady Bird, and she did not obey, immediately. Then Lyndon flat out ordered her—right in front of everybody—to go change her hose. Bird did as she was told.

Thereafter, whatever Lyndon said for her to do, Bird did; and her education stretched beyond nylons to politics. Soon after the wedding, Lyndon came home one day with a bunch of lists. "Bird, I want you to learn the names of all these counties," he told her. "These are the counties my boss, Congressman Kleberg, represents. These are county seats. These are the principal communities in each county, and one or two of the leaders in each. Whenever you travel around with me, when we get to this town, you want to know who Mr. Perry is . . ." and so forth and so on.

Setting up housekeeping in Washington, meeting the people, learning how to be the wife of a politician like Lyndon—Lady Bird's education advanced at the pace that Lyndon ran. She had married him in a rush, and now he took it for granted that she would do everything else he told her to do, and in a rush. He told her how to dress with better style and how to look good in her makeup; and if he did not like her look, he said so, in front of whoever happened to be listening. "I don't like muley-lookin' things," he told her.

Across a crowded roomful of expatriate Texans, he hollered at her: "Lady Bird, go get me another piece of pie!"

"I will, in just a minute, Lyndon," she replied compliantly.

"*Get me another piece of pie!*" he shouted at her.

Everybody else in the room felt sorry for Bird, but Lyndon got his pie, in a rush.

Bird told it on herself about some of Lyndon's other demands: "He early announced, 'I'd like to have [my breakfast] coffee in bed,' and I thought, 'What!?!? Me?!?!'" But Bird had a way of making any of Lyndon's demands seem reasonable: "I soon realized that it's less trouble serving someone that way [breakfast in bed] than by setting the table and all. . . ."

Moreover, she brought him the newspaper; laid out his clothes; properly filled each pocket with his pen, cigarettes, lighter (after making sure it was full of fluid), hanky, and money; and she shined his shoes. Lyndon was on his way up, and Bird understood her chores to be merely her part of their division of labor, a way of boosting busy Lyndon on up his ladder of ambition.

Friends wondered how Bird put up with it—Lyndon was rough as a cob to live with; and it made Bird unhappy, at times. On the day of FDR's funeral in 1945, when all of Washington lined the streets weeping to bid the chief farewell, Lyndon was so cast down that he took to his bed. Bird wanted to attend the funeral, but Lyndon browbeat her out of going. Timorous Bird failed that momentous day to walk the few blocks from their apartment alone to say good-bye to Franklin. She regretted having caved in. Later Bird would go ahead on her own when she knew she was right.

Virginia Foster Durr, a friend from the Johnsons' Congressional years, said that "Lyndon was wild about Bird and depended on her for everything. But you never heard Lyndon say it. Of course, he worked her to death! A lot of her women friends used to get mad at him. . . . He took her completely for granted, and he expected her to devote every waking hour to him, which she did. I don't know how she lived through it."

Any time spent feeling sorry for Lady Bird, however, was time misspent. Being raised by T. J. Taylor had naturally taught Lady Bird to like the kind of man that Lyndon was. Lady Bird was that unusual kind of unflappable person who could take the curves at any speed Lyndon cared to drive, and keep on smiling. After she worked in his congressional office for a while, Bird performed her special services for Lyndon even more wholeheartedly—the first-hand experience helped her, she said, to understand impatient Lyndon's "unnecessary irritations." Besides, Bird was getting something out of being married to Lyndon that she both needed and wanted: self-improvement.

Lyndon's effect on Lady Bird was to blast her out of that bashfulness from which she had always suffered. He improved on her good looks by getting her to bob her hair and wear high heels and bright colors. Lyndon did for Bird what Aunt Effie had failed to do: he taught her something about "dramatic style," the "art of clothing," and how she could show off her figure to best advantage. He lectured her: "You don't sell for what you're worth unless you look well."

Bird would placidly say: "Lyndon is the kind of man who stretches you. He always expects more of you than you're really mentally or physically capable of putting out. Somehow that makes you try a little bit harder, and makes you produce a little more. It is a very good fertilizer for growth; it's also very tiring." A desire for self-improvement came naturally to Lady Bird; however impatiently Lyndon made his demands, Lady Bird accepted them with patient composure as being for her own good.

Much later, after they were in the White House, Lyndon might still correct Bird in public, sometimes gently, other times less so. Once when she was late for a ceremony in the Rose Garden, he scolded her and told her not to let it happen again. In her diary, the First Lady called it a "measured admonishment" from a "dear man" who had stayed up all night wrestling with hard problems.

Harry McPherson, special assistant to the President, told a tale similar to the nylon stockings incident:

We'd be in a meeting—it might include the chairman of the Joint Chiefs and the Secretary of State and a couple of staff people from the White House—and in the midst of a very intense conversation on issues, interrupted by phone calls and all that, she'd walk through. And he'd suddenly stop and say, "Come here." He'd look at her dress and say, "I don't like the yoke on the back of that dress. You were wearing a pink dress last Saturday that had the right kind of yoke for your neck and shoulders. Turn around. Let me see the back." It was very unfeigned, unforced. He really related to her, and that's rare in my experience among public men. He loved her very much. Needed her. Depended on her.

Lady Bird knew that Lyndon's heavy hand was merely his rough way of saying "I love you;" but she had more to put with in Lyndon than just his pickiness or working around his impatience. All those promises he had made during their courtship to take Bird to "interesting places" were now out the window. There were no cozy evenings together, reading Lady Bird's best-loved books, nor even the *Congressional Record*, for that matter. Lyndon took in information the same way he did everything else—on the run; so, if Bird wanted Lyndon to read something, she followed him around their apartment reading it at him, whether he would stand still or not. When she wanted to go to the theater, Lyndon rarely went with her; he would accompany her to the door, and then go to his office: Lyndon never stopped working. Lady Bird was left to discover Washington on her own.

Lady Bird never knew when Lyndon would be home for supper, or how many hungry constituents he would bring with him. One morning after they were in the White House, Lyndon said: "Bird, let's ask Congress over this afternoon!" Lady Bird learned to prepare "expandable" meals and to hold continual open house for Lyndon's political hangers-on. Aunt Effie had not taught Bird how to cook, either; so, ever ready for a little more self-improvement, Lady Bird bought a Fannie Farmer cookbook and soon learned to spread the table for all comers. For the Texans and favored others, Lady Bird cooked barbecue, black-eyed peas, cornbread, homemade peach ice cream, and hot chili. (Bird herself, being from East Texas, preferred pork chops and sweet potatoes to CenTex molten chili.) As the company would be leaving, Bird would add the final touch of friendship at the front door: "Y'all come back real soon, now, y'hear?"

Lady Bird's style of hospitality won Lyndon legions of supporters, and it was her good cooking, as much as anything else, that first attracted "Mr. Speaker" Sam Rayburn. Fellow Texan, political Titan, and Lyndon's mentor, friend, and lifelong ally, "Mr. Sam," a bachelor, said that marrying Lady Bird was the best thing Lyndon B. Johnson ever did.

Then, there was the question of other women. It is no secret that Lyndon, both early and late, loved the ladies; and it would be idle speculation to try to figure out which ones he loved more than others, for Lyndon loved them all. What's more, he liked to brag about it. Lyndon's beer-drinking buddies told lots of stories about him—and some he told on himself—about being in bed with lots of women. That "avalanche of a man" (as Press Secretary Jack Valenti called him) had a bucking bronco for a sense of humor and took a Texas-brags approach to improving on the truth. "The elemental leader, reeking of human juices" (as historian David Halberstam described Lyndon), would do more than just show you the scars from his latest operation;

BEHIND EVERY SUCCESSFUL PRESIDENT

he'd whip out ol' "Jumbo" and boast about what *he* could do. Of course, Lyndon was also a gentleman, and Lady Bird was a lady; so Lyndon didn't talk that way in front of Lady Bird in public. Whenever he did talk rough, she would smile patiently and look the other way.

Lady Bird knew how to pick up her heels and have a good time, too. According to Chief Usher West, the Johnsons were "the dancingest First Family" of all. Nevertheless, Lady Bird was more reserved than Lyndon was. He was called the "Dancing President" and the "Kissing President," and he called all the women "Honey," including Jackie Kennedy. More than once, especially after Lyndon would get a little tight, Lady Bird just had to keep on smiling and looking the other way, while Lyndon went feeling and fondling his way across the honky-tonk dance floor of the best little White House in Washington.

The question has to be raised: How could a well-bred Texas lady like Claudia Taylor stay married all those years to a side-winding big-nosed long-eared ornery sonofabitch like Lyndon B. Johnson? Partly, Lady Bird's ability derived from her having been brought up in the house of a man like T. J. Taylor. Partly, it was just Lady Bird's innate goodness of heart. As one of our Texas poets has put it, Lady Bird Johnson was "a good-hearted woman in love with a good-timin' man."

The one time that Lady Bird came anywhere close to commenting on Lyndon and his ladies was in answer to Barbara Walters during a television interview. Lady Bird harbored her fair share of unspoken resentments, but, being the consummate politician with sense enough to keep her mouth shut when opening it would only lose votes, she was measured in her reply. Lady Bird told Barbara: "You have to understand, my husband loved people. All people. Lyndon was a people lover, and that did not exclude half the people in the world—women. You don't think I could have kept my husband away from half the people? Oh, I think perhaps there was a time or two. . . ." Then she paused and regrouped: "If all those ladies had some good points that I didn't have, I hope I had the good sense to learn a little bit from it." Finally, looking on her past through moist eyes, she concluded: "He loved me. I know he only loved me."

Most of those other women meant very little to Lyndon—he loved Bird, first, last, and in between; and she always knew that. One way she knew it was because Lyndon eventually got around to being as blatant in his affection for Lady Bird as he was loud about everything else: "As a sweetheart, a swimmer, a rider, and a conversationalist, she is the most interesting woman I know," he bragged. Whenever he had to be away from home for any length of time, the pain of separation would make his reliance on her ever more clear: "It was more difficult to leave you last night than I had anticipated. I have learned to lean on you so much. . . . Never have I been so dependent on anyone—Never shall I expect so much of any other individual."

All the way through his career, when Lyndon would find himself between a rock and a hard place, he would stop and say to his associates: "Let's ask Lady Bird!" Liz Carpenter, Lady Bird's press secretary, talked about how people made snide comments when Lyndon entered a room and started smooching on Lady Bird in front of everybody. Lady Bird, said Liz, "adored Lyndon's intense masculinity."

Nevertheless, they both suffered through his affair of the heart with Alice Glass. Alice was the mistress of one of Lyndon's wealthiest backers, Charlie Marsh. Lyndon's case of true love for Alice showed in telltale ways: Alice could

BEHIND EVERY SUCCESSFUL PRESIDENT

get Lyndon to mind his table manners, and he would even sit still and listen to her read the poetry of Edna St. Vincent Millay. The clearest proof of Lyndon's tender affections was that he did not boast about how good Alice was in bed, like he did about his casual women. Although Lyndon would leave Lady Bird alone weekend after weekend to be with Alice, he kept his feelings for Alice zipped up tight as far as everyone else was concerned; no point in ruffling Charlie Marsh's feathers. Only Lady Bird and Alice really knew what Lyndon was up to.

Lyndon had a problem: he had a lady that he loved as a wife, and a woman that he loved as a lady; but he had a career in politics that he loved more than he loved either his woman or his wife. He thought about leaving Bird and marrying Alice; and if his career in politics would not have gone down a sinkhole of scandal, he might have done so. But Lyndon was a passionately singleminded man, and politics was his passion. Politics—and Lady Bird's supernatural self-control—saved her marriage with Lyndon.

Lady Bird had time, God, and politics on her side. Even if Lyndon was loco over Alice, she was, after all, merely the other woman, whereas Lady Bird was the wife. She had a signed contract with Lyndon right out of the *Book of Common Prayer*. Moreover, Mr. and Mrs. Johnson were meanwhile buying property together and had been setting up a good life; and Bird knew perfectly well that not blood but politics ran in Lyndon's veins: "You know something of my ambitions," he once had written to her. So, while Lyndon was whipped over Alice, Bird bided her time. She read books. Because Charlie Marsh was preoccupied with Hitler, she read *Mein Kampf*. All one especially hard summer long, she chewed her way through *War and Peace*—and then, when she'd finished it, she started reading it again. She practiced her Spanish and learned to do the twist. Along the way, she worked on slimming some of the dumpiness out of her figure. Lady Bird was a champion self-improver.

Some of their friends laughed at Bird for her try-harder efforts and said that she seemed "out of place" in Washington. But finally, Bird won them all over—and kept Lyndon for good measure—by being calm and gracious, self-disciplined and self-contained. When anyone would "try" to be nice to her, Bird would be genuinely nice to them right back. She would put on her unquenchable smile and every day, one foot in front of the other, she would just keep on keeping on; and in the end, Lyndon got over Alice.

The Johnsons' marriage was an unusual one, and Lady Bird was an unusual woman. More than one historian made the assertion—marvelous to tell about anyone who was important in Washington—that "she had no enemies." Some found her dull and pedestrian; some said her inevitable sweetness made their teeth hurt; and many deplored her seeming willingness to behave like Lyndon's doormat. But these external judgments did not penetrate to the heart either of the woman or the relationship.

Jackie Kennedy's infamous dictum—that "Lady Bird would crawl up Pennsylvania Avenue on her hands and knees over broken glass for Lyndon" (or, in the other version, run down the same thoroughfare stark naked)—was not entirely wrong. Bird might well have done it, had she thought it would contribute to Lyndon's political stature and her own self-improvement. Alice Roosevelt Longworth hit even closer to the mark than Jackie: asked who in her time had been the best First Lady, Princess Alice replied without hesitation: "Why Lady Bird Johnson, of course. And what's more, she is *such fun!*"

She could confront her husband, when necessary. Once when Lady Bird had found just the house in Washington that she wanted to buy, she rushed in to tell Lyndon about it. He was talking politics with John Connally, and, when Lady Bird interrupted, Lyndon listened, said nothing, then went back to talking politics. But that wasn't good enough for Lady Bird: "I want the house!" she trumped in. "Every woman wants a home of her own, and all I have to look forward to is the next election!" She stormed out of the room. John Connally told Lyndon he thought he ought to buy the house. Lyndon did.

She could chastise him, when necessary. One time, when LBJ and LBJ were out riding together on the LBJ Ranch near Stonewall, Texas, ornery Lyndon leaned over and gave Bird's horse a poke. The beast leaped suddenly forward, nearly upsetting Lady Bird. Bringing her mount around, Lady Bird honed in on Lyndon with a withering look that he talked about for the rest of his life, and said: "I'll manage my own horse!"

Sometimes, she flat overruled him. The day Lynda Bird wed Charles Robb, when it came time for the family portrait and everyone was getting lined up, Luci's little white dog, named Yuki, frisked into the scene, attired for the festivities in a red velvet sweater.

"We've got to get Yuki in the picture," chortled capricious Lyndon, going for the dog. "We can't have a family portrait without him."

"That dog is *not* going to be in the wedding picture," interdicted the mother of the bride.

LBJ launched into a rebuttal.

But, as everyone knows, wedding days are for the bride's mother; and the First Lady turned the President's faucet off: "Mr. Brant," she summoned a White House aide, "get that dog out of here right now! *He will not be photographed!*"

The pretty bride sighed while the flashbulbs popped; for the veto stuck, and the aide ran away from the scene with the pup.

At other, even more serious times, Bird could gear up for independent, unilateral action. When Walter Jenkins, a trusted Johnson family friend and special aide, got arrested in the Washington YMCA men's room for "disorderly conduct," Bird came flying to his defense without consulting Lyndon.

"My God," said J. Russell Wiggins, then an editor for the *Washington Post*, "she was like a vessel under full sail. She came into that room, and she issued a statement declaring full loyalty to Walter Jenkins. She said she wondered if we would print it. It was a great statement, and we did print it, of course."

From the very beginning to the very end, Lady Bird was Lyndon's strong right arm and his most enthusiastic backer. His political career carried them through the years like a flash flood rolling down the Pedernales River, Lady Bird riding the crest: "Oh, the adventures we had!"

Starting out in national politics in 1935, with their work for the National Youth Administration, Lady Bird said: "I loved it, and Lyndon loved it." In 1937, she was the first to prime the pump of financial support when Lyndon decided to run for Congress. Lyndon needed $10,000. "So I called my daddy. . . ." said Lady Bird. She was so proud of having helped Lyndon, Bird carried the canceled check around in her purse for years.

As a Congressman's wife in Washington, she fed and watered Lyndon's colleagues, took his constituents on guided tours of D.C., helped Lyndon with his correspondence, made suggestions for his speeches, sat in on strategy sessions during his campaigns, and held the fort of his Congressional office for four months early in World War II, while Lyndon was away in the South Pacific with the Navy. Nights, Bird signed up for business courses, so she could do a better job.

During that time, she attended her first dinner at the White House, reveling in the excitement that a brush with the Presidency would cause a 29-year-old shy Congressional wife standing in for her husband. On February 13, 1941, Lady Bird made the following entry in her diary:

> Tonight, I went to my first (will it be the last and only!?!) Dinner at the White House! Everything managed with watchmaker's precision! . . . Was [seated] as far from the President as possible. . . . After dinner the ladies and Mrs. R[oosevelt] went to one drawing room and the men somewhere else. We had coffee and visited and Mrs. R. moved from group to group. Then we went upstairs and saw "Philadelphia Story"—big day!!

Lady Bird was improving herself daily, gaining the personal stature she needed as Lyndon's political equal. Moreover, she was learning why Lyndon so often seemed tired and tense and frustrated when he got home at night: ". . . dealing with a great variety of problems from the ten [Texas] counties and the three hundred thousand people takes a lot out of you." Texas Congressman Jake Pickle said that although Lady Bird was not the only Congressional wife who took over her husband's office during the War, "she was the only one who considered it a full-time job and did it." Lyndon said she did such a good job that "the Tenth District would happily have elected her over me, if she had run."

Claudia Alta "Lady Bird" Taylor Johnson

Before she became a mother, Bird became a business woman. In 1943, taking her recurring miscarriages in stride, Lady Bird and Lyndon spent her inheritance money from T. J. to buy Austin radio station KTBC from the Texas Broadcasting Corporation. Bird was more than merely a front for Lyndon—she ran the store herself. First off, she got a bucket and mop and cleaned the place up. Next, she cleaned up the sloppiness with which the staff had been managing the station, infecting them with her upbeat enthusiasm. Then, she brought to bear the good business sense she had inherited from her daddy and sharpened in night school. She kept the books herself, conferred professionally with every network official she could buttonhole, and laid the foundation for the Johnson electronic communications empire in Central Texas: "We couldn't have had the livelihood we've had and remained in politics except for the income from my TV business."

Lady Bird's $17,500 investment in 1943 was worth $9 million in 1969. Lady Bird, said one of her business associates, was "very rich and very frugal." Along the way, while Bird was building the Johnson fortune, she was also having their daughters: Lynda Bird was born in 1944; Luci Baines, in 1947.

When Lyndon ran for the Senate in 1948, Lady Bird, part of the war-time surge of working women in America, was ready to launch herself into a new career as an active political campaigner. She enlisted former schoolmates and friends, and arranged get-togethers in little towns all over Texas. On her way to a political meeting two days before the election, Bird had a car accident. She climbed out of the overturned car, thumbed a ride into town, borrowed a clean dress from the hostess, kept on smiling through the reception, shook hands with 200 women, and gave her

BEHIND EVERY SUCCESSFUL PRESIDENT

speech; then, she went to the hospital for X-rays and bandages. That evening, she told Lyndon: "All I could think of as we were turning over was, I sure wished I'd voted absentee."

On election eve, Lyndon told Lady Bird he was ready to go home and spend the night resting at the ranch.

"Oh no we're not!" she headed him off. "I'm going back to Austin," she told him, laying out her plan in characteristically deliberate detail, "and I'm going to get your mother, your sisters, your aunts and your uncles, your friends, and your cousins, and I'm going to take the telephone book and I'm going to assign one of them all the A's, one of them all the B's, one of them all the C's, one of them all the D's, right through the Z's, and we're going to call and say, 'Won't you please go to the polls and vote for my husband?' 'Won't you please go to the polls and vote for my son?' 'Won't you please go to the polls and vote for my brother?'—or 'my cousin?'"

Bird followed through; and the next day, thanks to her efforts and the family's—and a well-stuffed ballot box or two—Lyndon squeaked by in a hotly contested election, as close as a gnat's eyebrow.

In 1954, when Lyndon became Senate Majority Leader, and Lady Bird, still bashful, was getting more and more calls to make speeches, Lyndon finally goaded her into taking some speaking lessons. In fact, Lady Bird hounded Lyndon about some of his ways as doggedly as he had pursued her improvement. She attempted to supervise his health and smoking habits, his Scotch-drinking and his speechmaking, his overworking and overeating. She would hide the peanut brittle from him under the bed, but she was about as successful at doing that as she was with the rest; and heart disease would finally kill him. Whenever his speeches ran on too long, she sent him little notes: "That's enough" or "Close soon" or, more diplomatically, "Great speech, but time to stop." Sometimes Lyndon took her advice and stopped; other times he read the note to the audience, got a big laugh, and kept on talking.

But if she worried after him, she also came through for him. In 1955, after Lyndon's heart attack, Bird and Lyndon turned his sickroom into the Majority Leader's new office, and ran the Senate from the hospital. She did just as he asked, and always wore lipstick; they laughed a lot, and they held hands. "During those days we rediscovered the meaning and freshness of life." Bird whispered to a friend: "When this is over, I think I'll go somewhere by myself for about two hours and just cry."

In 1960, Bird was at first opposed to Lyndon's running for the Vice Presidency under JFK. Believing that her husband would make a "noble President," she was miffed that the Kennedy crowd had edged Lyndon out of the nomination for the higher office. Bird knew that those Kennedy boys did not respect Lyndon enough, and she forbade him to talk to Bobby Kennedy about the job offer. "If Jack wants to talk with you," Bird told Lyndon, "that's one thing, but I don't think you should see anybody else."

Once the campaign got under way, however, Lady Bird was right in there pitching. Jackie Kennedy was taken with Bird's campaign savvy:

> [Mrs. Johnson] and my sister and I were sitting in one part of the room, and Jack and the Vice President-elect [sic] Johnson and some men were in the other part of the room. Mrs. Johnson had a little spiral pad and when she'd hear a name mentioned, she'd jot it down. Sometimes if Mr. Johnson wanted her, he'd say, "Bird, do you know so-and-so's number?" And

she'd always have it down. Yet she would sit talking with us, looking so calm. I was very impressed by that.

In a concretely political sense, Lady Bird won the election for Jack and Lyndon as much as, or more so than, chic Jackie did. Hardy Bird traveled 35,000 campaign miles making speeches, making friends, making her folksy impression, and garnering votes. Democratic Party professionals called her "our secret weapon." She made four power trips across Texas; and when Kennedy narrowly defeated Nixon, Bobby Kennedy—JFK's campaign manager—declared it: "Lady Bird carried Texas for us!" A Democrat cannot win the Presidency without carrying Texas.

After Lady Bird got to be Second Lady, she was just as proud to be there as she had been with the other elective offices she and Lyndon had won. She announced her Second Lady's agenda: "To help Lyndon all I can; to lend a hand to Mrs. Kennedy when she needs me; and to be a more alive me." She became the Vice President's vice president—undertaking diplomatic assignments to foreign countries, greeting visiting dignitaries, and having a wonderful time. Learning about other cultures and peoples delighted the self-improver: "I had a ball. I loved it. I had a great time once I was in it."

Especially did the Second Lady "lend Mrs. Kennedy a hand." Jackie, notorious for not showing up where she was expected, called on Lady Bird to stand in for her; Bird became known as "Washington's No. 1 pinch-hitter." One night, Jackie was a no-show to receive a TV Emmy for public service. Lady Bird was already scheduled to attend a dinner in honor of Lyndon, but she managed both appearances. The Second Lady arrived with Lyndon at his dinner, stayed long enough for the opening formalities, sneaked out, took a cab to the second affair, stepped—like Superman—into a phone booth to prepare notes for her acceptance speech, received the award on behalf of the First Lady, made her speech, and then hightailed it back to the Vice Presidential dinner.

In 1963, in Dallas, LBJ's well-rehearsed exercise of elemental power and Bird's steady goodness were what the nation needed in face of the felling of the President.

Lady Bird helped Lyndon write the address he made to the nation immediately upon becoming President, and she issued her own First Lady statement. She invited Jackie to remain in the White House as long might be needed, and continued the special school that the Kennedy children attended. During the first months of the Johnson Administration, the two First Ladies and Lyndon engaged in a correspondence unusually rich in the annals of the Presidency. To Rose Kennedy, Lady Bird wrote: "We feel as though our heart is cut out, but we must remember how fortunate our country was to have your son as long as we did."

As mistress of the White House, Lady Bird's first self-assigned task was to take some "educational tours" of the 132-room edifice. Above all, she wanted to make the White House their home, a place where Lyndon could work productively.

Lady Bird summed up the challenge of becoming the First Lady with characteristic modesty: "A First Lady should be a showman and a salesman, a clotheshorse and a publicity sounding board, with a good heart and a real interest in the folks in Rising Star and Rosebud [little towns in Texas], as well as Newport and whatever the other fancy places are . . . Well, the last—real interest—I do have."

In 1964, Lyndon ran for his own term, and Lady Bird

BEHIND EVERY SUCCESSFUL PRESIDENT

was right out front. Her whistle-stop train trip—nearly 1,700 miles with 47 stops across 8 Southern States on board "The Lady Bird Special"—was the first such First Lady's independent campaign trip on behalf of her husband's candidacy.

Lyndon's 1964 Civil Rights Act had eroded support in the "solid South," and Lady Bird's work of erosion control was cut out for her: "Don't give me the easy towns, Liz," she told her press secretary Liz Carpenter. "Anyone can get into Atlanta—it's the new, modern South. Let me take the tough ones." Wherever she went, she spoke of her love for the South, said that she wanted the South not to be left out of the political process, said that Southerners were her kinfolk and friends; she called the train trip "a journey of the heart." Lady Bird talked Southern colorfully, with her accent and with an unaffected charm. The way Lady Bird put it, when she was with people she liked, she was "in mighty tall cotton." If she was planning to whistle-stop in some town, that would happen "if the Lord's willin' and the creeks don't rise." If her schedule got too full, Lady Bird was not merely busy; she was "as busy as a man with one hoe and two rattlesnakes." Aunt Effie's niece talked Alabaman as well as she talked Texan. Black and white together, Dixie gave Lady Bird a welcome home.

When she got to New Orleans—1,700 miles and 180 stops later—Lyndon was there to meet her for the grand finale. "I'm proud to be her husband!" said the President. On Inauguration Day, on the way to lunch after the swearing-in, Lyndon stopped in the middle of things and planted a big kiss right on Lady Bird's mouth. Bird glowed.

Jack Valenti, the President's special assistant, estimated Lady Bird's personal and political value beyond calculating:

She is a rare, unduplicatable human being . . . sure,

Claudia Alta "Lady Bird" Taylor Johnson

inexhaustibly steady pillar of strength to her husband. Her political judgments were sound.... She had definite opinions and she expressed them lucidly.... In a crunch, the President valued her considered opinion more than any of his counselors' because he knew that, alone among his entourage, she delivered her views without any self-interest or leashed ego.

Bird was more comfortable in her role as First Lady than her own words sometimes seem to indicate. She had come a long way from behind the high-school girl who prayed for smallpox to keep from making a speech. She could tell a Degas from a Matisse, and pick out a Renoir or a Toulouse-Lautrec from all the way across the gallery (although she admitted to having missed a Mary Cassatt, once). But, as far as Bird's insides were concerned, her long hard row of shyness never got any easier to hoe.

Lady Bird's enduring shyness did not, however, keep her from doing her job as First Lady. Her quiet wit was the best complementary antidote to the shyness. Lady Bird tabled her shyness by being hospitable. She held out a Texas ranch-style "howdy" and a "y'all come" farewell to everybody. French cuisine went up in the mesquite and live-oak smoke of Pedernales barbecue and pinto beans. A new bowling alley went in not only for Lynda's and Luci's teenager parties; the First Lady bowled her troubles away, exercising and meditating at the same time (while Lyndon took the press corps skinny-dipping in the White House pool).

Bird's struggle with self-esteem never let her graduate from the school of self-improvement. Whenever she had to make a speech—even a short one—she might work on it for hours, both with Liz Carpenter and alone, get the help of a speech coach, and polish it to perfection. Whenever she had to welcome state visitors from abroad, she would do her homework studying maps, reading briefing papers, learning the interesting details that enabled her to put the visiting dignitaries at ease. Before a state dinner, she would go over the guest list, learn something about each new person she was soon to meet, and prepare a personal word of greeting for use as an icebreaker in the receiving line.

Aside from hosting ordinary activities, Lady Bird had two pet First Lady projects: women and Beautification. When Lyndon would come home from a hard day's work in the Oval Office, Bird would greet him with: "Well, what did you do for women today?" Bird thought that the government ignored women; so, she rode Lyndon, organized luncheons, attended meetings, nominated female candidates for government jobs, and made speeches.

Lady Bird was a frontier woman, the Texas counterpart of the man of elemental power. Liz Carpenter described her boss as a lady with "a touch of velvet, with the stamina of steel." As LBJ practiced all his life the political use of raw power for the sake of poor people—from raising the dead so they could vote for him, to building dams and generating the Lower Colorado River Authority so Central Texas dirt farmers could have electricity, and finally to setting up the Great Society—so also did Lady Bird act the part of a human draft horse, stand by her man, and defend her land and people. Her soft-spoken ways made her the best ambassador of the Great Society's model cities and urban renewal, Medicare, Medicaid, child health, voting rights and racial equality, that rough-hewn Lyndon could have wanted; and Bird's Texan toughness paid off in handsome dividends when it came to her own, aesthetic dimension of the Great Society.

Lyndon told his First Lady that she should "work at the

Claudia Alta "Lady Bird" Taylor Johnson

project that will make your heart sing." Bird chose "Beautification." The word was an unfortunate one, she admitted, it sounded "cosmetic and trivial and prissy, [but] . . . we couldn't come up with anything better." Foreigners sometimes thought it meant how the First Lady did her hair. Bird set out to plant trees and flowers wherever they would grow. She planted so many trees—and was so proud of it—the First Lady said that her epitaph ought to read: "She planted three trees." Bird aimed to pull down every garbagey billboard and roadside sign she could get her hands on. She and Lyndon roped and hogtied the Congress —by a single vote—to get what Bird wanted, namely the "Highway Beautification Act" (1965), which people nicknamed "Lady Bird's Bill," and the equally controversial "Federal Aid to Highways Act" (1968).

So significant a part of the First Lady's work did Beautification become, Lady Bird was the first to hire a "projects manager" for the East Wing staff. Working especially with Secretary of the Interior Stewart Udall, and philanthropists Mary Lasker and Laurance Rockefeller, Bird launched her effort under the motto "Masses of flowers where the masses pass." Bird was working on two rattlesnakes with a single hoe: safeguarding and enhancing the natural environment while simultaneously making urban life more livable by making it more pleasant. The First Lady of Beautification saw a connection between ugliness and crime. She started by spiffing up Washington.

Lady Bird, as Eleanor Roosevelt had been, was a traveling activist: she poked into coal mines and ghettos, and visited with the Teachers Corps in Appalachia and Head Start programs in Newark's inner city: "I like to get out and see the people behind the statistics. It makes Lyndon's memos and working papers come to life for me."

BEHIND EVERY SUCCESSFUL PRESIDENT

Minnie Taylor's daughter prowled D.C.'s slums in an unmarked government car to gather intelligence for school improvement, Lyndon's "War on Poverty," and the Head Start Program. It was Lady Bird who urged Lyndon to appoint Walter Washington as the Capital's African-American mayor.

She led her Women Doers, armed with shovels and buckets, on clean-up expeditions to junky vacant lots around D.C., and then on to cherry-tree- and daffodil-plannting outings—Bird put a crop of two million daffodil bulbs in her D.C. patch. She took pride in her sore knees and the dirt under her fingernails. Later on, Columbia Island in the Potomac River would be renamed Lady Bird Johnson Park, parti-colored in the springtime with dogwoods and the flowers of Bird's plantings.

Leading her "Discover America" treks (a.k.a. "Lady Bird Safaris"), she toured National Parks and the small-town Midwest, gazed out from San Simeon high above the Pacific, and led the press corps on a rafting expedition down the Rio Grande. (Thanks in part to Bess Abell, social secretary, but especially to Liz Carpenter, press secretary, no First Lady ever sustained better relations with the media people than Lady Bird.) The Johnson Administration added a million acres to the National Park system, and fostered a total of 278 distinct conservationist measures. Enamored of America the Beautiful, the First Saleslady of the Great Society took 47 trips and traveled more than 200,000 miles on behalf of Beautification, planting trees and goodwill. Johnny Appleseed in a sunbonnet, Bird said: "Call it corny if you will, but I want to boast about America."

Bird knew how to take it easy in the company of other homefolks, too. Once, President-elect Richard Nixon called at the White House to keep an early appointment with

Claudia Alta "Lady Bird" Taylor Johnson

Lyndon, who was still in pajamas, having his coffee in bed. The lame-duck President and the leader-elect in this three-piece suit were going at it over Vietnam, when in walked Lady Bird in her dressing gown. She greeted Nixon in her warm way, then climbed into bed alongside Lyndon and joined in for the rest of the conversation.

Lyndon and Lady Bird had been on their way to carrying out FDR's promise of a New Deal, updated in theory with JFK's design for social democracy. The "Great Society" was becoming a reality, when the two LBJs got mugged in an back-alley war in Vietnam. "Mr. Johnson's War" lost Mr. Johnson his Presidency.

Twice Lyndon had to "wrestle with the demon" of whether or not to run for the highest office—once in '64 and now again in '68. The first time, Bird had boosted the idea all the way, and she probably had tipped the scales in favor of his running in '64. In '68, however, after talking it over, and over and over, Lady Bird and Lyndon agreed that he would not run. Lyndon's health was failing, the American effort in Vietnam was failing, and the polls said that a bid for a second term would also fail. Lady Bird wrote to LBJ:

> Luci hopes you won't run. She wants you for herself and for [grandbaby] Lyn and for all of us. She does not want to give you up. Lynda hopes you *will* run. She told me so this afternoon, with a sort of terrible earnestness, because her husband is going to war and she thinks there will be a better chance of getting him back alive and the war settled if you are president. Me—I don't know. I have said it all before. I can't tell you what to do.

Throughout Lady Bird's diary, whenever the subject of the war comes up, she pledges unthinking allegiance to Lyndon's proud but fatal Vietnam policy. When protestors

BEHIND EVERY SUCCESSFUL PRESIDENT

did a sit-in at the White House, shy Bird, instead of approaching them in her usual homey way, offering the kids some milk and cookies and sitting down and talking to them in good grandmotherly fashion, was too timorous even to "have a peek" at them. She typically ignored protestors and their protests, unless they became "extremely raucous." When she went to make a speech at Williams College in October 1967, she was met by picketers: "Confront the War Makers in Washington." But, instead of doing that, she sided with the war maker in Washington, agreeing with Lyndon against the "whiners, self-doubters, gloom spreaders."

Instead of grappling with the possibility that Lyndon's critics might have a legitimate complaint, Bird worried about his ratings in the polls, offering political advice rather than moral leadership. Although both she and Lyndon had taken the lead in Civil Rights legislation, when the all-black Mississippi Freedom Democratic Party challenged the all-white, but regularly elected, Mississippi Democratic delegation at the Democratic National Convention, Lady Bird took the politically safe, conventional route. Lyndon was up a creek about what to do, and asked Lady Bird to draft a statement for him. Had the President read the First Lady's words as his own, he would have sided with the white "legal delegation." The statement, however, was not read; and the Convention worked out a compromise solution more fair and more towards the middle of the road than Lady Bird's cautiousness.

In 1968, as the "miasma of trouble" swirled around her like a fog in the Big Thicket, Lady Bird felt alone: there was "almost nobody in the world that I can talk to." She called the anti-war riots a "virus," and she got her back up in loyal defense of her man.

At the same time, Lady Bird had to admit that she was learning something new, slowly. The time Eartha Kitt defied her to her face in the Rose Garden over the war, Bird must have learned a little more. And after a confrontation with anti-war protesters at Yale, she wrote: "I must not live only in the White House, insulated against life. I want to know what's going on—even if to know is to suffer."

Lady Bird felt herself emotionally becoming an isolationist: "I made a hotheaded statement about when we got the Vietnam war finally settled I didn't want to have another thing to do with any foreign country." Lyndon calmly corrected her by drawing an analogy between communism in Indochina and smallpox in the neighborhood—both need stamping out, something one can't accomplish by being isolationist.

Bird might have countered by saying that the way to cure smallpox is not by killing the people who catch it. She did, however, suggest in her quiet way that maybe somebody ought to send for a doctor. The point appears to have been too subtle for Lyndon. If Lady Bird's own mind had changed, or if she made other attempts to reason with Lyndon about the war, that is not recorded in the published version of her diary.*

---

*Lady Bird's 800-page volume, edited from the 1,750,000 words she spoke onto tape on almost a daily basis throughout her tenure of office, is the longest book yet to be written by a First Lady. The typescript was previewed by Lyndon, who mandated certain deletions. The unedited tapes, kept at the Johnson Presidential Library in Austin, are not yet available to the public. The hint that Lady Bird pressed Lyndon for a more humane resolution to the Vietnam crisis must wait for proof until after the full *Diary* becomes accessible—presumably after Lady Bird passes on.

BEHIND EVERY SUCCESSFUL PRESIDENT

Bird went to bed early on the evening of Richard Nixon's Inauguration, a line of poetry running through her mind: "I seek, to celebrate my glad release, the Tents of silence and the Camp of Peace." "And yet," she wrote in the diary, "it's not quite the right exit for me, because I have loved almost every day of these five years." The day they moved from the White House back to the LBJ Ranch, one tired-out Lady Bird sat down on a suitcase, threw back her head, and laughed: "The chariot has turned into a pumpkin, and all the mice have run away!" The next morning, they slept in.

Bird was glad to be home for good. Later on, she compared living in the White House to having climbed Mt. Everest: "Would you want to climb it again? No. But it's nice to remember."

Jacqueline Lee Bouvier Kennedy Onassis

*Classy Lady
in the President's House*

ACCORDING to almost any poll, Senator Jack Kennedy was the "most eligible bachelor in Washington." He could have any woman he wanted: he wanted Jackie. She was articulate and sophisticated; she could best him at word games and her palate was more refined than his; although he knew more about politics and American history, she knew more about European history, foreign languages, and the fine arts. Jack had thought about staying a bachelor—(Why limit oneself in any way?)—but if he was going to be President—and he *was* going to be President—the right wife would be a terrific political asset.

Bouvier money was older than Kennedy money, even if there was less of it. She was stylish; but there was something classic about her style. Jack was convinced that there was considerably more going on here than merely the stylish affects of a socialite who had been acclaimed "Queen Deb of the Year" at her coming-out. Besides, he was in love with the quick wit and the broad smile and the big, wide-set eyes in the beautiful face twelve years younger than his.

Jacqueline Lee Bouvier Kennedy Onasis

Her little-girlish, whispery, exuberant voice worked magnetically on Jack; he found her irresistible wrap-around mouth . . . irresistible. Doubtless, she had cultivated these celebrated features as carefully as she designed every other detail of her life, just like she straightened her kinky hair and fluffed it out into that trademark bouffant hairdo. But merely because the smile and the voice were artifices did not mean that they were artificial. Rather, they were *art*; Jackie —born Jacqueline Lee Bouvier on July 28, 1929—Jackie was an artist, and she herself was her own most artful creation. The flawless smile, the seductive voice, the perfect French accent when she spoke the Language of Civilization, the impeccable taste in clothes when she went out for the evening. And the ability to make anyone she talked with feel they were (at least for that moment) the only important person in her universe—it was all an artistic triumph.

As Inquiring Camera Girl for the *Washington Times-Herald*, Jackie, taking advantage of JFK's open office door policy, had walked in without being announced, interviewed, and photographed the junior Senator from Massachusetts. Interestingly, on the same day, she had also visited his Republican rival across the hall, Dick Nixon—their interviews and photos appeared side-by-side in the paper. But then, Jackie returned to turn the chemistry on in Jack's direction, and let the mutual attraction take its course.

The ambitious Senator proposed trans-Atlanticly to the Inquiring Camera Girl, whose newspaper had sent her to England to cover the coronation of a genuine queen. Their wedding at Newport, uniting two style-setting Catholic families, was the nuptial event of the season and one more aspect of the emerging Kennedy myth; it was presided over by Boston's Archbishop Cushing with a special papal benediction from John XXIII. In Acapulco, romantic Jackie wrote honeymooning Jack a poem, a parody on one of Stephen Vincent Benét's, in a way prophetic of the destiny she had married:

He would build empires
And he would have sons
Others would fall
Where the current runs
He would find love
He would never find peace
For he must go seeking
The Golden Fleece
All of the things he was going to be
All of the things in the wind and the seas.

They would be married for ten years. There would be one miscarriage, one stillbirth, and Patrick, who lived not quite two days; but there would be spry Caroline and handsome John-John. Lusty Jack would see the wedding as no reason to quit his womanizing ways, but Jackie would remain above all that, observing archly of Jack's "violent" independence that "I don't think there are any men who are faithful to their wives. Men are such a combination of good and evil." Jackie would almost always get what she wanted from Jack, except when it came to her extravagance at clothes shopping and her spoiled girl's way of unbalancing a budget. They would work White House receptions and other State occasions as a team, filtering democratically among their guests with easygoing elegance. They disposed of formal seating arrangements and the stuffy regality of the traditional, slow-moving receiving line. She cast herself in the role of adoring wife and protective mother; he would observe her with interest, avid for her matchless performance of whatever she set her mind to accomplish. Each profited from the other's unique style. She would teach him to dress better—tuck his shirttail in and comb his hair: Jack Kennedy would certainly never have gotten picked as one of the year's ten best-dressed men before Jackie re-did him. And, he would learn at least to *appear* to enjoy an evening of Pablo Casals at work on his cello. In turn, Jack would back Jackie's artistic *tour de force* that restored the President's dilapidated old White House into a national fashion plate of historic interior design. Each yielded to the other's needs, neither overpowering the other; together as two strong individuals they would achieve an enviable degree of maturity in marital companionship—truncated by Jack's assassination on November 22, 1963. The bright and shining moment the two effected in national history would be called "an American Camelot" by every political poet.

Jackie's father—the swarthy man for whom she was named—was "Black Jack" Bouvier, a.k.a. the Black Orchid, a.k.a. the Black Sheik, a not entirely successful Wall Street stockbroker and heir to a small fortune, whose Clark Gable good looks and genuine liking for women made him dear to many. He took his daughters on window-shopping sprees through Saks Fifth Avenue and Bergdorf Goodman, lecturing to Jackie and sister Lee on fashion and good taste. The great-grandson of a Frenchman who had made his fortune by purveying fine veneers and marble tabletops to the wealthy of Philadelphia, taught Jackie to develop a critical eye for color and line, to see what was wrong with a woman's outfit and to know what to do in detail to correct her look. Both girls felt the interior designer running in their veins, and Jackie would turn her daddy's love of female beauty into a pace-setting passion for her own good looks.

He also schooled Jackie in reserve and display, on how to give out and how to hold back, on how to make a grand entrance or how not to show up at all, but make everyone wish she had. Expert in the field, Jackie's first Jack taught her how to be desirable by being inaccessible. And, he let her learn that it is all right to love a man who makes love to more than one woman. At their first meeting, Bouvier and his son-in-law-to-be hit it off famously. "They talked about sports, politics, and women," Jackie acknowledged with understanding, "—what all red-blooded men like to talk about."

Jackie's second Jack was "Grampy Jack"—Grandfather John Vernou Bouvier, Jr., scion of the Bouvier family myth. In 1925, he published *Our Forebears*, in which volume of largely imaginative genealogy he related his line to ancient French noble houses out of sight and without proof. He was as indulgent with his granddaughter as he was generous with his history. When Jackie went away to Miss Porter's School in Farmington, Connecticut, she wanted to take her horse, Danseuse, with her—but Mummy and "Uncle Hughdie" said "no." Hugh D. Auchincloss was the man Jackie's mother had married a year before. His millions she was not yet ready to spend on room and board for a horse. So Jackie appealed to Grampy Jack. In his elegant diction, Grampy wrote back to her about "sumptuary extravagance," which, nevertheless, "spiritually provides a wholesome release from sordid worldly cares." He undertook for $25 per month to subsidize Danseuse's attendance at Miss Porter's, agreeing that he and Jacqueline were "in concurrence" on the "necessity" of this "indulgence."

Grampy Jack was also a major source of Jackie's interest in literature and letters. He critiqued her poems, of which there were many, encouraging her art. He composed annual birthday poems in her honor, replete with Classical allusions. On Jackie's fourteenth—just the age when a young girl dreams about such things—Grampy Jack penned a coronation ode to the future queen of the Western Camelot:

TO THE YOUTHFUL ARTEMIS

Diana, Mistress of the Chase
And of all sylvan arts the Queen
Performing with supremest grace,
The sports on which the healthful lean.

Favorites sometimes caught her eye,
And 'Tis to them her skill she lent;
All in the days that have gone bye;
Of Ancient Times, how long since spent.

But strange, sweet maiden, to relate
She has since crowned a modern Queen,
Nor did her ART one jot abate,
When 'twas bestowed on Jacqueline.

Congratulations, Gramps.

Jackie would profit a lot from the men in her life; but she learned from women, too. From her mother, Janet Lee Bouvier Auchincloss, she gained a mastery of the horse. "Go at the fences straight," Janet instructed the girl, and Jackie learned to clear the most difficult jumps without a ruffle and keep that newsworthy smile blazing—as one reporter burbled, "her dazzling smile was worth coming miles to see." Even when she took the rare fall, Jackie received praise in the grandstands and from the press. Once when Danseuse stumbled at a barrier, little Jackie, thrown flat on her back, held fast to the reins, controlling her mount. Another time after a tumble, spunky Jackie, trying to scramble back into the saddle on the wrong side, evoked amused applause from the crowd. Later, in the car as they were leaving, Jackie asked: "Mummy, why did they clap when I fell off?" Janet pulled the auto to a halt at the side of the road and gave her daughter a stiff lesson in good form: "Those were terribly silly people," she snipped. "They didn't know what really happened. You should be ashamed of handling your pony so carelessly. He might have been hurt." A photo of young Jackie in riding habit shows her leading a defeated pony from the field with an air of mastery and five-year-old *hauteur* that would become subtler with the years and more gracious, but not a particle weaker.

Jackie's artistic talents matured with the growing girl. She illustrated her many poems. Her junior year at Vassar was spent with a group from Smith, studying at Grenoble and the Sorbonne. She saturated her French soul with French literature and history, living with a French family and learning to speak the language without accent—a feat that even few of the French (those who live outside Paris) are unable to accomplish.

Jackie entered *Vogue* magazine's "Prix de Paris" contest. The contestants were required to submit four technical treatises on fashion, a plan for an issue of *Vogue*, a personal profile, and an essay on "People I Wish I Had Known." Jacqueline—at twenty-two and finishing her degree at George Washington University—wrote her essay on Diaghilev, who revitalized the Russian ballet by enriching it with other art forms—drama, painting, music; on Oscar Wilde, the English aesthete, wit, and dramatist; and on Charles Baudelaire, poet of *Les Fleurs du mal* and father of the French Symbolist movement and of modern French poetry.

Jackie won first prize, and was to have spent six months working for *Vogue* in Paris and six months back in

New York; but, she turned it down. Perhaps Jackie's family thought she was becoming too Francophile; perhaps taking prizes looked too much like accepting scholarships—something that poor people do. At any rate, Jackie said she needed to spend some time with her family and suggested that someone more deserving should receive the prize. Isn't winning, itself, more important than the prizes?

A year later, Jackie and her sister larked across Europe together, composing at the end of their tour a memento of thanks for their mother (published in 1976 by Delacorte Press, *One Special Summer*), comprising humorous narrative, poems, snapshots, and Jackie's delightful illustrations. The curlicues and embellishments are of the ilk one finds in the sketchings of many romantic young artists; but beyond the furbelows, one is surprised by the drollery of whimsical detail, the eye of the artist for human energy of the body in action, levity and grace in the forms of dancers, and a Strindbergesque quality to the cartoon line drawings. (Jackie's art has continued and, no doubt, matured. One wonders when her publishers will recommission the editor as illustrator.)

The prose tells of a meeting with Bernard Berenson, art critic and expert on the Italian Renaissance, that was for Jackie one of those moments when youth meets maturity and is changed forever. Wisdom that she carried away from Berenson included knowing that "anything you want, you must make enemies and suffer for," and "he would so much rather make enemies than be loved by all." Berenson "set a spark burning" in Jackie—actually he blew the spark that had already been burning into a blaze. She remembered that he made a distinction between "Life Diminishing and Life Enhancing people;" and the advice he offered about the difference became her *modus operandi*: "Don't waste your life with diminishing people who aren't stimulating—and if you find it's often you are with unstimulating people, it must be because you yourself are not stimulating." Jackie had added yet another dark and older man to her collection.

Jackie's wit, the passion for appropriate detail, and her love of beautiful things were all still with her when she got to the White House—as was also her ability to hold a bolting horse by the reins. "The one thing I do not want to be called," she instructed her secretary after the Inauguration, "is 'First Lady.' It sounds like a saddle horse." She said she felt like a moth hanging on the windowpane of the Presidency or like someone living in a fishbowl, but with all the fish on the outside looking in; she identified with Martha Washington, who had declared herself a "prisoner of State." These hesitations were only aspects of settling in; by the time Jackie discovered that her true work as Presidential woman was to be more than merely wife and child-bearer, her obsession for decoration became a national mission to bring elegance and grandeur to "the dreary Maison Blanche." Jackie reflected: "When I knew I'd be living [in the White House], it wasn't a matter of wanting to restore it or not; it was something that *had* to be done, just as one had to do something about the food." Before she was finished, poet Robert Frost could say and rightly: "There have been some great wives in the White House—like Abigail Adams and Dolley Madison—so great that you can't think of their husbands, Presidents, without thinking of *them*. It looks as though we are having another one now."

Jackie's sense of the aesthetic found the Mansion in a shockingly drab state—without decent pictures on the walls and without an appropriate library or even cases to put books in, had there been any. ("Doesn't any President *ever* read?") The ashtrays were too few and too ugly; the potted palms, a vegetable hazard. Monroe silverware, Lincoln china and a Lincoln chair (one leg missing), Teddy Roosevelt rugs, and the desk fabricated from timbers of the H.M.S. *Resolute* and presented by Queen Victoria to Rutherford B. Hayes—among other priceless historic treasures—were uncatalogued, lost in unmarked storage, or being misused and abused. The curtains were all too short, the bottom twelve inches having been scissored off without regard for style or proportion—one of Eleanor Roosevelt's efficiency moves to speed up floor-mopping and keep the curtains clean.

Within a month of moving in, Jackie launched herself in research and discovery. Without having to think, she abolished "Mamie Eisenhower pink." With the help of the Library of Congress, she began to ascertain what the 132 rooms had looked like originally, and what it would take to restore the ones that had once been beautiful, and perfect the others. Jackie established her standard of quality: "Everything in the White House must have a reason for being there. It would be a sacrilege merely to 'redecorate'—a word I hate. It must be *restored*, and that has nothing to do with 'decoration.' That is a question of scholarship." (French Minister of Culture André Malraux once enchantedly described Jackie as a "certifiable egghead.")

Jack was "largely unenthusiastic, at first," Pierre Salinger, the President's Press Secretary, acknowledged later. Jack remembered what it had been like with Jackie in a redecorating fit when they lived in Georgetown: "Dammit it, Jackie, why is it that the rooms in this house are never completely livable all at the same time?" She would not only move the furniture more times than necessary, she would change the new paint-job from white to off-white or the wallpaper three times at whatever expense to taut budget or frayed nerves, till her passion for decorative detail was satisfied that everything was just right. Besides, Jack knew that public opinion was conservative regarding changes to the Mansion. When word got out that an artist was loose in the White House, fears began to be expressed that Jackie would hang crazy modern art all over the venerable white edifice or paint it any strange color she wanted.

To stanch criticism and insure that she had the best possible advice, Jackie organized the Fine Arts Committee for the White House, comprising some of the most prestigiously knowledgeable experts on historic art in the country. She appointed the first White House curator, Lorraine Pearce, who, with Jackie's help (and that of John Walker of the National Gallery and Melville Grosvenor of the National Geographic Society), produced *The White House: An Historic Guide*. Sale of the guidebook would help defray the costs of restoration. Gifts of appropriate (and some not so appropriate) pieces to fill the rooms were made easier with the passage of Public Law 87-286, which established the "museum character" of the Mansion, reassuring donors that their treasures would be cared for properly and not sold off at auction by the wagon-load, as had happened after some previous Administrations.

In came upwards of seventy-five thousand letters offering for free or for sale Presidential memorabilia from Andy Jackson's spittoon and Victorian chamber pots to a bust of Washington, optimistically evaluated by its owner to be worth $200,000. Ninety-five percent of the offerings had to be turned down as "inappropriate" or redundant; but Jackie couldn't resist some antique, pictorial Zuber wallpaper, steamed off the walls of a Maryland house and rehung in the Mansion for the embarrassing sum of $12,500. The matchless Rembrandt Peale portrait of Jefferson and the David Martin of Franklin were gratefully received, without cost.

Jackie transformed the undistinguished Monroe Room into the Treaty Room, now an experience of American history made visible in period pieces and facsimiles of the numerous treaties signed in that room. She hung a Cézanne in the Green Room. Jackie, wife and mother, also improved the second-floor Presidential living quarters, adding an upstairs kitchen (so the food could be served hot) and a playhouse for Caroline. With the help of Yale University Librarian James T. Babb and his committee, a library of 2,700 volumes of Americana was stood on ample new shelves. (Lady Bird Johnson and her husband the Vice President donated one of Lincoln's "Appointment Books.") The finishing touch to the Mansion's new look was Jackie's dictum about flowers: no more formal sheaves of rigid roses stuck upright in tall vases, but "Flemish" bouquets of colorfully mixed blossoms in more natural, relaxed arrangements. *Life* magazine devoted a special edition to the process, and CBS telecast a tour of the results, with Jackie as hostess, on St. Valentine's Day, 1962. By the time the other two networks also aired the film, fifty-six million Americans (one-third of the national population) had toured the White House via TV, and Jackie was a hit. Not a cent of it had come out of the taxpayer's pocket.

Too little has been said about Jackie's maturity as a Presidential wife. She was only the third youngest ever to live in the White House, and in her early thirties. In contrast to the matrons who had preceded her, she seemed younger than she was. Whereas enough has been said about her shopping sprees and elitist tastes, too little understanding has been brought to bear on her personal style and its impact on the American consciousness.

Luxury was Jackie's natural habitat, a pattern running consistently throughout the fabric of her life. She was not a politically oriented Presidential wife, nor one mindful of the social welfare. One would be amiss to ask what she thought of Jack's Bay of Pigs. And this Democrat in a Republican fur was capable of Eleanor-like concern for the Appalachian poor only on a theory of trickle-down economics: When "The President's House" crystal pattern that Jackie selected from the Morgantown Glassware Guild caught on, she said, "I thought it was nice to help West Virginia and nice that people should see that those simple glasses were pretty enough for the White House." The upbringing that had trained the thoroughbred from East Hampton was the same schooling that ingrained a love for beautiful things in Jackie. Her savor of the patina of old, fine, rubbed wood or her ability to hear a whole culture ticking in a delicate, antique mantel clock was also the refinement of taste that enabled her (and her like-minded associates) to deliver the Mansion, restored and perfected, in public trust to the whole people as a national treasure-house.

For a person in whose eyes beauty is uppermost, fine style of every kind is the personal superlative. Jackie extended her touch to the White House food and brought in a French chef. White House parties became casually elegant but lavish affairs, and receptions for foreign dignitaries became theatrical extravaganzas.

The only problem was that somebody had to pay for Jackie's champagne taste. The more she traveled and the more she grew into her role as Presidential wife, the more extravagant her wardrobe had to be. In 1961, when Jack's salary was $100,000, Jackie spent $105,446.14. In 1962, she spent $121,461.61. And the bills for "Food and Liquor" and

"Miscellaneous" kept stacking up higher. "Clothing" was the budgetary item Jackie could not whip; nor was it all pillbox hats. When confronted with a choice between mink or a much more expensive leopard, Jack told her to think mink, but Jackie just couldn't resist the leopard. Steaming, Jack led her away: "Let's go back upstairs and go over the books!" (Later, when Jackie was married to Ari Onassis, she would spend ten times Jack's salary in one year on clothes alone—and Ari would grouse about it ten times as much as Jack had.)

Jackie tried—really she did, on everything but "Clothing"—to economize. She ordered less smoked salmon and paté for the guests and cheaper bubblebath for herself; gift turkeys sent to the White House kitchen she now directed into the freezer instead of to charity; and she availed herself of a promising-looking S&H Green Stamp Gift Catalog. By mid-1963, Jackie had shaved only $700 per month off the White House budget by application of her somewhat uneven budgetary policy. For example, her secretary had spotted some nice-looking $8.95 sweaters at a wholesale outlet that Jackie thought she might buy for the horde of Kennedy cousins for Christmas; for herself—Jackie was already hinting to the right people—she hoped everybody would go together and get her something she'd really been wanting: a fur bedspread. Jack, urging further austerities, had less trouble with Congress.

Just because Jackie was a bird of paradise did not mean that she was not Jack's dutiful ally. She more or less put up with his family (she got along with his father, "the Ambassador," very well). She tended Jack when he was flat on his back and—some people thought—dying of his football/war-wounded back. She had helped him with his book, *Profiles in Courage,* and one night she sneaked Grace

Kelly, pretending to be a nurse, into his hospital room. And, like Caesar's mother, tough Jackie was having her premature babies the hard way. She cared little for politics—Jackie had been raised in a Republican family among whom "Kennedy" was a dirty word. While Jack had reveled in his ticker-tape parade in Manhattan, Jackie had gone gallery hopping. And she jealously guarded her privacy to the point of refusing to give media conferences. All that notwithstanding, she had helped her husband get elected President. On his behalf, she had written thousands of letters (in longhand—Jackie doesn't do typing), had composed a weekly newspaper column, "Campaign Wife," and had risked her own health and the baby's she was carrying during the frenzy of the last weeks of the campaign.

But far beyond duty, Jackie's style of reception of foreign visitors was becoming Jack's—and the country's—status symbol. Speaker of the House John McCormack once toasted her as "a great diplomat and a great ambassador—who has given an image of America which has made the world smile again!" Jackie's private vacation trip to India and Pakistan was greeted with such warmly positive response that "the American Maharani" became a major subject of foreign relations and a jewel in the crown of America abroad. In Latin America, she spoke Spanish and was wildly welcomed. In Vienna, she had Khrushchev eating out of her hand.

Jackie in Paris was a natural: the capital of fashion, the home of art, the city of beautiful women capitulated without a struggle. Her perfect French diction, her appearance at Versailles in a Givency tri-color, and her stated preference for a Manet nude caused fifty million Frenchmen to cry "Jacquii! Jacquii!" wherever the Presidential couple appeared. That night at Versailles, Jack indicated that he had taken another look at his Presidential wife. When he stood up to make his speech, after the conventional address to everyone important who was present, he continued: "I do not think it entirely inappropriate to introduce myself to this audience. I am the man who accompanied Jacqueline Kennedy to Paris, and I have enjoyed it!" The applause and laughter roared like a 101-gun salute. But Jack would not live to see Jackie's sense of style at its most dramatic expression on his behalf.

A few critics caviled that at the funeral the widow Kennedy was a bit much. Veiled in black, she walked regally in the lead of the elected and crowned heads of both hemispheres behind her dead husband. Then, she prompted John-John to remember to make that heartrending salute to the flag-draped casket. Later, she lit an "eternal flame." However, Jackie long before—once for her pony, once for her dad—had rehearsed well the dramaturgy of high honor for the cherished dead.

When Danseuse had died, young Jackie compiled a photographic history of the jumping pony in whom she had invested so much of herself, annotating the homemade book with comments about "Donny's coat that glinted in the sun when she was brushed and shining," and the "soft, pink spot at the end of her nose." "She was such a lady," her mistress inscribed, and "she knew how lovely she was and flicked her tiny feet out in front of her as she trotted."

When Jack Bouvier had died all but friendless, Jackie resolved that her father, so important to her—although sometimes neglected by her—in life, would be honored in death, if by no one else, then properly by her. She sent her husband, then Senator, to deliver in person a photo of her debonair progenitor to the *New York Times* to insure an obituary worthy of the society page. She filled St. Patrick's

Cathedral not with funeral wreaths, but with baskets of wildflowers and garlands of summer flowers, and decked the casket of the man who had lived a carefree life with white daisies and blue bachelor buttons. No more than two dozen attended the funeral, and fewer than that drove two hours out to the Hamptons to see Jackie at the burial site, strewn with thousands more bachelor buttons, drop the last little blue flower on the grave.

Inside the airplane in Dallas, while Johnson was taking the oath of office, Jackie was steeling herself for the final display of the qualities that had made her worthy to be the wife of a President. She refused to take any sedatives, knowing she would have to rise early and be clear-headed to order the funeral arrangements. Against pleas and protests, she refused to change out of the blood-spattered shocking-pink skirt and blood-spattered stockings. The world must see the blood and know the horror and share the agony. She sat beside the coffin during the flight to Washington.

That night, Jackie did not want to sleep alone; so dear Uncle Hughdie lay down beside her and held her while she tried to sleep. On the day of the funeral, she received dignitaries in the morning, led them in stoic mourning at the St. Matthews parish church and at Arlington National Cemetery, then returned to the White House to receive the Prince of Wales, the Presidents of France and Ireland, and the Emperor of Ethiopia—sixty-two heads of state in all.

That done, she saw to it that Caroline and John, whose birthdays fell that week, were not deprived. John-John's birthday celebration took place on the night of the funeral —presents and fun and candles on a cake for a little boy who could not have understood the cancellation of a birthday party. On Jackie's last night in the White House, she wrote on prayer cards bearing Jack's likeness a personal note of thanks to every member of the White House staff.

Jacqueline's influence on both her husband and the nation as a whole was, finally, of a political nature, regardless of her disdain for the issues and the infighting. Jackie's values, as reflected in everything she did and in the way that she projected herself on the national and the world stage, helped to integrate the country—bring it together in something resembling national pride within the framework of elegance and high culture. She embodied the country's coming of age, its maturing into *civilization*, its evolving respect not for finery per se but *sensitivity*. If nothing else, Jackie, emboldened by her preeminence, promulgated sensitivity as something worthy of respect, and personified a beauty that was as tough as it was delicate.

Camelot was half Jackie's realm, and some think the better half. Politics is at the very least half style—witness the galvanizing effect that charismatic leaders have purely by virtue of their charisma—and Jackie's efforts to galvanize the country against the kitsch and slapdash insouciance of the past—can appropriately be called *political*. She exemplified, moreover, an independence in women that was achieved and solidified in and tempered by the fires of the material world, the rough-and-tumble world of politics, and she gave hope to millions of women who identified with her. But she also gave solace to millions of men who were able to appreciate her independence and her strength without being threatened by it.

Miss Ethel Stringfellow had been headmistress at Miss Chapin's School for Girls when Jackie attended there. Jackie was a reputed outlaw, "very artistic, but full of the devil," considered "the very worst girl in school." Her specialty was stealing warm cookies. But one day Miss Stringfellow got through to Jackie: "I know you love horses and you yourself are very much like a beautiful thoroughbred," said Miss Stringfellow. "You can run fast and you have staying power. You're well built and you have brains. But if you're not properly broken and trained, you'll be good for nothing." Of that properly trained thoroughbred on her saddest day, General Charles de Gaulle, the President of France, said: "She gave an example to the whole world of how to behave."

After having been married to the "most powerful man in the world," Jackie, "the most well-known woman in the world" (according to the polls), allied herself with "the richest man in the world": Greek shipping tycoon Aristotle Onassis. Working out patterns that would make Sigmund Freud blissful somewhere in the heaven of psychology, Jackie had attracted another man like Black Jack Bouvier. Onassis was a darkly scintillating, if not entirely trustworthy, diamond-studded beau. He *said* he had broken off his relationship with Italian opera diva Maria Callas, when he married Jackie. He fed his yacht crew cheap spaghetti while his guests ate caviar; his deckhands called him "The Shark."

Apart from all that, Jackie and Ari understood one another, just as Jack and Jackie had; and, too, they liked each other. After Jack's assassination, Jackie had become overly anxious—she was fearful that Caroline and John would be kidnapped, or worse. "I just couldn't live anymore as the Kennedy widow. [Marriage to Onassis] was a release, freedom from the oppressive obsession with me and the children." And, she might have added, freedom from the clannish Kennedys, whom she once described, at play in their numerousness on the lawn at Hyannisport, as a lot of "gorillas falling over one another." She still needed protection—more than the kind that Secret Serviceman give; and above all, she needed seclusion—the kind she could find on Skorpios, Ari's island. She needed money, of course, and especially she needed the emotional support she had always derived from strong, dark men. Ari provided all that and more—Ari was fun, and he left her free to come and go. Said Ari:

> Jackie is a little bird that needs its freedom as well as its security and she gets them both from me. She can do exactly as she pleases—visit international fashion shows and travel and go out with friends to the theater or any place. And I, of course, will do exactly as I please. I never question her and she never questions me.

Jackie's marriage to the melanous foreigner did not play well in Middle America. She had become a national icon, a vision of noble, suffering American womanhood, who—according to many—should have been content to go through life as the personal shrine sacred to Jack's memory. But that was not the kind of woman Jack Kennedy had married in the first place; and Jackie, not yet middle-aged when Jack was killed, was not ready for her existence to become either a museum or a memorial. Ari gave her a new name, the occasion to display a new identity, and an opportunity to escape the burden of being a flesh-and-blood Ms. Liberty.

Jackie's statement after Ari's death clarified their relationship precisely. Something short of everlasting love, they had enjoyed some good times together, and Jackie was grateful: "Aristotle Onassis rescued me at a moment when my life was engulfed with shadows. He meant a lot to me. He brought me into a world where one could find both happiness and love. We lived through many beautiful experiences together which cannot be forgotten, and for which I will be eternally grateful."

At middle age, Jackie selected another powerful and wealthy, if somewhat less ostentatious, man: Maurice Tempelsman, a Belgian gold and diamonds magnate who quietly advises Jackie on how to invest her millions and affords her the masculine support she always craved. The spice of scandal still tingles: Maurice no longer lives with his wife, since he became Jackie's friend. But Jackie no longer defines herself in terms of the men in her life, as once was the case.

Jackie entered upon her mid-life years as career woman: a book editor, first for Viking Press, beginning in 1975, and then for Doubleday, beginning in 1978. At first, her eye for opulence led her to big, colorful coffee-table books, such as (quoting Abigail Adams) *Remember the Ladies*—a lavish celebration of 18th- and 19th-century American women, which did not sell particularly well. Jackie has also edited a book about Russian culture and another of Russian fairy tales. As Senior Editor in Trade Books at Doubleday, she now specializes in celebrity biographies—such as Michael Jackson's, the one-gloved musical wonder who sings like Jackie talks. Who better than Jackie to get other reclusive superstars to write about themselves—she who refuses to grant interviews or, thus far, to write her own memoirs.

At the same time, she continues to pursue other interests consistent with her life's previous patterns of richness. Jackie perdures as an attentive mother to Caroline and John, rides to the hounds at a New Jersey hunt club, surveys Central Park through her telescope, keeps at her painting (sketches, still lifes, street scenes, landscapes), has expanded her interests to bird-watching and horticulture, and—as she did for the White House—devotes herself to the cause of fine art and historical restoration. As apolitical as ever, Jackie has refused to espouse the Equal Rights Amendment for women—a cause of consternation to politically activist women, who see Jackie as a paradigm of the emergent, independent woman. But Jackie adopts her causes selectively: she raises funds for the Metropolitan Museum of Art, is big at the New York Municipal Art Society, and is taking a lead with the 42nd St. Development Corporation and the movement to restore Times Square into a national theater center.

Mary "Mamie" Geneva Doud Eisenhower

The Pink First Lady

𝒜N INAUGURAL gown in Renoir-pink silk, glittering on the outside with 2,000 pink rhinestones, fortified underneath with multitudinous pink petticoats; pink gloves, pink shoes, and a pink silk bag embroidered with pink rhinestones, pink pearls, and pink beads—and that's not all: a pale pink bedroom in the White House, a pink satin ribbon in her hair, and daintily ruffled pink pj's. "Mamie—born Mary Geneva Doud on November 14, 1896—was about to become a symbol of the First Ladyship. President Ike, the Conqueror of Europe, looked at his girlfriend in bangs and all that pink, and he said: "By golly, Mamie, you're beautiful!"

Ike became President, first by leading the Western Allies to victory in World War II in Europe, then by whistle-stopping his hero's way across America. When the train stopped so he could make a short speech to the crowd, Ike would walk out on the rear platform, grin his mile-wide grin, offer his proverbial wisdom, and then say: "Now I want you to meet my Mamie!" The crowds went wild. On

Mary "Mamie" Geneva Doud Eisenhower

the campaign trail and later during White House receptions, Mamie always smiled and shook hands—not just fingertips, either—and chatted and quipped her great one-liners and made the people happy, as though she had not just done it with a thousand others and still had a thousand more to go. Ike was their war hero; Mamie was their pink sweetheart rose, an American Beauty; and the era was the "Togetherness Decade" of the 1950s.

If you were ordinary folks, it was hard not to like Mamie. Only if you had something against the color pink or bangs as a hairdo, or held some arbitrary notion that the First Lady ought to be an arbiter of intellect or high style or refined taste did Mamie's two terms seem longer than eight years. Exciting front-page news during the Eisenhower Administration was when the First Lady decided to receive guests with her right glove off—better for shaking hands. With General Ike, the man from Abilene (Kansas), and his gal Mamie, born in Iowa and raised in Denver, Middle America came to the White House for a long and comfortable stay.

Mamie started life as the privileged daughter of a well-to-do meat packer and his first-generation Swedish wife. John Doud had a thing about motorcars. Each year, he would load his family into his newest driving machine and head out for the Douds' summer home in San Antonio, Texas (the servants and the electrical car having been sent ahead by rail). Thanks to her father, Mamie Doud and her three sisters grew up both on the ample lap of Denver's social season (Mamie attended the "very katish" Miss Wolcott's school) and also on the highroad to vacation-time adventure.

Mamie grew up as well with an absolute respect for her father's values: she developed patience to keep the accounts, sensibleness to run a household, and self-control to live within a budget. She was also exposed to a demand for punctuality, a part of the picture that always remained fuzzy for Mamie; nor did she grow up learning how to cook. Mamie did grow up, however, wearing a diamond ring that Santa gave her on her sixth Christmas. She cruised around Denver in "Creepy" (the electrical coupe), could play all the latest tunes on the piano by ear (not by the discipline of musical learning), and dated all the swellest guys in town. One evening, when Mamie was fox-trotting her way across Denver, and the band started jazzing it up, high-flying Mamie and her date had to be intercepted: "The management requests that you dance a little less spectacularly."

In the fall of 1915, as the Doud family was packing to head south with the geese, one of Mamie's many suitors lamented: "Suppose you fall in love with some guy in San Antone?"

"I won't do that," chirruped Mamie. "There's nobody in Texas that I especially like."

Mamie first met Ike Eisenhower at Fort Sam Houston, near San Antonio, on a Sunday afternoon in October 1915. She was sitting in front of the Officers' Club with some of the women, when the Officer of the Day—a tall, handsome, earnest Second Lieutenant from Kansas—came striding across the street on his way to make his rounds. Mamie's friend called to the good-looking soldier to come meet some people, and finally persuaded him to deflect his attention to duty long enough to be polite. "The woman-hater of the post!" Mamie's friend whispered aside, as the paragon of spit-and-polish marched up to do his social duty.

Mamie watched Ike approach: "He's a bruiser!" she thought. And then she thought: "He's about the handsomest male I have ever seen!"

While the introductions were being made and the polite talk gotten out of the way, the man of action, too, was quickly assessing the field of engagement: Mamie "attracted [his] eye instantly." She was "a vivacious and attractive girl, smaller than average, saucy in the look about her face and in her whole attitude." Second Lieutenant Eisenhower asked Miss Doud if she would care to accompany him on his rounds. She accepted, although Mamie was not fond of taking walks.

The next day when Mamie returned from a fishing trip, Ike had been calling all afternoon. The phone rang again: Second Lieutenant Eisenhower was inviting Miss Doud to go dancing. Unfortunately, popular Mamie's date calendar was booked solid for the next four weeks.

"I'm usually home about five," she softened the blow. "You might call some afternoon."

"I'll be there tomorrow," said Ike.

Ike did arrive at the Douds' the following afternoon, and for most afternoons thereafter. When Mamie was out, Ike spent the time enjoyably and profitably with her parents. He proposed marriage on Valentine's Day of 1916, four months after their first meeting.

Back in Denver, Mamie's friends and some of the neighbors warned her against marrying the Army fellow. She was marrying "down," they said, and she would never have a home of her own, they said. For two utter romantics like Mamie and Ike, however, marrying "up" or "down" was meaningless. During more than fifty-two years of marriage, while following Ike around from Panama to the Philippines to Paris—one year, they moved from Army post to Army post seven times—Mamie lived in at least two dozen different places, and, she said "in everything from shacks with cracks to palaces." In the end, Mamie proved the neighbors wrong and did finally get a house of her own, after they vacated the government housing unit at 1600 Pennsylvania Avenue in Washington, D.C. The farm home of their retirement at Gettysburg was the first and only house the Eisenhowers ever owned.

The wedding took place in the Douds' Denver Mansion on June 1, 1916—the day Ike became a First Lieutenant. After a two-day honeymoon in the mountains west of Denver, the newlyweds entrained to Abilene for a visit with Ike's family. And in Abilene, Mamie and Ike had the first of many memorable "spats."

It had been a long time since Ike had spent time with his Abilene buddies, so the afternoon poker game ran on past suppertime. Against her mother-in-law's advice, Mamie got on the horn and rang up the boys. Ike was appropriately apologetic; but, said he, he never quit a game the loser, and, asking for understanding, explained that, at the moment, he was behind.

"Come *now!*" Mamie telephoned his orders to her AWOL husband, "or don't bother to come at all." Then she hung up the receiver with ear-drumming finality, remarking to Ike's mom: "That'll fetch him." Mamie had a quick, sharp tongue.

"Don't get too upset if it doesn't," Ike's mom gently, knowingly replied.

When Ike did come home sometime around two the next morning, Mamie was lying in ambush. Grinning his big grin, Ike proudly showed her his winnings: "It took a little while longer than I thought, but . . ." Mamie went up in pink smoke. They retired behind the bedroom door, and the "spat" lasted until dawn. Ike had a temper to match Mamie's tongue. There would be lots of "spats" in the years to come, most of which the Eisenhowers would hold in private. Ike had been right about one thing: she was "saucy," all right.

Mamie had her own version of boot camp to get through. Precisely one day less than a month after their wedding, Ike received orders to move out. He came home to get his gear together.

"You're not going to leave me this soon after the wedding day, are you?" Mamie was in tears, and Ike was rustling his equipment in shape behind the piano, where he had stowed it in their Fort Sam Houston quarters.

Ike stood up, came over to Mamie, put his arm around her, and said: "Mamie, there's one thing you must understand. My country comes first, and always will. You come second."

That night, Mamie cried herself to sleep, as she would do on many other occasions. Years later, Mamie remembered: "It was quite a shocker for a nineteen-year-old bride." Ike's parting words were stenciled on Mamie's mind like "U.S. Army" on every piece of military matériel in the camp. That day, the Army bride became an Army wife.

Ike had already told Mamie the way it must always be. Their money would be hers to spend as she saw fit—he would not interfere; raising the children would also be primarily her responsibility. When he was ordered to move, she could pack and follow, conditions permitting; otherwise, she would have to stay behind, alone. Looking back, Mamie said: "It used to anger me when people would say, 'You're an Army wife, you must be used to Ike being away.' I never got used to him being gone. He was my husband. He was my whole life." Mamie and Ike would spend much of their life together in writing letters to one another.

Ike's return was Mamie's reward for waiting, whether

BEHIND EVERY SUCCESSFUL PRESIDENT

from all-night duty on post or from years of duty overseas. Ike's promotions were Mamie's glory; Ike's love was Mamie's joy. Ike's career was the controlling theme of Mamie's life, and her source of borrowed satisfaction. After he became famous, she liked reading the newspapers about him—it was the best way Mamie had of keeping up with Ike's movements. But she did not enjoy watching newsreels; movies of Ike always made her cry. She told how:

> I knew from the day I married Ike that he would be a great soldier. He was always dedicated, serious and purposeful about his job. Nothing came before his duty. I was forced to match his spirit of personal sacrifice as best I could. Being his wife meant I must leave him free from personal worries to conduct his career as he saw fit.

Mamie had been taught at home and at school to put her husband first, and that is what she did; but nothing in her upbringing had prepared her to compensate for the bittersweet life of being a great man's wife. Because they moved often, there was no point in her putting down roots. Mamie was uninterested in higher education (while living in Paris, Mamie did not bother to learn French); she undertook only a few causes; she evinced no desire for a career of her own outside the home. Mamie played her piano, read novels and mysteries, knitted, enjoyed watching football games, and spent uncountable hours talking girl-talk and playing mah-jongg with other Army wives. Otherwise, when Ike was away, Mamie tended to decline social invitations; she had no recipes to swap (except one for fudge), as Ike was the chef in the family. Mamie craved nothing more; she would remain content with her lot as Ike's Mamie.

Mamie's boot-camp training included jumping other

hurdles besides just learning how to live alone. She also had to clear cooking fitness, handgun efficiency, moving-day preparedness, brass polishing, automobile driving readiness, and military hero training.

Mamie washed out in cooking. "I was a cooking-school dropout," joked Mamie, after she flunked a course at the "Y." She learned how to make mayonnaise, and, with the years, would do her duty on K.P. as needed; but, she said, Ike was "the world's best cook"—a master at grilled steaks and vegetable soup. "Ike cooks anything better than anybody; that's why I hate to work hard over a meal."

When Ike was made Provost Marshal at Fort Sam, with the responsibility of keeping rowdy soldiers in line, he worried about Mamie's safety on account of her being alone so much of the time. So, he gave her a .45 and taught her how to shoot it; and, a few days later, he put her through her paces.

"Mamie, let's see you get your pistol out—as if there were somebody trying to break in through the front door."

Mamie sprang into action, but first she had to remember where she had hidden the thing. She went rummaging behind the piano, inside a roll of bedding, under a stack of his and her other articles. Ike came to the conclusion that it would be easier for him to make the soldiers behave than it would be to teach Mamie how to protect herself: "She couldn't have gotten it out in a week, much less in a hurry."

At first, Mamie was almost as bad at moving house as she was at cooking and shooting. When Ike was transferred from Fort Sam Houston to command of the Tank Corps at Camp Colt, near Gettysburg, it was Mamie's job to get their stuff from Texas to Pennsylvania. A friend advised her not to clutter her life with a lot of *things*, as she and Ike would always be on the move. Accordingly, Mamie sold off to new arrivals the household goods that she and Ike had bought, thinking that she could buy more at the other end of the line. She sold $900 worth of new furniture for $90: "How could I have been so gullible!" Mamie finally became able to laugh at herself: "I know I was young, but not *that* young. . . . It's a wonder Ike didn't wring my neck."

Worse than the furniture, in Ike's mind, was what Mamie did with his two, almost new, civvy dress suits tailored for him on graduation from West Point: she sold them both for a ten dollar bill. But on this item, Mamie was unrepentant: she considered the suits "horrid eyesores" and was glad to be rid of them. Ike cooled off, after a while.

Nor, in the beginning, was Mamie any better at polishing brass than she was at cooking or shooting or bartering. During an inspection tour at Camp Meade, near Baltimore, the Secretary of War, Newton Baker, happened to stop by the Eisenhowers' quarters. Mamie made her guest at home and they exchanged small talk.

"What does your husband do best, Mrs. Eisenhower?" asked the Secretary of War.

"Oh," said the Commander's wife, "he plays an awfully good game of poker."

When Ike heard about it later, first he groaned, and then he laughed. "What possessed you to say such a thing to the Secretary, Mamie?"

She brightly replied: "I took it for granted he knew you were a good soldier."

When it came to "smoothing the edges off the rough-and-ready Kansan" and to "teaching him some of the polish that later put him in good stead," said son John Eisenhower, "she takes full credit." With Ike presiding over the steaks, Mamie applied her Denverite social flair to hostessing, charming Ike's fellow officers, the brass, a few crowned heads, and, later on, Ike's political constituents. The Eisenhowers' quarters, whether at Fort Sam, in Manila, or at NATO headquarters in France, came to be known as "Club Eisenhower." Mamie gave good parties; people relaxed and enjoyed themselves—playing cards, stuffing themselves at the buffet spread, and joining in singing old favorites while Mamie tickled the ivories and kept an eye on the Supreme Allied Commander: "Now, Ike, no bellowing!" John Eisenhower wrote of his mother's ability at polishing the rough-cut: "Every bit of an aristocrat, she taught him by example and, on occasion, direct instruction, the manners of the higher born." Ike would be good at winning wars, but it took Mamie to make him presentable to kings and queens and the American voter.

All in all, Mamie passed the boot camp of her early marriage with colors flying, and was rapidly promoted to the civilian vehicle corps in 1919. Ike was involved in an experimental, coast-to-coast convoy of Army trucks, aiming to prove that motor vehicles could outdo horses. Mamie and her dad loaded up the Packard in Denver and set out, Conestoga wagon fashion, on unpaved roads across the uncharted prairie to North Platte, Nebraska, where they rendezvoused with Ike's convoy. (During the Eisenhower Administration, America would begin to build its vast network of Interstate Highways.) Mamie was tough to tumble; and in this same year, at Ike's invitation, she became the first woman (as far as we know) to ride in a tank. "Checked-out in tanks!" Mamie boasted.

Mamie's victory on land sealed Ike's future. Ike planned for his career to take off with the Army Air Corps; but Mamie was terrified of flying and too much of a worrier to allow her husband to do much of it, if she could keep him from it. Very early on, Mamie grounded Ike with her own ultimatum: "Flying or me." Ike stayed on the ground, to become one of the greatest land tacticians in military history.

In January 1921, the Eisenhowers sustained the profoundest sorrow of their life. Their first son, Icky (pronounced "Ikey"), died of scarlet fever at Christmastime, when he was only three. The Eisenhowers' marriage had been going well—better, even, than Ike's career. (Ike was disappointed that he never got overseas during World War I; and the pace of his post-war advancement was slow.) Under Ike's schooling—he was a natural historian—Mamie had been developing an interest in the Civil War battlegrounds near where they were camped.

But when Icky died, Mamie wasted herself with self-reproach over the only two categories that really counted for her: wife and mother. What more might she have done to keep the boy alive? Mamie rolled the question over and over again inside her head.

Ike, for whom the little boy's death was to be an everlasting sadness, plunged into a depressive mistrust of life itself and a loss of freedom to be joyful, his nerves stretched to the fraying point. There would be no more growling on all fours on the floor like a bear, or playing horsey.

During stony silences, tired of blaming themselves, the bereaved father and mother at times blamed each other. It would be literally years before either Mamie or Ike would be able to talk to anyone else about Icky. Knowing Ike's grief, and suffering for him, only made Mamie sadder. Later on, she would say that Icky's death was worse than Pearl Harbor. When the second boy came along, Icky's death made Ike and Mamie overly strict. To young John, his father seemed too stern and demanding, too West Point in his discipline; his mother was overprotective and a worrier. After John grew to manhood, Mamie asked his forgiveness for her "smother love" when he had been a child.

Icky's death was a permanent defeat for Ike and Mamie, and their marriage almost became a casualty of war. Living in the Canal Zone in 1922 only made matters worse. Mamie hated the melting heat, the mold and the mildew in everything, the bugs—cockroaches and ants and mosquitoes and other things that they have only in Panama —and, above all, bats in the bedroom. On their second night there, Mamie heard a flutter above them, turned on the lights, covered her head with the sheet, and shrieked: "Ike! There's a bat in the room! Kill it!"

Ike tried to explain why he ought not to do that. The bats were prized because they ate the mosquitoes, and it was against the law to kill them.

"Law or no law, kill that bat!" screamed Mamie.

Ike unsheathed his ceremonial sword and proceded to fence with the bat. Later on, when Mamie's memory of Panama had been eased by better times and cooler temperatures, she recalled: "Ike was so grim and earnest. I didn't dare laugh. His long leaps and fancy sword-play on the furniture was a riot."

"Got him!" cried the victor. Mamie said that Ike had reminded her of Douglas Fairbanks, "the great leaper and jumper and swordsman of the movies. Only Fairbanks didn't fight bats."

In Panama, Ike buried himself and his sorrow over Icky in his work. Mamie spent more and more with other Army wives. Virginia Conner, wife of Ike's commander, tiring finally of Mamie's hours of rambling self-pity, told Mamie bluntly that she was going to lose her husband if she

BEHIND EVERY SUCCESSFUL PRESIDENT

didn't use her feminine strategies to save her marriage.

"You mean that I should *vamp* him?" Mamie asked in surprise.

"That's just what I mean," Virginia replied, advocating the firepower of the Feminine Mystique. "Vamp him!"

That was when Mamie took to wearing bangs. Flirtatious Mamie Doud, who had been a shaker and mover in the Denver teenage social set, re-emerged in the ladies-magazine image that would define the pre-feminist, "modern" ideal of feminity through the 1950s. In her mid-thirties, Mamie seduced her romantic soldier-boy into falling in love with her again, and would keep it up till she was in her seventies. The bangs became a permanent attraction, because "that was the way he liked it." With a little help from some reddish brown tint along the way (and in later years the occasional visit to an Arizona fat farm), Mamie stayed sexy the way Ike liked it. The vamping worked.

Mamie's motherly, stay-at-home, penny-pinching approach to life paid off in an unexpected way for the Panamanians while she lived in their country. Mamie and Virginia Conner were moved to active pity at the sight of Panamanian mothers giving birth and caring for their newborns under dreadful conditions, both medical and natural, that prevailed in the country. The two Army wives organized an effort among the U.S. military personnel to build a lying-in clinic for the nationals. As money was in short supply, Mamie turned her knack for hostessing to sparking a fund-raising campaign: dances, casino nights, bridge tournaments, white-elephant sales, and "ginger-ale evenings" (Prohibition was then in force, even in the sweltering U.S. Canal Zone).

After Panama, the Army moved Ike and Mamie back to the States. She raised young John, who had been born in

Mary "Mamie" Geneva Doud Eisenhower

Panama, partly in Fort Leavenworth, Kansas, and partly in Washington, D.C. When Ike was posted out to Manila in 1935 as Douglas MacArthur's assistant, Mamie thought about going, remembered Panama and the heat—and groaned. After holding back for a year in D.C. to see Johnny through the eighth grade, Mamie resigned herself to life in the tropics of the Philippines.

Her first experience confirmed Mamie's dread. When Ike stepped up to greet his wife at the pier in Manila, and took off his hat, Mamie was shocked: her husband had gone completely bald in only one year. He lamely explained that he had to crop his hair to keep cool.

"Crop what?!" she sauced him.

When the great and famous MacArthur returned to Manila after a brief time away, a welcome dinner was being given in his honor, and the Eisenhowers were in their rooms getting ready. Suddenly, Mamie felt dizzy.

"I feel queer, Ike! What is it?"

"It's not you," he reassured her. "It's an earthquake. By golly, it's a humdinger!"

When the room and its furniture had settled down, and Ike removed his protective arm from around Mamie, with the suggestion that they could finish dressing, Mamie smiled weakly and asked bravely: "Does this always happen when Mac comes back?"

Next, the tropics attacked Mamie with a stomach disorder; but, after a gall-bladder operation in 1938, she regrouped. The Eisenhowers moved into air-conditioned elegance at the Manila Hotel. "Club Eisenhower" was in business again, and Mamie was soon charming both the American military crowd and the ranking Filipinos with her mah-jongg and bridge parties, fancy dinners and teas. In 1939, when President Manuel Quezón awarded Ike the

BEHIND EVERY SUCCESSFUL PRESIDENT

Distinguished Service Cross of the Philippines, he handed the medal to Mamie: "You pin it on," said the President, "for you helped him to earn it."

In the summer of 1941, the Eisenhowers came full circle when they were posted back to Fort Sam Houston in San Antonio—they arrived on their 25th wedding anniversary. Mamie's Lieutenant was now a Colonel, and life might have been looking pretty good, except for December 7, 1941. Mamie remembered Pearl Harbor as "the next most terrible night of my life." Only Icky's death had been worse for Mamie.

It was Sunday afternoon at Fort Sam, and Mamie was sitting by the radio, listening to a football game, and knitting. Ike was taking a nap, having worked since dawn. Mamie was thinking about plans for Christmas vacation and a visit with John at West Point. Suddenly a news announcer interrupted the sports broadcast: "Pearl Harbor—Japanese planes attacking—Battleships in flames!" Mamie turned up the volume and woke Ike. "Nichols Air Field, Manila, the Philippines, and Clark Field ablaze!" the radio voice continued shouting. Mamie shuddered: she and Ike, only a year before, had lived there; they had friends there.

The phone rang. Still half asleep, Ike picked it up. "Right away!" Ike's voice saluted along the telephone lines, as he slammed the receiver down. To Mamie: "The Japs have hit us. That's it—that's war."

She watched him pull on his shoes, grinding his teeth in anger, his neck cords pulsing. He jerked around, patted her arm, and was gone. One by one, the other Army wives whose husbands had also received a telephone call came to Mamie's quarters. Mamie kept thinking about all the people she knew in Manila. The women agreed that, this night, they did not want to be alone. They stayed together, hugged each other, tried to eat something, listened to the radio, and wept. A few days later, Ike and Mamie were moved to Washington.

Mamie called World War II "my three years without Eisenhower." From 1942 to 1945, she was alone longer, and more lonely, than ever before. As always, Mamie was proud and supportive of her soldier-boy, now a Lieutenant-General; but the Army bride who had become an Army wife now became an "Army widow." She kept up with Ike the way everybody else did—through the media. One evening in 1942, Mamie was at his brother's—the Milton Eisenhowers'—trying to keep her mind off things with another game of mah-jongg. The radio was on, too loud, and Mamie had trouble concentrating on her game.

"Please turn that darn thing off!"

Brother-in-law Milton, however, was unwilling. Then, suddenly, the music was interrupted by a deep, radio voice: "We interrupt this program for an important announcement: American and British troops under the command of Lieutenant-General D. Eisenhower are landing at several points on the coast of North Africa. . . ."

Meanwhile, Mamie's ill health—weak from her operation long ago and from life in the tropics, and exacerbated by a fall—deteriorated into lethargy. Too many headaches and colds, insomnia and her perennial stomach trouble, and dizziness caused by an inner-ear problem drove her to her bed. Mamie had only Ike's picture for comfort. But then she rallied: "I finally told myself I couldn't carry on that way." "Worried sick" about Ike, she tried to shuck off her anxiety over his safety by putting her problem in God's lap: "I came to feel that God was not going to let anything happen to Ike until he had done what he was intended to [do]." She threw herself into Red Cross work; she hostessed at the Stage Door Canteen; she showed up at social gatherings where she might be able to foster goodwill for Ike; and especially she undertook to answer the many letters written to her by wives and mothers of men under Ike's command.

In January 1944, Ike, unannounced, slipped in on a quick and secret leave. Mamie and Ike went up to West Point to see John, and then on to West Virginia for a short vacation. As Ike was preparing to return to Europe, Mamie told him: "Don't come back again till it's over, Ike. I can't stand losing you again." And when she told him good-bye, she thought her heart would break. Years later, Mamie told her granddaughter-in-law Julie Nixon Eisenhower: "There were a lot of times when Ike broke my heart. I wouldn't have stood it for a minute if I didn't respect him. It was the kind of thing where I respected him so much, I didn't want to do anything to disappoint him."

Mamie's earnest desire not to disappoint Ike was operative during John's West Point graduation. The son was marching in his father's bootsteps; but Ike, at war, could not be present on the proud occasion. Mamie watched the glittering parade, memorizing the scene for Ike: "I knew one day [Ike] would ask for every detail," she wrote. "Johnnie's graduation was to have been one of the great personal moments of Ike's life. Writing him about it would help, but later he would expect to hear me describe everything, so I had to keep alert."

Mamie described the effect of the military ritual on herself as if "the drums of my mind tattooed, 'Ike in battle, Johnnie going toward battle.'"

She clipped the newspapers and magazines to build a scrapbook of Ike's feats, detailing his rise to become

Mary "Mamie" Geneva Doud Eisenhower

Commanding General of U.S. Forces in Europe and, ultimately, as Supreme Commander of Allied Expeditionary Forces at Normandy, France, on D-Day, 1944. She decorated her bedroom at the Wardman Park Hotel in Washington with photos of Ike, and she spent a lot of time looking at them. She sent airlifts of birthday, anniversary, and Christmas presents to him; and she headed stuffed top-secret diplomatic pouches Ike's way with such "classified" items as pajamas without holes, paperback Westerns, packets of instant noodle soup, and a recording of "Abdul, the Bulbul Ameer." Above all, she wrote him reams of letters full of newsy chitchat—anxious Mamie's version of brave face and stiff upper lip.

Mamie did not disappoint Ike. Did Ike disappoint Mamie? Wartime and distance take their toll on any marriage, and the threat to peace between the Eisenhowers was the Kay Summersby interlude. Kay Summersby, a former model with Irish good looks and English airs, was one of Ike's drivers during the War. They were frequently photographed together; they became confidants and, possibly, not entirely successful lovers. According to the rumor mill—including a couple of choice bits ground out by Ike's political foe, Harry Truman—Ike had a blazing affair, dashing about Europe and North Africa, contemplating divorce of his wife, and fantasizing marriage with his glamorous driver. Meanwhile, patient Mamie, faithful Army wife, grieved at home, jilted, jealous, and pickled.

Later rumors that Mamie became a drunk stemmed from the Summersby era, when, in fact, Mamie did nurse her worries from a bottle. Mamie's sociable habit had been to stretch a single drink through an entire evening; but, worried about Ike, and especially upset by the gossip, Mamie's habit expanded to maybe three stout drinks and feeling no pain. Eventually, when she saw the direction her drinking was tending, she pulled herself up and out of it by tugging on the same bootstraps that she had pulled on to combat her lethargy. Mamie went back to her one-drink rule. Her unsteadiness of foot and her bumping into things, both then and later in the White House, was caused not by alcoholism but by Ménière's syndrome, an inner-ear condition characterized by, among other symptoms, a dizziness and loss of balance. Mamie also suffered from chronic headaches, asthma, and claustrophobia. She was recommended "a day a week in bed" (for women over 50).

What was really going on between Ike and Kay from 1942 to 1944 was to be understood in view of what happened years later. In 1948, Kay Summersby published an innocuous volume of memoirs, *Ike Was My Boss*, in which there is no hint of wartime romance, much less a proposal of marriage from her boss. Nevertheless, the rumors, abetted by Harry the plain-speaking Democrat, persisted during Republican Ike's Presidential campaign in 1952. After Ike died in 1969, the Truman comments surfaced again; and this prompted Kay Summersby—who was dying of cancer at the time—to write *Past Forgetting: My Love Affair with Dwight D. Eisenhower*, published in 1976, after Kay had died in 1974. Kay denied that there had been a proposal of marriage, but she acknowledged that she and Ike had on three disappointing occasions attempted sex.

One can either argue that Kay, terminally ill, needed money to pay her medical bills, or one can accept as fact that Kay was making a deathbed confession of the truth. John Eisenhower, knowing that the Summersby book was in the offing, edited a counterthrust. *Letters to Mamie* (1978) is a selection of Ike's wartime correspondence with his wife (her letters to Ike are not extant), and, by its silence on the affair, it seems to prove Ike's fidelity. Ike's former aides and others came forward in number to deny the Summersby allegations. In 1979, the mass media made a buck first with an ABC mini-series premised on Summersby's *Past Forgetting*, and then on a novel based on the made-for-TV movie.

"Of course I don't believe it!" Mamie told a friend. "I know Ike." But Mamie was worried, chewing on it as she drank. Finally she got up the courage to mention it in letters to Ike.

Ike wrote back and admitted that Kay was a likeable person; but in letter after letter, he reassured Mamie: "I have *never been in love with anyone but you.*" He cautioned her against believing gossip and lies; he encouraged her to rise above the rumors and "smile at anything" people were saying; he told her he wanted nothing other than for the war to be over and for them to be together again.

Ike's replies, however, never quite seem to hit the critical question head-on: Did he or didn't he? Did they or didn't they? One of Ike's typical letters of reassurance leaves open ample room for speculation that it might very well have been Kay's beauty and youth that proved to Ike in stolen moments the shortcomings of his advancing age. Kay, after all, did not claim that much had happened—only that they had tried.

Ike to Mamie: "Darling, stop worrying about me. The few women I've met are nothing—absolutely nothing compared to you, and besides I've neither the time nor the youth to worry about them. I love you—always. Yours, Ike."

Ike, presumably, could have made the familiar distinction between loving one's spouse and enjoying one's friend, and thus could have stuck to his bottom line to Mamie without lying: "You are my only girl. I love you and I can say no more than that." Any "spats" between Ike and Mamie over Ms. Summersby were held in private.

None of Ike's letters mentions the area Mamie ought to have worried about: Kay was a far better bridge player than Mamie was. Mamie preferred chatting to concentrating. Ike, like some other steamed-up bridge-playing spouses, once threw down his hand and walked away from Mamie at a bridge table. Ike, it seems, preferred concentration in his bridge partners, if not in his wife.

On the other hand, Mamie had a preference for snappy dressers in her English lords, if not in her husband. For Mamie, the Summersby episode ended finally in wit; she had her own imagined peccadillos to savor. Lord Mountbatten, English hero of the war, was charmed by Mamie, and she by him. "He was such a perfect English gentleman, so witty, so charming, and so cultured. And so handsome in his English hand-tailored suits." Ike, in civvies, was a notoriously drab dresser, not at all up to Miss Mamie Doud's sartorial standards. Ike dressed well enough for the White House, but would have raised eyebrows at Denver's Brown Palace. "If I had one thought that there was an iota of truth in the Kay Summersby affair," Mamie grinned saucily, "I would have gone after Monty. And believe me, my friend, I could have gotten him!"

Mamie and Ike came through World War II with their marriage intact; and Mamie, who had lived her life for the sake of her hero, had a lot to be happy about: "Imagine how I felt, hearing presidents, prime ministers, kings, and generals praising Ike to the whole wide world! I was so happy I could hardly breathe." In private, she knew how to rib him: after a heady New York-sized welcome-home, ticker-tape parade, she dished him up some more of her sauce: "May I touch you?"

Not all the kudos went alone to Ike, however. When the French presented Ike the Grand Cross of the Order of Malta in gratitude for the liberation of France, they also presented Mamie the Cross of Merit with Crown: for the "exquisite good will, delicate charm, and intelligent kindness" that she "personally added . . . to the mission of the Commander-in-Chief of the Allied Forces," and for her "noble soul and generous heart."

Their life and relationship continued as before: Mamie making the necessary moves to keep up with Ike. In 1947, when Ike was being honored at Columbia University, adoring Mamie rose with the rest of the audience as Ike came down the aisle. But Ike stopped, stepped out of line, took Mamie's hand, and earnestly said to her: "Don't you ever stand up for me, Mamie!"

They lived in New York while Ike was President of Columbia, then moved to Paris in 1951, when Ike took over as Supreme Commander of NATO. Wife now of a politically famous man, Mamie learned her first and enduring lesson in management of the media when she let slip to the press the substance of a "spat" she and Ike had been having: he had approved their living in some posh quarters, but she had vetoed the idea. By the time the newspapers finished kidding the Supreme Commander's supreme commander, Mamie had resolved never again to give ammunition to the press by making public statements that could ricochet and hit Ike.

When Mamie could get over her fear of flying sufficiently to accompany Ike, she brought the homey touch to his hobnobbing with European royalty. In England, visiting in drafty Balmoral Castle, Mamie endeared herself to the Queen when she revealed that she traveled with a couple of hot-water bottles at the ready. So did the Queen.

Once when the Eisenhowers were entertaining Lord and Lady Halifax at tea, and just as Mamie was about to pour, Ike offered drinks to anyone who preferred. The British former Ambassador to the United States, the Lord Halifax, hesitated between tea and Scotch.

"No you don't!" Mamie sauced his lordship. "I went to all sorts of trouble to get the sort of tea Ike told me he used to have with you in England. Now, you take your tea, and after that you can have a drink."

In Stockholm, the Eisenhower entourage was spending an evening with the King and Queen of Sweden. (Mamie had insisted that her mother—who loved flying—and sister "Mike" accompany them as an antidote to Mamie's aversion to airplanes.) After dinner, Mama Doud (née Elvira Carlson, of Boone, Iowa), Mamie and Mike—with Ike cheering them on—tuned up to sing the Swedish folksongs that had for years been sung in the Doud family. With shining eyes, Queen Ingrid held out her hands and exclaimed her pleasure at hearing Swedish blood singing in American veins.

In 1952, when Ike became the Republican candidate for the Presidency, Mamie's life changed. "Helping Ike" now meant that Mamie had to become publicly more active than before. Ike, as he was coming to the decision to run, told Mamie that he knew he was asking her to go against her inclination to be a stay-at-home.

Mamie said later that she was about to reply: "Of course, I'll do anything you want," when he went on to tell her the reason behind his political commitment: the children —all children, everywhere, born and unborn. Ike was

Mary "Mamie" Geneva Doud Eisenhower

thinking of their own children, both the dead boy and the living one, but especially he was thinking of the waifs of war whom he had seen in Europe by the thousands. Behind Ike's commanding military presence beat a heart of pure mush; and Mamie knew it. "I was so proud he wanted my help. I knew it would be hard to change from a home-body, but I was perfectly willing to alter my life if and when he received the nomination."

Mamie met Pat Nixon for the first time at the Republican National Convention. When she first saw Pat, Mamie exclaimed in her affable way: "You're the prettiest thing!" Mamie was feeling a little groggy that night, having taken a painkiller for a toothache. She and Pat sat in the convention hall chatting about Mamie's toothache, while the Republicans nominated their husbands to head the next Administration.

Mamie's new duty assignment meant that she marched at quickstep. Instead of waiting out Ike's wars in solitude at home, or unpacking and repacking the baggage train and bringing up the rear, Mamie now found herself on the front lines. As she told one reporter: "This comes naturally. I've been training for it for 36 years. When you're in the Army, you get used to chasing after your husband."

She dazzled and shone like troops on parade, greeting the public from stages, at parties, and on train platforms whenever Ike introduced "my Mamie."

"I don't understand politics," she said, time and again; but she did understand people. She knew how to put them at ease and make them happy. The good effect of politics on Mamie was that she found it "exhilarating." The good effect of Mamie on Ike's political image (as a reporter told her) was that Mamie was "the best politician of the lot!"

Whistle-stopping through North Carolina, the

Eisenhower train pulled into a little town early one morning just as the sun was rising up and the Eisenhowers were getting up. A couple of hundred people had gathered to cheer.

"Come on, Honey! Let's say hello to them." Ike was still wearing his dressing gown.

"Like this?" Mamie had her robe on, too, and her hair up in curlers.

"Sure!" said Ike. "You're pretty as a picture."

The two stepped out onto the platform, and Ike greeted the crowd. A woman in the audience, seeing Mamie in her morning attire, called out: *"She's going to get him elected!"*

Later, at breakfast, it came out that of the three press association photographers covering the campaigns, only one had been up early enough to snap any pictures. The other two, caught sleeping at the switch, might be in "bad trouble," their jobs on the line.

"We can fix that," cried Mamie. "I'll get my hair in curlers again and we'll re-stage it."

"Dynamite" pictures of the Eisenhowers in their bathrobes and curlers appeared in the press nationwide. James Reston of the *New York Times* estimated Mamie's political value to be at least 50 votes in the Electoral College. Ike agreed, and said so.

Mamie had other campaign jobs to do. As she had once answered letters of concern about Ike's soldiers, she now employed two secretaries to write letters to Ike's supporters: "I get up with letters, I go to bed with letters. I guess I'm what you would call a well-lettered woman."

Mamie helped Ike with his speeches. She would listen and make suggestions as Ike read his drafts aloud. The train was headed towards Detroit, and Ike was only a few sentences into his address—an address that speech writers had written for him.

"Ike, you can't say that," Mamie interrupted. "It's not in character."

Ike kept on reading.

A few sentences later: "Ike, that simply isn't *you!*"

Irritated, Ike kept on reading.

For another twenty minutes, she broke in every few sentences to register her frank displeasure with the un-Ike-like speech. Finally, according to Kevin McCann (later Ike's Presidential aide), Ike "threw the speech down and slammed his way into the bedroom of the train so hard I thought he'd throw the train off the track." But he got over his mad soon and wisely enough he discarded the alien speech; he spoke effectively and extemporaneously instead. After this "spat," Ike introduced his wife not by saying, "Meet my Mamie!" but more formally: "And now I want you to meet Mrs. Eisenhower."

Once after a speech that had moved Mamie to tears, she told Ike: "Don't change a word, Ike." He beamed his Eisenhower grin at her approval. When someone told her that according to some scientific poll, Ike was considered to be the greatest living American, Mamie replied with a smile: "They didn't have to go to all that trouble. I could have told them."

The night they won the election, Mamie was again crying her tears of joy and inspiration: "It's inspiring, the way people look at him with such affection, interest, and hope." Seeing the people's confidence in Ike's leadership, said Mamie, kept her "cloud-high all the time."

Inauguration Day, 1953, was an emotion-packed day

BEHIND EVERY SUCCESSFUL PRESIDENT

for Mamie. She was not keen on moving into this next government barracks, even if it was the White House; Mamie wanted a home of their own. But when Ike took the Oath of Office, she broke into tears. Then, her "boyfriend" —as Mamie called her Second-Lieutenant become President —helped his Mamie achieve one of her few First Lady firsts. After he took the Oath, the new President turned and kissed his wife on the cheek, his first official act. No President before had kissed his First Lady in public at his Inauguration —and it was the best kind of recognition for a job well done, and a life well lived, that Mamie could have wanted. Following that, Ike insisted that Mamie, instead of the Vice President, ride beside him from the swearing-in to the White House and the reviewing stand for the Inaugural Parade.

The parade lasted five hours, and Mamie's feet in her high-heel shoes got tired of standing so long in the open car. She sat down, slipped off her shoes (Mamie always had trouble finding shoes that fit, especially since she insisted on buying them off sale racks), and the rubbing her arches. The news photographers swooped in for a shot. Let them shoot away, Mamie laughed; every woman in America will sympathize with aching arches! While General President Ike stood at attention, saluting the flags passing by, Mamie crawled in under a blanket with Herbert Hoover. The former President and the new First Lady sat together laughing, enjoying the parade, and keeping warm.

After this unconventional beginning, the Eisenhower years proved socially humdrum. Ike was glad, for the first time in his life, to be able to stay at home in the evenings, have dinner with Mamie from a couple of TV trays, and maybe watch a movie. As for Mamie, she had few First Lady projects: "I never intended to be anything but Ike's wife. . . . I have only one career, and his name is Ike."

Mary "Mamie" Geneva Doud Eisenhower

Even if Mamie's First Ladyship did not come up to the standards that Washington's social columnists would like to have set for her, she simply adored being First Lady. She was thrilled at having Ike around the House: "I've got *my* man right here, where I want him!"

Mamie was not tall; and, loving to be at the center of attention, she was afraid that people would miss seeing her at receptions. "So everyone can see me," she had the White House carpenters build her a little platform on which to stand while receiving; but it proved dangerous: "We almost lost me," she said the next day. "They nearly jerked me off the platform."

At the next reception, she tried standing on the landing of the great staircase in the Green Room; but waving at the people as they moved past felt too far away. Next, she tried the bottom step near the lobby, flanked by four leading Republican women on the next step up behind her. The First Lady was having trouble finding her own place: the other women were too close, Mamie thought, "Nobody knows who is *me*!"

Whenever Mamie rode around town in a White House limousine, she would wave her friendly greetings to anyone who recognized her. In parades, Mamie sometimes rode in the car behind the President's; when people would shout: "Where's Mamie?" she would roll down the window, stick her head out, and shout back: "Here I am! Here I am!"

Mamie was always ready with some of her sauce. During a festive dinner to honor General George C. Marshall, the emcee for the occasion misspoke himself: "General Marshall wants nothing more than to retire to his Leesburg, Virginia, home, with Mrs. Eisenhower."

The company at her table made merry with the gaffe, while the emcee tried to recover himself: "My apologies to the General!"

As the laughter subsided, Mamie brought down the House by asking, "Which General?"

Mamie organized her First Ladyship from her pink bedroom, sitting in her pink bed, dressed in her pink dressing gown. It was her morning command post: there she planned her day, conferred with her staff, sorted her mail, and passed out orders for the White House routine. The White House staff found the Army wife in pink a demanding taskmistress: occasionally imperious, with a spine of steel, efficient and knowledgeable, and a crack personnel supervisor. Mamie took a spit-and-polish approach, and would run her white-gloved fingers along window sills to make certain that they had the shine she wanted. She hated to see footprints in the deep pile of the carpets, so the staff learned to walk about the edges of the rooms to keep from having to vacuum the rugs unnecessarily.

When Mamie moved she proceeded with ruffles and flourishes: "When I go out," ordered the five-star general's wife, "I am to be escorted to the diplomatic entrance by an usher. And when I return," she commanded, "I am to be met at the door and escorted upstairs."

Chief Usher J. B. West summarized Mamie's style: "She knew exactly what she wanted, every moment, and exactly how it should be done. And she could give orders, staccato crisp, and detailed, and final, as if it were she who had been a five-star general. She established her White House command immediately."

One of the butlers was more awed in his view, and invested Mamie with the powers of percipience that a child ascribes to its mother: "Mrs. Eisenhower knows every single thing that goes on in this house, who's here, what they're doing, and why."

At the same time, Mamie was a kindly chief of operations. She took personal interest in the staff's lives. Sick people received flowers; birthday people got presents and a cake from the White House kitchen. She was lavish in her praise for work done well. At her first Christmas in the White House, Mamie personally bought and wrapped gifts for everyone in the Mansion.

"Well, I've finally done it!" She was viewing the Christmas tree with pride, commenting to Mr. West. "It's been my desire all my life to be able to give a Christmas gift to *everyone* who works for me!"

After they bought their Gettysburg farm, the Eisenhowers had the entire Mansion staff out to the farm for a grand party. The Eisenhowers were the first Presidential couple to host a party—it took two parties, in fact, to accommodate everyone—just for the people who worked at the White House. "She wants to be everybody's godmother," commented one of Mamie's workers.

Ike and Mamie had a clear agreement on separation of powers in their division of labor: "Ike took care of the office; I ran the house." Once when Mr. West presented a luncheon menu for the First Lady's final glance, she caught him up short:

"What's this? I didn't approve this menu!"

"The President did, two or three days ago," explained the Chief Usher.

"I run everything in my house," General Mamie informed her second-in-command. "In the future all menus are to be approved by *me* and not by anybody else!" That included the President.

Mamie planned the menus, shopped the newspapers for sales and coupons (and then sent the staff out to cash in on the bargains), and—above all—kept the White House running on a comfortable, hospitable basis. In other words, Mamie was doing at her House what every other middle-class American housewife in the 1950s was doing at her house.

Mamie bought her clothes off the rack and her jewelry off the counter; she presented her coupons at the grocery store check-out counter, watched the Soaps, and was a "demon" at canasta (the middle-class game of preference, a more sociable diversion than bridge, and less complicated than mah-jongg). On holidays, Mamie gussied up the Executive Mansion with the same Early Hallmark touch they were using out in the suburbs on the split-levels: candy canes at Christmastime, witches and skeletons and jack-o'-lanterns at Halloween, and green top hats for St. Patrick's Day. White House cuisine was American foursquare, too: Mamie's favorites were corn-on-the-cob, fried chicken, baked beans, corn bread, and apple pie.

The Eisenhowers were the First Family in the purest sense of American sentiment. On June 1, 1959, on Ike's and Mamie's 43rd, the oldyweds (with two other couples, old friends) renewed their marriage vows in the White House. They had the works—white veils and bouquets, Wagner and a minister. When grandson David married Julie Nixon in 1968, the grandfolk's wedding present was an inscribed brass plaque: "God Bless This Home." On the back, Mamie had written: "This hung in the White House during the eight years your grandfather was President." Mamie loved children, and had always looked forward to becoming a grandmother. She re-instituted the Easter Monday egg rolling on the White House lawn, which had been discontinued during World War II.

Even Mamie's sense for the appropriate, however, was

not unerring. She did far better at hostessing informal teas and coffees—which she thoroughly enjoyed—than she did, for example, at receiving Latin American dignitaries, whose culture she failed to understand. (If only Mamie had taken advantage of her Spanish lessons at the White House during Bess Truman's days!)

Mrs. López Mateos, wife of the President of Mexico, called at the White House with an entourage of ten other women. Mamie, taken by surprise at their numbers, blurted out that not enough places had been set at the table. Some of the Mexican women politely slipped away.

Mrs. Mateos then presented Mamie with a giftbox, beautifully wrapped. Inside was an elegant pin wrought in costly gemstones of the Mexican and American flags intertwined. Mrs. Mateos had done her diplomatic homework flawlessly; it was just the kind of jewelry that Mamie favored. (Mamie's two favorite pins were an expensive ruby-diamond-sapphire American flag and an identical other in convincing-looking paste. The latter she wore all the time; the former she kept for special occasions.)

Mamie offended Mexican custom by not opening the package immediately and exclaiming over the gift. Instead, she tossed the box to a White House usher, saying: "Put this on my desk."

Señora Mateos departed shortly thereafter, her face as gravely set as the visage of an Aztec god at Tenochtitlán. It was not Mamie's best day in the White House.

Consistent with the Eisenhowers' division of labor, Mamie left the running of the country up to Ike. Ike, however, was a smart husband—he told his Cabinet now and again, regarding some new idea, that he wanted to "try it out on Mamie first." He considered her a "pretty darn good judge of things." He discussed appointments with her, relying on her shrewd judgment of character. In 1956, Mamie intervened effectively against the "Dump Nixon" campaign among the Republicans. Mamie saw Nixon as loyal and therefore deserving of loyalty in return.

Presumably, Mamie made her opinions on politics and policy clear to Ike, but not in the Oval Office. James C. Hagerty, Ike's Presidential press secretary, commented: "She'd argue with him plenty of times about his policies—but upstairs, in the privacy of their living room." For Mamie, their division of labor was rooted in a separation of sexual powers: "When Ike came home, he came home. He left all his work at the office. I never went to his headquarters when he was an army officer. I only went to his White House office four times—and I was invited each time."

Reflecting on his wife's First Ladyship, Ike wrote that "Mamie's biggest contribution was to make the White House liveable, comfortable, and meaningful for the people who came in. . . . She exuded hospitality, no matter how tired she was."

At state dinners, Mamie arranged the throne-like mahogany chairs in which she and Ike sat side-by-side, so that she could sit next to, not across from, the President. She wanted to be near Ike.

Once, when unpunctual Mamie arrived later than usual for dinner, always-punctual Ike called her on the carpet: "Do you realize that you have kept the President of the United States waiting?"

"Why no," the demure imp replied. "I've been busy making myself pretty for my husband."

After Ike suffered his heart attack in 1955, and it appeared that he would be unable to run for a second term, it was Mamie who, after her initial hesitation, encouraged him to continue in office. Whatever Ike wanted was just fine with her. Ike wrote in his memoirs:

> She felt and said that it would be best for me to do exactly whatever seemed to engage my deepest interest. She thought idleness would be fatal for one of my temperament; and consequently, she agreed that I should listen to all my most trusted advisers and then make my own decision. She said she was ready to accept and support me in that decision no matter what its nature.

Mamie, as she characteristically did, put it more succinctly: "I just can't believe that Ike's work is finished. . . . He still has a job to do." They lived in the White House for four more years.

Mamie oversaw the building of their retirement home in Gettysburg—a lot of it done in "Mamie Pink." There, Ike wrote and painted, golfed and played at being a dairyman, while Mamie continued doing what she had always done. She ran the household, shopped for bargains with her coupons, and took her turn in the check-out lines as though she had never been the First Lady. Speaking of their retirement, but commenting on their entire life, she said: "I knitted and he painted. There was never any competition between us." The focus of Mamie's life was still Ike: whenever Ike was absent from the farm, she said, "the house sagged. When he came home, the house was alive again."

On June 1, 1966, the Eisenhowers celebrated their golden wedding anniversary. Mamie offered her recipe for a happy marriage, sending ideological shudders through feminists and gender egalitarians everywhere. She does not mention where "spats" fit in; presumably, they are fair fights to be fought out in private, whereas family solidarity is to be maintained in public: "Young women today want to prove something, but all they have to prove is that they can be a good wife, housekeeper, and mother. There should be only one head of the family—the man."

Mamie verbalized her gender politics consistent with the life she had lived. She comprehended neither student nor sexual revolution. She said that, in her opinion, women did not need "liberating." The abbreviation "Ms." was a mystery to her. She said that she "never knew what a woman would want to be liberated from." Mamie summed up her theory of the woman's threefold role in life almost as succinctly as a Confucianist might put it (Mamie forgot to mention having been John Doud's daughter): "I was Ike's wife, John's mother, the children's grandmother. That was all I ever wanted to be. My husband was the star in the heavens. It wasn't that I didn't have my own ideas, but in my own era, the man was the head of the household."

After Ike suffered another heart attack in April 1968, and was living out his last year at Walter Reed Hospital in Washington, Mamie moved in beside him. She pinked their hospital rooms—installed a pink phone and a pink toilet seat—continued with her knitting, and, best of all, held Ike's hand.

She also engaged enthusiastically in Republican politics: Mamie was a Nixon booster all the way. During the Presidential campaign that year, she kept a glass bowl full of Nixon buttons by her chair and handed them out to the doctors, nurses, and visitors. Later on, she preferred George Bush to Ronald Reagan. Mamie said that Ike had picked George out as "Presidential material . . . when Bush was low man on the totem pole."

During the Nixon Presidency, Mamie was often invited to the White House to enjoy girl-talk with Pat, a cordiality that she freely returned in time of need. The two Presidential families had become happily related through the marriage of Mamie's grandson David and Pat's daughter Julie. During the Watergate miasma, Mamie invited Pat out to the Gettysburg farm.

> Pat Dear—
> This is not an engraved invitation but I would love to have you come up here when the President goes away—you could rest, walk, read, and gossip with me—now please everything would be on the QT. What fun we would have—have told Julie and David they could come too—Come a running—
> Love, Mamie E.

On other First Ladies, Mamie held pronounced opinions that corresponded as much to her gender politics as to her Party preference. Fellow Republican Pat Nixon always remained "one hundred percent" in Mamie's book; two Democrats she deplored; two, she favored. Mamie considered Jackie Kennedy to be "brazen and frivolous," thought that she spent too much time away from home, and "had no respect for money at all." Rosalynn Carter, according to Mamie, was too given to "grandstanding," and ought not to have tried to help run the government as a "kind of Assistant President." Bess Truman and Lady Bird Johnson, on the other hand, Mamie respected; they had kept themselves in the background, stood by their men, and played their role with grace and quiet dignity.

Among Ike's last words were these to John: "Be good to Mamie."

"When Ike died," Mamie told granddaughter-in-law Julie, "the light went out of my life." To friends, she said: "I miss him every day."

When Jimmy Carter was President, he paid a call on

BEHIND EVERY SUCCESSFUL PRESIDENT

Mamie, in her early eighties, at the farm. As he was leaving, he gave her a kiss.

"My Lord!" said ever-saucy Mamie afterwards, "I didn't know what to do. I hadn't been kissed by a man outside of the family since Ike died." Nor, by a Democrat.

Mamie Eisenhower died on October 1, 1979.

Elizabeth "Bess" Virginia Wallace Truman

No-Comment Bess

"*N*O-COMMENT Bess" was the wife of "Give-'em-Hell Harry." He was a Democrat and the plain-speaking, straight-talking commoner from Independence, Missouri, who failed at wheat farming, lead and zinc mining, oil-well drilling, Kansas City haberdashering, and just about everything else, except elective politics and winning the woman he loved. Bess—born Elizabeth Virginia Wallace on February 13, 1885—was the golden-haired goddess of Harry's childhood devotion: he knew already in 1890 that he was everlastingly in love with her, when he was six and she was five. She was the girl with "golden curls" and "beautiful blue eyes," whose family—more refined than wealthy—lived in the big fine house at 219 North Delaware Street. Five years later, when he first got up the courage to speak to her, the courting started and continued from the fifth grade right through high school and beyond. But true love must leap over many obstacles.

Sometimes Bess let Harry carry her books home from school, and sometimes they studied Latin together. But

Elizabeth "Bess" Virginia Truman

"Four-Eyes Harry"—young to wear glasses—was a book-reading, piano-playing indoor boy, who worked his way through school by doing odd jobs and by being a dry-dirt farmer. Bess' mother, the "queenly" Madge Wallace, could hardly be expected to approve of such a suitor. Bess, quite the opposite of Harry, was an athletic outdoor girl, who roller-skated, climbed trees, and could out-whistle any boy in town. She was a horsewoman, downright lethal on the tennis court, almost as ferocious with a basketball, and loved baseball. Bess enjoyed going fishing: Harry felt sorry for the fish.

Moreover, her Grandfather Gates saw to it in 1905 that Bess went to Barstow, a finishing school in Kansas City. Bess was a hit at school, as she had been at home: she made top grades, became a star basketballer, and won the shot-put contest; and, she could have her pick of the young men. Back in Independence, Bess was in no hurry to marry. Grandfather Gates had given her a splendid black horse to ride and let her drive his Studebaker—the first one in town. She spent her time enjoying tennis, bridge, the Needlework Guild, and going to parties. Bess had, furthermore, effectively assumed much of the responsibility for her family of mother and brothers, her father having died when she was eighteen. What did Bess need with a husband!

Then, in the summer of 1910, Harry Truman came to town from his farm at Grandview for a visit with his kinfolk. Harry's aunt mentioned that she needed to return a cake plate to Mrs. Wallace. Harry grabbed it "with something approaching the speed of light" and sprinted towards 219 North Delaware. Two hours later he returned with a smile of triumph: "Well, I saw her!"

Courting Bess in earnest now, Harry had no better luck than before. He was poor, and knew he was a country bumpkin, but he had high hopes. The first time he proposed to Bess, he admitted that he was "a kind of good-for-nothing American farmer," but offered her a "sneakin' notion that some day maybe I'd amount to something." She turned him down; but Harry lived with it—she was still his friend and she had not made fun of the proposal: "You see," he said, "I have never had any desire to say such things to anyone else."

Bess Wallace was a hard woman to convince on any score; and Harry was up against more than he could know. But he knew he was beginning to make progress when she allowed him to start calling her "Bess" instead of "Miss Wallace." She accepted his photograph. He was invited for Sunday afternoons, and she even visited him at Grandview. They went fishing together, and she made fun of his squeamishness. She even gave him her photo. And in 1913, she acknowledged that, if she ever were to get married, it would be to him.

Harry was exuberant: an "ordinary gink" was unofficially engaged to "the best girl in all the universe."

Again, he hinted at a promise: "How does it feel," Harry asked Bess, "being engaged to a clodhopper who has ambitions to be . . . Chief Executive of the U.S.?"

The next-to-last obstacle to be hurdled was "queenly" Madge. Harry won over his mother-in-law-to-be when he scraped together enough bucks to buy a second-hand, open touring car. Madge thought Bess looked fine being squired around town in that Stafford. The last obstacle was World War I. Although Bess was finally willing to marry him in 1917, seven years after his first proposal, Harry put wedding plans on hold: he would marry when he returned from the trenches. Bess agreed, and sent him off to war with a new photo of herself, inscribed: "Dear Harry, May this photograph bring you safely home again from France—Bess."

Harry's side won the war and he made it home again. He and Bess were married in June 1919, after a nine-year-long courtship; Bess was 34. They settled in the house on North Delaware Street; and Harry, with an Army buddy, went into the haberdashery business in Kansas City. That first year set the pattern for the Trumans' married life: Harry worked out front, and Bess worked behind the scenes—she planned advertising, took inventory, and kept the books. When postwar depression caused the business to fail, Bess and Harry agreed not to take the easy way out; instead of declaring bankruptcy, they cut back expenses and gradually squeezed out the total repayment of all their debts, although it took them years to clean up the financial sabotage.

Harry decided that he preferred politics to selling hats, and took a turn into the business of public service—a change of lifestyle that heightened the differences between him and Bess more than any other could have. Harry was a born public figure, with a down-home yarn for every occasion and an astute opinion on everything for everybody. Bess restricted her opinions, equally astute, to expression at home and for Harry only; she met the outside world with cool indifference. Throughout the course of Harry's public career, Bess would invest almost an equal amount of effort in her career—staying out of the public glare.

Harry enjoyed playing poker and sipping high-grade Kentucky Bourbon with the boys (though he was a more honest politician than most of them); he was an affable rover and a rip-snortin' politico who loved the grime and the heat and the handshaking of election time. Bess was an independent-minded, reserved homebody who played bridge and savored the quiet life of her house on North Delaware in Independence. She would concede the crowd nothing more than a one-line greeting; and, especially, the snoopy people from the press, both then and later, she would intimidate with a consistent "No comment."

She cared little for Harry's colleagues. Like a lot of other people, she mistrusted Harry's chief backer, the Democratic boss of rough-and-tumble Kansas City politics, Tom Pendergast. Politicians, like the press, seemed to think that they could invade Bess' home and her privacy any time they liked. One noisy fellow, with a clown-red nose, walked up on the porch in 1924, picked up Bess' two-year-old daughter Margaret, and gave the baby a politician's kiss; whereupon the toddler grabbed the colorful nose and gave it a pinch. The man hollered, put Margaret down, and retreated. "Served him right!" said Bess.

Nevertheless, Bess backed Harry in her quiet and resolute way, exchanging daily letters with him and sending him local newspaper clippings when he was away; at all times, she kept her mistrustful eye on his constituency and the political machines. Bess trusted neither crooked Democrats nor the self-righteously Republican *Kansas City Star*. Later on, she would train her sights on FDR as sharply as she watched Pendergast's wheelings and dealings.

In the evenings before bedtime, Bess and Harry retired first to his study for a discussion of the day's events, the morrow's duties, and the issues of their time. Harry was an optimist; Bess was a pessimist and a ticking worry clock. He trusted people, sometimes too much; she saw through them with a critical glance. No one knows what Bess and Harry said to one another during those years of private discussion, or how they said it. She told him what she thought, critiqued whatever he had to say, but never disagreed with him in public or criticized him to anyone in private.

In 1934, when Pendergast ran Harry for the U.S. Senate, Bess agreed to stand on the platforms with Harry while he made his speeches; but the most anybody got Bess to say was this: "A woman's place in public is to sit beside her husband, be silent, and be sure her hat is on straight." When Harry won the election, Bess said she was "thrilled to be going to Washington"; it would, she thought, "be a change" from Delaware Street.

The reason Bess hesitated to take public part in Harry's career had nothing at all, contrary to what Bess said, to do with "a woman's place" or silence or hats. In fact, Bess had firm and settled opinions about the strong hand a wife ought to take in her husband's affairs. Talk about "a woman's place" was just some of Bess's camouflage. One might speculate about her highly individualistic nature, find in her partial deafness or her chronic and troubling arthritis an explanation for the flipflop from the outgoing, sports-loving young girl to the aloof adult.

As a youth, Bess had been dismayed to watch the effects of notoriety on the life and affections of her best and lifelong friend, Mary Paxton. Mary had early success as a daredevil newspaper reporter, but it made her seem unacceptable as a demure bride to her true love, Charlie Ross, and to Charlie's mother. In later years, Mary would like to say, "I was born liberated." But in losing Charlie, she had paid dearly for her freedom in a day when "ladies didn't do such things." Bess had seen her friend nearly waste away, before Mary regained a sense of self-possession.

Bess had also watched the destruction of the Swope family who lived next door in Independence. A Swope son-in-law poisoned a good number of Swopes in order to protect his hoped-for inheritance from dissolution. The sensationalist press and corruptible courts dismissed the perpetrator before the bar, and tried the innocent family in the newspapers instead, scattering Swopeses to sorrow, poverty, and California.

All of this only reminded Bess of what had happened to her own mother. When Bess was eighteen, her beloved father, a cheerful, forthcoming fellow and well-liked Missouri politician—saddled in the Depression of 1903 by heavy debts and heavier drinking, sat down in his bathtub and shot himself. The front page of the Jackson County *Examiner* almost made the reader hear the lead bounce on the porcelain: "The ball passed through his head and out of the right temple and fell into the bathtub." Madge Gates Wallace, Bess' mother, reacted to this shock, to the garish media curiosity and public gossip, by becoming a recluse in self-imposed exile inside her drafty Victorian mansion. Bess would protect and care for her emotionally fragile and politely demanding mother for the next fifty years—this being one of Bess' main reasons for preferring Missouri to the District of Columbia.

Out of these experiences of the world's unkindness, Bess had learned to be wary of the prying public.

Of course, Bess never told any of this to anybody. Margaret conjectured that her mother had early rejected altogether the traditional separation of the woman's sphere from the man's sphere. But Bess had resolved that when she found her man, she would share his whole life, however painful. Quiet loyalty and absolute reliability made Bess Harry's supremely valuable confidante as he worked his way up from being a County Judge overseeing the building of roads and public buildings, to U.S. Senator, and then to Vice President, on his way to keeping his engagement

Elizabeth "Bess" Virginia Truman

promise to Bess.

At first, Senator Truman's family—Bess and Margaret and Madge—did a lot of Washington sightseeing. One thing about Washington that Bess did not like was the laundry establishment—too expensive and not careful enough. As postage was cheap in those days, Bess sent their laundry to K.C. to be done!

Bess soon distinguished herself by working shoulder-to-shoulder with Harry, but quietly, in the background, as his anonymous office help. Harry made noise enough for both of them in the Senate, first by serving on the Railroad Commission that went after the tycoons who behaved more like outlaws than patriotic industrialists. Then, during World War II, he headed the Truman Committee that rode herd on the greedy big-business crowd, out to fleece the taxpayers in the profitable game of Military-Industrial Complex.

This was the kind of politics Bess liked best, so she settled in for a long tenure as a crusading Senator's wife. She thrived on Harry's victories at the polls, and she rooted for his reformations in the political arena. When Harry won a second six-year term in 1941, he put Bess on the payroll; she earned $2,400 per year for being on his staff and for continuing to do what she had always done. Bess read and answered Harry's mail for him, researched critical issues, read the *Congressional Record* every day, and every night debated the issues with Harry the same way she would have pressed her advantage at the net in a smashing game of tennis.

Staying part of the time in Independence, she kept up with the hometown newspapers, and kept her Senator in D.C. informed on the backyard maneuvers of known enemies and questionable allies on Harry's Missouri flank.

And, she kept a weather eye on FDR, whom she judged to be manipulatively disloyal to his political friends—an unpardonable offense to a personal stalwart like Bess.

Although Bess' status as paid employee was not uncommon for Congressional wives, Republican Congresswoman from Connecticut Clare Boothe Luce picked an election-year fight with Harry in 1944, calling his bride and prize staff member "Payroll Bess." Time and again, Harry came to "the boss'" defense: "She earns every cent I can pay her. She helps me with my personal mail, helps me with my speeches and with my committee work. I don't know where I could get a more efficient or willing worker." Like a stubborn Missouri mule, Harry permanently held Luce's political cheap shot against her.

Later, after he had become President, Harry stated his position plainly and in no uncertain terms to Henry Luce, publisher of *Time* and *Life*, and Congresswoman Luce's husband: "No one has a right to make derogatory remarks about Mrs. T. Your wife has said many unkind and untrue things about her. And as long as I am in residence here, she'll never be a guest in the White House."

In 1944, when the Democrats proposed that Harry run for the Vice Presidency, he nixed the idea straight off: "I talked it over with Bess," he said, "and we've decided against it." The reason he gave was that the limelight is no good place to raise a daughter. Privately, he said he had no wish to "drag a lot of skeletons out of the closet." When asked what skeletons he had to hide, Harry's lame response was that he had "the boss" on the payroll, and he did not want her name "dragged over the front pages of the papers and over the radio." A little more specifically, he feared that "Mother Wallace" would be brought up as an issue—a reference, as Margaret later speculated, to the reason behind Harry's hesitation, namely, Bess' morbid fear of having her father's suicide flaunted and the family name defiled in the press.

But then, FDR put the pressure on, and Harry was nominated. Bess was opposed at first, but, at the end of the Convention, told the media people that she was "almost reconciled" to the idea. As the screaming delegates were crushing them, the importunate press accosting them, and the police manhandling people to rescue them from the Democrats' convention hall, Bess acidly queried the nominee: "Are we going to have to go through this for the rest of our lives?"

Harry, still protective of Bess' anxious concern for privacy, told Margaret: "This is going to be a tough, dirty campaign, and you've got to help your dad protect your good mama."

Back in Kansas City, the candidate's wife found her privacy eroding fast; Bess was becoming public property, and she didn't like it.

Fortunately for Bess, Harry was mistaken, and the campaign was not a dirty one (except for Congresswoman Luce's dollop). On election night, Bess went to bed before the results were in, resigned to becoming the Second Lady of the Land. And, just as she had thought, being the wife of the Vice President turned out to be less enjoyable than being a Senate wife had been. Now, they were expected to attend the endless round of ritual appearances, standing in for the Roosevelts, who, by 1945, were almost totally out of the social picture. Three cocktail parties and a big dinner in one day was not Bess' idea of a fun time.

Moreover, Harry, no longer a shy lad, seemed to be enjoying himself way too much. At a National Press Club party, piano-playing Harry sat down to render some

BEHIND EVERY SUCCESSFUL PRESIDENT

requests, and movie star Lauren Bacall slinked up onto the piano and struck a vampish pose. The flash bulbs popped, and the next day's photo journalism revealed the Vice President looking the other way—but grinning. Harry said it had embarrassed him; Bess said she thought it was time for him to quit playing the piano.

Bad as the Vice Presidency was, it lasted a mere 82 days; and then things got worse. On April 12, 1945, Mrs. Roosevelt summoned Harry to the White House and told him of the President's death. When Harry phoned home and told Bess, she broke into sobs at the sad news. Her first action, however, was not to rush to Harry's side, but to condole, in person, with the grieving Eleanor. Then, Bess went to stand by Harry. As he was taking the Presidential Oath, Bess appeared to be a "woman in pain." In spite of that pain, she helped Harry write the Presidential address that consoled a war-worried, weeping nation.

One of Bess' first acts as First Lady was to protect Eleanor's memory and run interference for her work. Harry's White House secretary Eddie McKim observed some of his staff stenographers replying to the thousands of letters of sympathy Mrs. Roosevelt had received after Franklin's death.

"So, this is 'My Day'!" McKim quipped, referring to Mrs. Roosevelt's daily newspaper column. "Stop it!" He stopped the work and fired the stenographers.

When Bess heard about it, she was outraged and told Harry. The next morning, McKim found himself transferred to other duties, and the secretaries continued their work.

A day or two after he became President, Harry was awakened in the middle of the night by Bess' sobbing. "Bess cried most of the night and it wasn't for joy, either," Harry told reporters from the *Kansas City Star* next day. He then had some explaining to do to "the boss."

Later, Bess wrote to her friend Mary Paxton: "We are not any of us happy to be where we are but there's nothing to be done about it except to do our best—and forget about the sacrifices and many unpleasant things that bob up."

One of the first and most unpleasant things to bob up was Bess' first (and last) press conference. Eleanor Roosevelt had made such extensive and effective use of the media, and had for twelve years so endeared herself to the corps of female reporters, it was expected that Mrs. Truman would follow suit. Dutifully, Bess scheduled her first interview; and then, to everyone's shocked surprise, cancelled it at the last minute: "I am not the one who is elected. I have nothing to say to the public." That ended the First Lady press conferences.

Relenting a little, Bess agreed to entertain the newswomen at tea, and to attend their luncheons, always claiming that anything she said was off the record. She occasionally entertained questions, but only if they were submitted to her first in writing. Her answers were invariably brief, almost uninformative; and any tricky or controversial question—and many perfectly innocent ones—was met with Bess' stock-in-trade reply: "No comment."

In addition to her pure dislike of publicity, Bess found the questions from the ladies of the press trivial and boring. American attitudes were still quite traditionally sexist in 1945, especially to a mind like Bess', unconcerned as she was with fashion or gossip or Washington society. To a rivetingly interesting question posed on one occasion: "What will Mrs. Truman wear to the tea for the United Council of Church Women today?" Bess told her secretary, Reathel Odum, "Tell 'em it's none of their damn business!" Reathel sensibly conveyed the First Lady's message as:

"Mrs. Truman hasn't quite made up her mind, yet." Bess Truman's press policy, stated to her staff as plainly as Harry could have said it, was this: "Just keep on smiling and tell *them* nothing."

Another unpleasant thing that bobbed up was the flap with Adam Clayton Powell that got Bess' First Ladyship off to a rough start. She had accepted an invitation from the Daughters of the American Revolution to a tea in her honor at Constitution Hall on Columbus Day. Powell, the flamboyant Congressman from Harlem, sent Bess a telegram, protesting her attendance: ". . . If you believe in 100 percent Americanism, you will publicly denounce the D.A.R.'s action." The D.A.R., more than occasionally stuffy, had barred Marian Anderson because of her color from singing in Constitution Hall in 1939. More recently and more pertinently, Powell's wife, Hazel Scott, a pianist, had similarly been denied permission to perform there.

Bess was neither race-prejudiced nor a segregationist, but she disliked being told what to do. She insisted on going to the tea, and Harry backed her all the way. Powell was right, however, and he outmaneuvered both Trumans in public: he retaliated by calling Bess "the Last Lady of the Land." Chivalrous Harry became furious, and the White House guest list of *personae non gratae* was now at least two names long: neither Clare Boothe Luce—who had not improved her reputation with Harry by calling Bess an "ersatz First Lady"—nor Adam Clayton Powell was ever invited to the Mansion, not even to Congressional receptions, so long as Harry Truman had a say in the matter.

Bess would have to live down this bad beginning before she could enjoy being the President's wife; and it was only when the Truman Administration integrated the U.S. Armed forces and consistently supported civil rights that

Harry was able completely and clearly to disentangle personal animosities from residual suspicions of racism in the first First Family from Missouri.

Other unpleasant things bobbing up were more routine, such as large dinners and formal receptions. Uncharacteristic for a First Lady, Eleanor Roosevelt had been essentially uninterested in fashionable sociability, a lack of concern that had intensified as Franklin's condition had worsened. After the global war, the standard duties of a President's wife approximately doubled: with so many new nations emerging, there were twice as many ambassadors to entertain. Shaking hands with all those people—hundreds at a time, thousands in a few days—made Bess' arm swell up and inflamed the arthritis in her hand. When people asked her how she stood it, she bragged that she had "a strong tennis arm."

What with Eleanor's heavy travel schedule and war rationing, the White House had run down terribly. Bess now made war on the cobwebs, and evicted the only permanent residents of the Mansion, the rats. Ultimately, the antique building required a total restoration—including the addition of a hotly debated back porch that gave the Trumans an upstairs island of seclusion, ideal for sitting and rocking and chatting on wilting Tidewater evenings. The "Great White Jail," as Bess and Harry called the President's House, now seemed a little more like home.

Although Bess had proved unapproachable at first, the Washington press applauded what they perceived as a thaw in the First Lady freeze when she invited the entire Independence Tuesday Bridge Club—all ten ladies, including her two sisters-in-law—to D.C. for a four-day weekend at the White House. Earlier, out in Missouri, Bess had already set the girls straight about formalities. When Bess had walked into the room on their first occasion together in Independence after Bess had become First Lady, the bridge club all rose.

"Now stop it, stop it this instant!" fussed the First Lady. "Sit down, every darn one of you!"

When she got the girls to Washington, Bess put them through a whole social season in one long weekend—visits to Congress and the Smithsonian, nightly dinners with the President presiding, bridge aboard the *Williamsburg* cruising the Potomac—all to the utter delight of Washington's social columnists: No-comment Bess was a human being, after all!

Bess as First Lady did what she had always done for the Truman and Wallace families, acting as the general overseer of family affairs. For the sake of the taxpayers' and the Trumans' pocketbook, she did the bookkeeping, planned the menus, tallied the grocery bills herself, and otherwise kept an eye on expenditures—all of which set her on a collision course with the imperious Executive Cook, Mrs. Evelyn Nesbitt.

When Bess went to Denver to tend to her alcoholic brother, Harry and Margaret were left to Mrs. Nesbitt's merciless menu. One evening, Mrs. Nesbitt served the President a bowl of Brussels sprouts. Harry pushed them away, and Margaret explained that her dad didn't like Brussels sprouts. The next night, Mrs. Nesbitt served Brussels sprouts again. Again, Margaret informed Mrs. Nesbitt that the President did not eat that vegetable. When Mrs. Nesbitt put Brussels sprouts on the table the third night, Margaret put through an urgent telephone call to Denver, and told her mother to come home and "do something about that woman, before I throw a bowl of Brussels sprouts in her face!"

Elizabeth "Bess" Virginia Truman

Mrs. Nesbitt might have succeeded in keeping Harry and Margaret up a tree, but when she crossed Bess, she had made her last mistake in the White House. Bess was on her way to a bridge club potluck, and wanted to take some butter. When she stopped by the kitchen to pick it up, Mrs. Nesbitt confronted her.

"Oh, no!" cried the tyrant of the kitchen, "We can't let any of our butter go out of the House. We've used up almost all of this month's ration stamps already."

Bess struck an alliance with H. G. Crim, the Chief Usher. "Our housekeeper tells me I can't take a stick of butter from the kitchen," she informed him.

"Why, of course you can!" Mr. Crim was taken aback. "She is entirely out of order!"

"Then," said Bess, sending Mrs. Nesbitt to the showers, "I think it's time to find a new housekeeper."

Bess and the other two Trumans were all popular with the White House staff. On account of their personal closeness, they were called "the Three Musketeers." First Lady Bess sent the maids home for half-holidays on Sunday afternoons, saying: "I can turn the beds down perfectly well by myself."

Margaret, at first, had a tendency to enjoy being the President's daughter too much to suit her mother. On a shopping spree to celebrate her singing debut on the radio, when Margaret blithely told the saleslady to charge the best mink scarf she could find to "Mrs. Harry S Truman," Bess trumped in: "Oh no you don't. You bought it, you pay for it. You're making your own money now."

Margaret went dancing at El Morocco a number of times with a chap who had been mentioned in the gossip columns on other counts, and the newspapers were already licking their chops over a First Family furor. Mother called daughter and, after brief preliminaries, came to the main point: "How did you happen to be dancing with So-and-So the other evening?"

"He asked me,"—daughters can be devious—"I couldn't be rude."

"I should think once would be enough to take care of manners." Mothers can be shrewd.

Harry had gotten so busy being the Chief Executive, Bess felt left out. He went off alone to Potsdam for a Big Three conference in the summer of 1945, and she went off to Independence, alone and moody and mad. He called her from across the ocean, and she accused him of having ignored her since he had become President. Their harsh words and the separation made him "blue as indigo." He wrote and called her every day, just as he used to do when he was politicking through Missouri and she was at home. He promised to make amends.

But after he got back to Washington and while he was preoccupied with one of the most momentous decisions of his—or any—Presidency, Harry continued to ignore his wife. When President Truman ordered the atomic bomb dropped on Hiroshima on August 6, 1945, Bess found out about it only after it had already happened. Her irritation at being treated like an outsider now exploded; Harry had broken their connection and breached her trust. Bess moved to Independence in high dudgeon, and a mushroom cloud of a different sort rose over Missouri, too.

The dreadful new weapon troubled Bess. She questioned the need for its use against Japan, and would have argued against dropping it, had Harry asked her counsel. It is unlikely that she could have persuaded him not to drop the bomb. At the time, the awesome use of atomic power seemed the quickest way to end the war and save the greatest number of lives on both sides. The upsetting issue as far as Bess was concerned, and more important than use of the bomb, was that Harry had taken so drastic a step without discussing the matter with her first. The news of Hiroshima and Nagasaki took the uninformed First Lady by surprise. He had not been merely a busy Chief Executive inadvertently ignoring his wife, he had uncharacteristically shut her out. She terminated their working partnership for a number of weeks. If she had been angry with him before Potsdam, her temper now had reached near critical mass.

Despite Bess' slow burn during this most troubled period in their life, she did her public duty as First Lady. On November 27th, she and Margaret were the star attractions at the opening of the Metropolitan Opera in New York. When they took their place, the orchestra volunteered "The Star-Spangled Banner," and all opera glasses were trained upon the Presidential box. Margaret, still preening on being the President's daughter, suffered deflation under a single "sardonic glance" from Bess. "I realized that I . . . would probably never hear the last of it from the teasing Truman," wrote Margaret.

Harry flew home to the battle zone in Independence on Christmas Day.

"So, you've finally arrived!" she said, as he walked through the door. "I guess you couldn't think of any more reasons to stay away. As far as I'm concerned, you might as well have stayed in Washington."

Christmas of 1945 at 219 North Delaware Street was not a merry one. They fought for two days; then Harry flew back to Washington on the 27th, mad as hell. As soon as he got to the White House, he wrote Bess an atomic letter and dropped it on her, special-delivery.

Next morning, the half-life of his anger having proved

short, Harry called Margaret and did something that Presidents cannot do with bombs: he called back the letter. Harry told his daughter about the "very angry letter," told her to get the help of the Independence postmaster, and "burn it." Margaret did as she was asked, and Harry wrote another, calmer, somewhat apologetic letter. In it, he lamented being there alone in the White House, "the great white sepulchre of ambitions and reputations." He regretted the Christmas fight. He acknowledged how important Bess' approval was to him: "You can never appreciate what it means to come home as I did the other evening after doing at least one hundred things I didn't want to do and have the only person in the world whose approval and good opinion I value look at me like I'm something the cat dragged in." Since he was now "No. 1 man in the world," even if he "didn't want to be," he concluded by asking Bess for her help: "If I can get the use of the best brains in the country and a little bit of help from those I have on a pedestal at home, the job will be done."

Bess' mood of isolation changed, and Harry gradually regained her cooperation; he was careful not to alienate her again. Over the next two years, Harry kept Bess briefed on the international situation, and they worked on the Marshall Plan together. She again offered advice on his speeches, Presidential appointments, Congressional legislation, and standing down the Russians.

During those first, almost four years, Bess had not been happy in the White House. She could play hardball when she had to, whether it was the White House cook or the President himself who was at bat; but the proof that Bess was not an "ersatz First Lady" could come only if she and Harry won their own full term of office. Bess was doubleminded about the prospect. She admitted that First

Elizabeth "Bess" Virginia Truman

Ladyship had its "enjoyable spots," but, she said, these were "in the minority." When they asked her how she liked it in the White House, Bess answered: "Oh, so-so."

During the 1948 Presidential campaign, Bess played the backstage part she had always played, and came to the footlights only when Harry insisted. She took part in campaign strategy sessions, helped Harry with his speeches, and saw to it that he ate right and got enough rest. She also kept a supply of aspirin on hand for headachy news people, and sewed buttons back on coats for Harry's staff. But all the while, she wondered: "Does he really believe that he'll be elected?" The polls and the papers all predicted a win for the New York Republican, Thomas E. Dewey. Only self-confident Harry himself—and the common, ordinary voter—was not surprised at the outcome.

During Harry's whistle-stop campaign—thousands of miles back and forth across America on the railroads and hundreds of speeches from a back platform—Bess always made only her single, one-line speech. After Harry had shot from the hip for a few minutes with the folks, he would ask: "How'd ya like to meet my family?" The crowd would roar its approval, and Harry would drag Bess and Margaret out onto the platform with him and introduce Bess as "my boss," and Margaret as "the boss's boss." The crowds ate it up. Bess, however, never had liked being called "the boss." (When Harry *really* wanted to get Bess' goat, he called her "Miss Lizzie.") Margaret, too, made these non-musical appearances under duress. Harry finally stopped his orneriness only when Bess threatened to get off the train if he did it one more time.

After a five a.m. Texas breakfast of white-wing and mourning dove, bacon, ham, fried chicken, scrambled eggs, and hot biscuits, Uvalde honey, peach preserves, and barrels of coffee at the home of former Vice President John Nance "Cactus Jack" Garner, Bess smiled and saluted the five thousand or so Southwest Texas ranchers with: "Good morning, and thank you for this wonderful greeting." That was a long speech for No-Comment Bess.

Bess' most outstanding contribution to the Truman Administration was what she gave Harry—the strong emotional support that he needed, and somebody to talk things over with at night. Margaret said: "Bess never hesitated to try to influence Harry Truman's decisions, but she never attempted to control him." She nagged him on one point only: his naughty language.

When Arkansas Senator J. William Fulbright criticized the Truman Administration's Reconstruction Finance Corporation, Harry shot off his mouth at a press conference and called Fulbright an "overeducated s.o.b.," and dubbed Fulbright's critical report on the RFC "asinine." Reflecting later on what Bess said when he got home to the White House that night, Harry owned up that "The Madam thinks I shouldn't have any more press conferences."

Bess saw to it that Harry's bumptiousness got neither herself nor him into more trouble than was necessary. Once at a reception, when a prickly anti-Truman politician was working his way forward in the handshaking line, Harry egged Bess on, daring her in whispers to trip him up.

Bess whispered back: "Shush! Remember, he is a guest in our house."

An example of Harry's chivalrous lack of objectivity came up when a Russian diplomat, in a pique about the seating arrangements, declined a White House invitation at the last minute. Harry flew off the handle and took it as an insult to Bess. Alone with Undersecretary of State Dean Acheson, Harry was ranting about having the Russian

Elizabeth "Bess" Virginia Truman

blacklisted—like Powell and Luce—and deported.

"Why?" asked Acheson.

"He insulted Mrs. Truman by turning down that invitation at the last second," raved Harry, "I'm not going to let anyone in the world do that!"

Acheson suggested that they get the First Lady on the line. She calmed Harry down a bit, and then asked to speak with Acheson. The Undersecretary of State explained the diplomatically delicate nature of the situation and asked for the First Lady's suggestions. Bess replied in sober terms, proposing that Acheson fib to Harry and say that nothing could be done about it for twenty-four hours, suggesting that the President would be able to laugh about it after he'd slept on it.

Acheson, however, while keeping an eye on the President, interpreted her message out loud to the Oval Office in the following diplomatic terms: "'Above himself' —yes. 'Too big for his britches'—I agree with you. 'Delusions of grandeur'. . . ."

"All right, all right!" Harry grabbed the phone and spoke to the First Lady: "When you gang up on me, I know I'm licked. Let's forget all about it!" He and Bess hung up.

Putting down the receiver, Harry picked up the photo of Bess on his desk, and said to Acheson: "I guess you think I'm an old fool, and probably I am. But look on the back." It was the inscribed picture that Bess had sent with Harry to France during World War I to help him come home safely.

After Harry had patched things up with Bess following the atomic bomb fallout, he was able again to call her his "chief adviser" who had been in on all his major Presidential decisions [except one]. Overstating the case slightly, he bragged about Bess: "I discussed all of them with her. Why not? Her judgment was always good." He called her "a full partner in all my transactions—politically and otherwise."

Although Bess left the government up to Harry in public, she did take a few visible politically significant steps. Convinced that closer friendship in the Western hemisphere depended on being able to communicate with Latin Americans, she instituted Spanish classes at the White House. (Mamie Eisenhower was one of the class members.) Bess learned more Spanish than all the other ladies put together.

In some ways more of a democrat than Harry was, Bess opened the White House during the Korean War for the kind of teas and receptions that *she* enjoyed—with less pomp and greater congeniality. She invited the wounded vets in, a hundred at a time, to sit on the Presidential furniture, drink coffee from Presidential cups, and eat cake from Presidential plates. Harry warmed quickly to Bess' wartime policy, and suggested that she add beer to the menu, which she did, and everyone had a good time. Bess' Presidential entertaining throughout most of Harry's second term was curtailed due to the major repairs underway on the decaying Mansion, during which time the First Family lived in the much smaller Blair House.

Bess helped the President in other public, but subtle, ways. Once during a dinner party, she sent Harry a note: the quiet woman sitting next to him whom he was ignoring, she said, was Dr. Lise Meitner, the distinguished atomic scientist. Harry perked up.

Exercising her caution against unreliable people, she warned Harry about Jimmy Byrnes, though neither firmly nor soon enough. Harry appointed Byrnes, one of FDR's holdovers, to be Secretary of State, and had nothing but trouble from Byrnes, who was always grandstanding for the sake of his own political reputation at Harry's expense.

Bess saw Douglas MacArthur as another potential political troublemaker, and proved right again—Bess hated personal disloyalty. Harry concurred. In the classic struggle between a civilian Commander-in-Chief and a loose cannon of a military hero, Harry sacked MacArthur for insubordination when the Conqueror of Japan bombed communist forces in China across the Yalu River during Harry's "police action" in Korea. (Madge Wallace, Bess' mother resident in the White House at the time, gave Harry hell for firing MacArthur.)

Bess had an eye for reliable lieutenants as surely as she could spot the troublemakers. George Marshall was, to Bess, the outstanding figure of a public servant, as loyal to the President as he was good for the country and the world. Something similar could be said for her opinion of Dean Acheson, who succeeded Marshall as Secretary of State.

The full degree of Bess' direct influence on American policy cannot be known; but daughter Margaret speculated that Bess coined the term "Fair Deal"—the banner of Harry's domestic Marshall Plan for America, a program to share postwar prosperity with small business people, farmers, and racial minorities. Bess was always looking for a way to distinguish Harry's Administration from the previous one, and the "Fair Deal" was her emendation of FDR's "New Deal."

A few of Bess' direct involvements are known. By encouraging Blevins Davis, a former English teacher from Independence who had become a successful Broadway producer, Bess fostered a theatrical experiment to send a troupe of American Shakespeareans abroad to perform *Hamlet* in Denmark's Elsinore Castle and prove to the snobbish Europeans that Americans could produce culture as well as win wars. This was followed by a touring

BEHIND EVERY SUCCESSFUL PRESIDENT

company of *Porgy and Bess*; and by the mid-'50s, Bess' novel idea of cultural outreach had become State Department standard fare.

Bess' impact on America was even more direct and more pervasive in terms of national health. At the suggestion of Florence Mahoney (a relative of one of Harry's backers and a friend of Mary Lasker, who contributed millions to medical research), Bess became convinced that the National Institute of Health could become America's war-machine in the all-out campaign against cancer and other major diseases. When Harry took office in 1945, the NIH budget was about $2 million; when the Truman partnership left office in 1952, the NIH had $46 million to spend. Bess' effectiveness as a lobbyist can be measured in proportion to her treasured anonymity.

The Truman years—from World War II to the Cold War to Korea—were years of strife. To keep sane, the Truman family occasionally turned the Mansion into Monkey Island. Bess, who was not a morning person, would come to the breakfast table in a state of theatrical grouchiness, barbing Harry and Margaret about any misbehavior of the night before, and actually growling. The breakfast staff joined the play and developed a scale of measurements to keep tabs on Bess' morning moods: was she wearing one gun or two, and—when Bess was riding high—were the guns smoking?

On an occasion when the First Lady was supposed to christen an Army C-54 hospital plane, someone had forgotten to score the champagne bottle so it would break easily. Rather than shattering when Bess swung the bottle against the plane's fuselage, it dented the aluminum hull. Swinging again and again, Bess just about dug herself a hole in that plane. A gallantly pragmatic mechanic finally

Elizabeth "Bess" Virginia Truman

stepped over and shivered the bottle with a wrench, showering both the nose of the airplane and the First Lady with champagne. The frustrated First Lady was immortalized in a wonderfully funny newsreel.

Bess had once said that the qualifications for being First Lady are "good health and a well-developed sense of humor." One night at dinner in the White House, the Trumans had watermelon for dessert. Without warning, Harry thumb-flipped a watermelon seed across the table at Bess. Bess returned the fire. Margaret joined the fray. Instantly, a gleeful battle-royal of flying watermelon seeds ensued. When a waiter came through the door to clear the table, he was barraged with a hail of watermelon seeds from all three assailants. Beating a quick retreat, he waited outside the door until the Presidential food-fight subsided.

In 1952, Harry was sorely tempted to run again. A war against communism was on in Korea, and a war against anti-communism and McCarthyism was on in America. On the strength of the political proverb that it is not good to change horses in the midstream, Harry could perhaps have won. But Bess put her foot down!

"Four more years?"

"Well," laughed Bess, easy in her job at last (and already fairly certain that she would soon be on the train to Independence), "I stood it for seven years!"

The Trumans in retirement at their old homeplace enjoyed fifteen more good years together. Bess gladly returned to being a private homemaker and grandmother. She enjoyed watching Margaret's musical career develop and the four grandchildren grow. She played bridge, listened to baseball games on the radio, watched TV, and read whodunits. She was tired of politics, for a while, and played the old game with Harry only to the extent of helping him with his memoirs.

The first volume, *Years of Decision*, was published in 1955. Harry paid part of his lifetime debt of gratitude to Bess in the preface. He thanked her for the "counsel and judgment" on which he had "frequently called." But within the text of the book, as in all of his writings, the references to Bess were sparse indeed. *She* had edited every word of the pre-publication manuscript and so preserved her anonymity forever.

Bess Truman died on October 20, 1982.

Anna Eleanor Roosevelt Roosevelt

Mrs. President FDR

"*I* NEVER wanted to be a President's wife, and I don't now." That is what Eleanor—born Anna Eleanor Roosevelt on October 11, 1884—said when Franklin became President in 1932; and about herself, she said: "There isn't going to be any First Lady. There's just going to be plain, ordinary Mrs. Roosevelt. And that's all. . . . I shall be myself, as always." She went on:

> I was happy for my husband . . . After all, I'm a Democrat, too. . . . But as for myself I was deeply troubled. As I saw it, this meant the end of any personal life of my own. I knew what traditionally should lie before me; I had watched Mrs. Theodore Roosevelt and had seen what it meant to be the wife of a President, and I cannot say I was pleased at the prospect.

In a room at the end of the hotel corridor on the night following Franklin's victory, an associate discovered Eleanor weeping. When asked what was wrong, she moaned, feeling sorry for herself as she sometimes did: "Now I'll have no identity!" Eleanor was afraid she would be devoured in the White House mill that threatens to grind First Ladies down to ceremonial powder. But, after she dried her tears, Eleanor joined the victory celebration and even toasted Franklin's Presidency with a sip of champagne (Eleanor was a Prohibitionist); she had, after all, worked awfully hard to get him elected.

Young Eleanor thought of her mother as "one of the most beautiful women I have ever seen." But Anna Hall Roosevelt, New York socialite, called her gangly, bucktoothed, old-fashioned daughter "funny child" and "Granny." Her mother tried, Eleanor remembered, "to bring me up well so my manners would in some way compensate for my looks, but her efforts only made me more keenly conscious of my shortcoming. . . . I wanted to sink through the floor in shame." (Later, Franklin insensitively picked up on the "Granny" nickname.)

Eleanor was raised in the religion and starch of late-Victorianism; and what little self-confidence she might have had was wrenched away when her father, Elliott Roosevelt (Teddy's younger brother), seemed just to drop out of her life. The man who called Eleanor his "little golden hair," the darling of her childhood, died of alcoholism when she was ten years old. Eleanor's mother had died of diphtheria two years earlier. From then on, Eleanor was raised by her grandmother, Mrs. Valentine Hall. Shy, withdrawn, fearful, and unloved, Eleanor turned to books, the French language, and horses for friendship; she read and wrote and studied hard in order to earn approval of the grown-up world. Her "real education" began, she said, only when she was sent in 1899 at age fifteen to England and Marie Souvestre. Eleanor remembered the three years at Souvestre's Allenswood

School (near London) as the "happiest years of my life."

Marie Souvestre was unlike anyone the teenaged aristocrat had met before: she was politically liberal, a religious freethinker, who challenged Eleanor to think actively and as an adult. She taught her how to unbend her rigidity, to dress attractively, to be outgoing and poised; she took her for holidays to the Continent, and taught Eleanor responsibility by requiring her to handle the travel arrangements. Eleanor at age seventeen had a mastery of French, German, Italian, Latin, and her special interest, English literature, and also had a budding mastery of herself.

Back in New York, Eleanor put up with the social engagements requisite for her coming-out, but she did not enjoy them. She danced poorly and blamed herself for not being the belle of New York society that her mother and grandmother had been. More to Eleanor's taste was her teaching at the Rivington Street Settlement House, and her work with the Consumers League, for whom she investigated working conditions in sweatshops and garment factories. She was regarded as the hardest worker in the Junior League.

At one of the burdensome social functions, she danced with Franklin Delano Roosevelt, a dashing Harvard man down for the season, a distant cousin whom she had known when they were children. Franklin's insistent courtship culminated in the offer of his charming self for marriage: he proposed to her, he said, because he "would amount to something some day."

"Why me?" Eleanor implored. "I am plain. I have little to bring you." She described herself in those days as a woman of "painfully high ideals and a tremendous sense of duty . . . entirely unrelieved by any sense of humor or any appreciation of the weakness of human nature."

Uncle President Teddy Roosevelt gave the bride away on March 17, 1905, grinning, "bullying," and stealing the show. With a wedding ceremony under the domination of one overbearing Roosevelt, to a marriage under the domination of another, to life in proximity to a third—namely, Franklin's mother Sara Delano Roosevelt—Eleanor detoured off the high road on which Marie Souvestre had set her. Eleanor raised five children (one other died) more or less successfully—Anna, James, Elliott, John, and Franklin Jr.—more without Franklin's help than with.

Eleanor toughed out her role as daughter-in-law to the kind of woman about whom mother-in-law jokes were first invented. Sara dominated her only child's adulthood, and his marriage, as thoroughly as she had dictated his boyhood. She had a house built for Franklin and his family right next to hers at Hyde Park, with passages in between, the better to supervise their life. Eleanor said that she never knew when Sara was going to pop out of one of those passages. Sara bought Eleanor her new furniture and hired Eleanor's servants. Eleanor, whose typical response was a deferential "Yes, Mama," and "No, Mama," wrote: "I was beginning to be an entirely dependent person. . . . I was not developing any individual taste or initiative. I was simply absorbing the personalities of those about me and letting their tastes and interests dominate me." When Franklin caught Eleanor having a cry about it, he thought she was quite mad and told her so. Eleanor bit her lip.

When Franklin ran for the New York State Senate in 1910, however, a bat squeak of interest in politics evoked an echo in Eleanor's soul. Listening to one of his speeches, she was shocked to find that her husband advocated the vote for women: "I took it for granted that men were superior creatures, and . . . knew more about politics than women."

BEHIND EVERY SUCCESSFUL PRESIDENT

Since, however, wives were supposed to agree with their husbands, Eleanor changed her mind to conform to Franklin's advocacy of female suffrage; in this passivity she began her active political career.

During legislative sessions, the Roosevelts lived in Albany, where Eleanor was free of her mother-in-law's controls: "I had to stand on my own feet now, and I think I knew that it was good for me. I wanted to be independent. I was beginning to realize that something within me craved to be an individual."

Eleanor made the late-night sandwiches, poured the beer, and brewed the coffee that fueled Franklin's political machine—and she began to take her own notes on politics. She put up with the poker games and cigar smoke and booze that came with Franklin's cronies, and she otherwise embodied the ideal of wifely subordination that fed Franklin's ego. She studied politics by watching politicians, attended working sessions of the New York Assembly, learned how the State and Federal governments worked, and went with Franklin to the 1912 Democratic Convention in Baltimore. It was the beginning of what some would later proudly call, and others would sneer, the "Franklin-and-Eleanor team." Already Eleanor was becoming Franklin's conscience and his watchful eye.

During the next years, she overcame her dislike of Louis Howe, who had become Franklin's secretary in 1913. Louis was a chain-smoking politico from the underclass, who Eleanor thought looked like a gargoyle, but he was Franklin's best political adviser. Eleanor took Louis as her own mentor. Louis saw unaffected majesty in the stately, shy woman who, though surrounded with people, remained lonely within. Eleanor drew on Louis' savvy and learned from her new confederate how to calculate success.

Years later, Louis would quip: "Eleanor, if you want to be President in 1940, tell me now so I can start getting things ready."

When Franklin was appointed Assistant Secretary of the Navy in 1913 during the Wilson Administration, Eleanor marshaled the many moves of her household—"army on the march"—between Albany, Hyde Park, New York City, Washington, and Campobello (their island retreat in the Bay of Fundy). All the while, Eleanor's political education continued: she made the Cabinet-level social calls *de rigueur* in Washington, went with Franklin on inspection tours of Navy facilities, entertained the Navy brass and their wives, and listened in on the rip-roaring political talk of Franklin's cohorts. On Sunday nights at the Roosevelts, Eleanor scrambled the eggs. In the summertime, while the witty, energetic, and oh-so-attractive Franklin dazzled Washington, the demure, self-effacing Eleanor vacationed at Campobello with the children, trying to balance her theory of child rearing between the strict discipline she had endured in her own youth and Sara's grandmotherly spoiling.

When World War I came, Eleanor went to work for the Red Cross. She knitted and sewed; helped organize the Railroad Canteen, where she made and served a lot of sandwiches—this time not for politicians but for doughboys; distributed gifts among, and talked with, wounded sailors.

This war work led Eleanor stumbling into her first major political gaffe. In 1917, Mrs. Roosevelt was picked as a "model for other large households" in the effort to "Hooverize" (economize). The newswoman who reported on the Assistant Navy Secretary's wife's food-saving methods in the *New York Times* wrote about the work of

BEHIND EVERY SUCCESSFUL PRESIDENT

Eleanor's cook, her laundress, and the other servants making good use of "leftovers," and quoting Mrs. Roosevelt: "Making ten servants help me do my saving has not only been possible but also highly profitable."

While Washington snickered, Franklin roared with teasing mirth; he called her "newspaper campaign" a "corker," and said how proud he was to be "the husband of the Originator, Discoverer and Inventor of the Household Economy for Millionaires! Please have a photo taken showing the family, the ten cooperating servants, the scraps saved from the table and the handbook. I will have it published in the Sunday *Times*."

Eleanor had learned her first not-to-be-forgotten lesson about how to take charge of a media interview: "I will never be caught again, that's sure, and I'd like to crawl away for shame."

The following year and to greater effect, Eleanor savored her first taste of victory at getting the government to reform society. Appalled by the terrible conditions she had observed in government for shell-shocked sailors, Eleanor sent a report to the Secretary of the Interior. Her effort resulted in congressional appropriations for St. Elizabeth's Hospital, which consequently was improved into a model institution for the mentally ill.

At war's end, Eleanor accompanied Franklin on a tour of European battlefronts, visiting hundreds of wounded military men in hospitals, and sweeping First Lady Edith Wilson up into the activity with her. Eleanor with Franklin observed the Paris Peace Conference, and then returned to America in company with Woodrow and Edith Wilson—four internationalist Democrats intoxicated during the crossing by salt spray and the heady ideal of a League of Nations united to foster world peace.

In 1918, because Franklin had returned from Europe ill with pneumonia, Eleanor began opening his mail for him. Some letters from Lucy Page Mercer (later, Rutherford), an attractive young woman from Maryland who had been Eleanor's secretary since 1914, revealed that Franklin and Lucy had been lovers for some time. Eleanor was devastated, and the marriage almost ended: "The bottom dropped out of my own particular world, and I faced myself, my surroundings, my world, honestly for the first time. I really grew up that year."

By the time their last child was born, in 1916, Eleanor had already left Franklin's bed. Their relationship had become more a working partnership than a marriage, with affection, but with little or no romance. To Eleanor, sexuality was "an ordeal to be borne," as she once stated to daughter Anna. So, while Eleanor had vacationed at Campobello with the kids, Franklin had been summering with Lucy. (Cousin Alice Roosevelt Longworth meowed: "Franklin deserved a good time; he was married to Eleanor.") Before Eleanor achieved "little by little" the self-control and wisdom of years, both her own and others' hormonal powers were an offense to her. She had tied young Anna's hands to the bars of her crib to keep the girl from masturbating.

Eleanor offered Franklin a divorce. He refused—counting the costs to his political career and the children, and considering Lucy's Catholic impediment to marrying a divorcé. Sara engineered an arrangement between Eleanor and her son for the sake of his career. Eleanor forgave, and Franklin promised to break off the relationship with Lucy.

When Franklin ran unsuccessfully for the Vice Presidency, Eleanor went out campaigning with him; and, with Louis Howe, she took a hand in advising Franklin on his

BEHIND EVERY SUCCESSFUL PRESIDENT

speeches and planning campaign strategy. She announced her support for the League of Nations. She learned to type and write shorthand. She joined the League of Women Voters, and began to author the League's monthly reports on Congressional legislation. She gladly took Franklin's political advice and enjoyed the power that his expertise availed her.

In the summer of 1921 at Campobello, life together for Eleanor and Franklin changed radically when, at age thirty-nine, Franklin's legs were suddenly and permanently paralyzed by poliomyelitis. Eleanor took turns with Louis, massaging the stricken limbs to keep the blood circulating, until Franklin could be ferried to a hospital.

When his mother took Franklin's illness as her opening to regain control of him from Eleanor and "that ugly, dirty little man" (Louis Howe), she would have indulged her crippled boy in permanent invalidism. But Eleanor, backed by Dr. George Draper, withstood Sara and demanded that Franklin follow a prescription of exercise, a return to action, and a renewed interest in life: "His illness finally made me stand on my own two feet in regard to my husband's life, my own life, and my children's too." Had she not done so, Eleanor thought she would have become "a completely colorless echo of my husband and mother-in-law . . . [and] might have stayed a weak character forever."

Dispirited, Franklin lamented, "I have only a few bright prospects now." Showing tough optimism, Eleanor replied: "I have faith in you. I'm sure you'll really amount to something someday." It was not the last time that Eleanor would save Franklin for the nation.

While Franklin convalesced, Eleanor learned to swim, pitch a tent, paddle a canoe, and take her boys on camping trips. She moved Louis into their home to keep Franklin keen on politics, and she brought politically minded and socially active people to the house to meet Franklin, keeping him abreast of the issues. Coached by Louis, Eleanor got over a nervous habit of giggling in public. Louis lectured her: "Have something you want to say, say it, and sit down!" Eleanor had learned that she could make speeches.

She linked up with political and social activists Nancy Cook, Marion Dickerman, and Caroline O'Day to organize the women of New York's Democratic Party. Eleanor took charge of the hardest part—fund-raising. She learned to drive, and chauffeured voters to the polls on Election Day. She co-edited (with Louis) the *Women's Democratic News*. Sounding a lot like Franklin, she began to write; on the subject "Why I Am a Democrat," Eleanor wrote: "On the whole, the Democratic Party seems to have been more concerned with the welfare and interests of the people at large and less with the growth of big business interests."

She became an activist in New York City through various women's organizations. She monitored the State Assembly in Albany, staged political debates, and stalked male politicians who dismissed the idea of women's equal involvement in Democratic Party politics as female foolishness. When Eleanor and another well-honed female volunteer followed a Democratic county chairman to his home, they were told by the man's wife that he was "not at home."

"All right," replied impatient Eleanor, who had learned to bide her time on much colder front porches than this one, "We will just sit here on the steps until he comes."

After an hour or so, the wife tried again to dislodge them, saying that she had no idea when her husband might return.

"It doesn't matter," smiled Eleanor, waiting with a new kind of patience, and holding a strong suspicion that her prey lurked within. "We have nothing to do. We will wait."

After another hour or so, the elusive Democrat came out of hiding to hear Eleanor lilt her points regarding women in the Party, her toothy smile beaming.

Following the Republicans' Teapot Dome scandal, Eleanor pursued the Republican candidate for Governor of New York along his campaign trail in a car that she Democratically fitted out to look embarrassingly like a teapot and that spouted real steam as she drove.

Characteristic of Eleanor's swings of balance, she claimed to Franklin during these years: "I'm only being *active* until you can be again." Expressing the lack of self-awareness that she outgrew only gradually, Eleanor affirmed on another occasion that she had no "great desire . . . to serve the world." Nevertheless, she was finding her own voice—and it was rather a high-pitched, trilling one that sounded like music if one agreed with her, and grated on the nerves if one did not.

> It is always disagreeable to take stands. It is always easier to compromise, always easier to let things go. To many women—and I am one of them—it is extremely difficult to care about anything enough to cause disagreement or unpleasant feelings, but I have come to the conclusion that this must be done for a time, until we can prove our strength and demand respect for our wishes.

The "Franklin-and-Eleanor Team" was in action again in 1924, at the Democratic National Convention in New York. Eleanor presented a number of women's planks to the Resolutions Committee, and together they backed Al Smith for President, Franklin making the nominating speech that was the high point of the Convention. They repeated their act in 1928. Working out of New York Democratic headquarters, Eleanor campaigned sturdily for Smith, who, although he lost to Hoover nationally, won in New York. Franklin, too, despite his paralyzed legs, won the governorship of New York in 1928. Eleanor was returning to Albany as the victorious First Lady of the Empire State.

Eleanor, with her friends Cook and Dickerman, had purchased in 1927 the Todhunter School for girls in New York City, to which she now commuted from Hyde Park and Albany to serve as vice-principal and teach English and American literature and civics. To combat the Depression (which started on the American farm before the Crash of '29 on Wall Street), also in partnership with Cook and Dickerman, Eleanor founded a furniture factory in Val-Kill, near Hyde Park, to give work to unemployed Dutchess County farmers. All these and her other activities Eleanor continued as the Governor's wife, but now she added State visits to public hospitals, prisons, mental institutions, and other places where Franklin's legs would not let him go.

While Franklin kept the bureaucrats busy entertaining the visiting dignitaries, riding around the grounds in the gubernatorial limousine, it was Eleanor's job to go poking into dark places behind the official scene:

> It was [Franklin] who taught me to observe. . . . My first reports were highly unsatisfactory to him. I would tell him what was on the menu [of some institution] for the day, and he would ask: 'Did you look to see whether the inmates were actually getting that food?' I learned to look into the cooking pots on the stove and to find out if the contents corresponded to the menu. I learned to notice whether the beds were too close together, and whether they were folded up and put in closets or behind doors during the day, which would indicate that they filled the

corridors at night! . . . Just sitting with him in the observation car of a train, I learned how to watch the tracks and see their condition, how to look at the countryside and note whether there was soil erosion, and what condition the forests and fields were in; and as we went through the outskirts of a town or village, I soon learned to look at the clothes on the washlines and at the cars, and to notice whether houses needed painting. Little by little I found I was able to answer my husband's questions after I had taken a trip alone and give him the information he would have gathered had he taken the trip himself. . . . It was the best education I ever had.

This Rooseveltian social empiricism was the method appropriate to Franklin's and Eleanor's common style of political compassion. She actually met the multitudes whose causes she championed. She knew from firsthand observation exactly what they needed. She was not so much a feminist as she was fair-minded, believing that hardworking women ought to get paid equal money for equal work; not so much a pacifist as she was compassionate, suffering with the tens of thousands of war-worn men she visited in front-line hospitals; not so much a racial activist as she was a tender conscience who could not bear to think of black people being ravaged by lynch mobs, or left uneducated and unemployable. Eleanor was not so much a socialist as a populist—a person who believed less in economic theory and more in all the many people she met, at whom she looked searchingly and to whom she listened attentively.

An Episcopalian faithful in her church attendance, Eleanor was not a Quaker, although she contributed generously to the work that Quakers did. (Better that, Eleanor figured, than pay out tax money to the uncaring Republican Administration!) She was both a social democrat and a Party-loyal Democrat, absolutely and proudly. In every way she could, Eleanor took on the cares of Depression-sick America as her own.

After two terms as the husband-and-wife Governor of New York, Franklin and Eleanor had become a functioning, efficient team unlike any pair before them in American politics—she was, as she said, "his legs and eyes." Philosophizing on the "Wife's Job" in 1930, she employed the egalitarian language of partnership that best described the Roosevelts' way of making things work: "Today, we understand that everything else depends upon the success of the wife and husband in their personal partnership relation." With their election in 1932, this partnership made of Eleanor and Franklin a pair of Presidents.

The day that Mrs. Hoover invited the First Lady-elect over to the White House for an inspection tour, Eleanor declined the offer of an official car and an aide; instead, she walked over from the Mayflower Hotel after breakfast.

"But Eleanor darling," protested the Chief of Protocol (who was also Eleanor's cousin by marriage), "you can't do that! People will recognize you! You'll be mobbed."

From the very beginning as First Lady, no one knew what to do with Eleanor. She astounded the White House staff with her energy and egalitarian ways. Never quite able to keep her balances level, Eleanor wrote in her autobiography that she had never wanted to be a Presidential wife, and then described on the next page the vigor with which she attacked her first day in office. She began by organizing "the household and the secretarial side of the office which did the work for the President's wife;" then she "went over the White House from basement to attic, looking into closets. . . ." Next, she shocked the ushers by insisting on running the elevator for herself. After that, she moved Mrs. Hoover's wicker furniture, plants, and birds out of the solarium and converted that wide hall into an extra sitting room, ". . . and in order to hurry things along I helped with the moving and placing of the furniture, much to the horror of the household staff." After tidying up the House, she reorganized the nation; and in order to hurry that thing along, helped with the moving and placing of the Presidency, much to the horror of a great number of traditionalists. These jobs finished, she went to work on the world.

She trotted at a pace others had to run to keep up with, and seemed never to burn low on energy. The First Lady who objected to her title achieved in her lifetime more revolutionary accomplishments than many national governments in their entire history. The press corps, at prayer about Eleanor, beseeched: "Let me pray the prayer they say that Franklin prays. Just for one day, PLEASE make her *tired!*" The grateful female press corps also waxed theological about Eleanor, saying that she was "God's gift to newspaper women." Not only was she the first First Lady to hold press conferences on her own, but also she usually invited women reporters only. At first, male news reporters jeered, and then they were jealous—Mrs. Roosevelt not only turned out to be good copy herself, but also proved to be a major voice of the Administration. This media innovation contributed mightily to professionalism among female journalists, of which profession Eleanor was herself a proud member.

She astonished state guests by meeting them at the front door, instead of waiting until everyone was inside the Mansion before making her own grand entry. She astonished the Secret Service by maintaining the independence of action that she had announced she would maintain: she drove her own car without escort, walked alone where she pleased, and more or less successfully resisted the Service's attempt to guard her. When, after the assassination attempt against Franklin in Miami in 1933, the President wanted to assign someone from the Service to protect her, Eleanor retorted: "Don't you dare do such a thing! If any Secret Service man shows up . . . and starts following me around, I'll send him right straight back where he came from." And when they did, she did, stating with her characteristic idealism (and an ingenuousness no longer thinkable): "No one's going to hurt me. . . . Make your mind easy on that subject. Americans are wonderful! I simply can't imagine being afraid of going among them as I have always done, as I always shall." When she did finally learn how to use a pistol for self-defense purposes, she carried it unloaded.

Eleanor was no housebound First Lady. Franklin's "legs" kept on jogging, and she was the first to use airplanes in the ordinary exercise of her office. In her first year, Eleanor traveled 38,000 miles; in her second year, 48,000. She toured the back alleys of Washington and the slums of Puerto Rico, work camps, women's prisons, coal mines and mental hospitals, sharecroppers' camps and camps of protesting vets. When the Bonus Army boys (on whom the U.S. Army under the Hoover Administration had opened fire and forcibly driven from Washington) returned during the Roosevelt Administration to demand their World War I pensions, Eleanor herself went out to greet them, took her coffee pot along, and joined the doughboys in singing a round of "There's a Long, Long Trail Awinding."

"Hoover sent the Army," cheered the vets, "Roosevelt sent his wife."

BEHIND EVERY SUCCESSFUL PRESIDENT

She took Congressional wives on her tours of the Capital's slums, and got them to working on their husbands; she worked on Franklin and kept at it until money was appropriated for a housing project and the relocation of destitute families. She bullied Congress into cleaning up mental hospitals in Washington, upgrading school lunches, and reforming children's welfare programs. She invited some girls convicted at least three times of vagrancy, shoplifting, or prostitution to a White House garden party as a media event to focus national attention on their plight.

Franklin's prying "eyes" looked into everyone's business, read (and personally answered most of) 300,000 pieces of mail in the first year, and carefully tracked and critiqued the alphabet soup of the New Deal's many programs: it was Eleanor who saw to equal pay for women and consumer representation in the NRA codes; and Eleanor, working with Labor Secretary Frances Perkins and CWA Administrator Harry Hopkins, who oversaw work projects especially for women and young people; and Eleanor who saw to the employment of artists—poets and painters, musicians and actors—by backing the Federal Theater Project and the Federal Writers Project of the WPA. And, it was Eleanor who put a stop to the mindless policy of the AAA: the destruction of agricultural surpluses in an attempt to raise farm prices by creating an artificial scarcity.

"My missus goes where she wants to," crowed Franklin, "talks to everybody, and does she learn something!" Once when the President did not know where his wife was off to that day (she had gone to Baltimore to inspect a prison), and asked where she was, Eleanor's secretary replied: "She's in prison, Mr. President."

Franklin cackled with laughter. "I'm not surprised! But

what for?" he asked

Franklin's "hands" took a hand in everything, ladled out soup to the unemployed, settled a strike, and shook hands by the thousands. On top of all her other, unprecedented activity, Eleanor also carried off, as successfully as necessary, the social functions of her First Ladyship, although gadabout Eleanor was not much of a housekeeper. A woman who had soiled her white gloves on a White House balustrade wrote to complain to the First Lady of the "disgraceful" condition of the Mansion and to suggest that "instead of tearing around the country," she ought to "stay at home" and see to the cleaning.

During 1939, the President's partner was hostess in the White House to 4,729 people who came to dinner. Another 323 stayed overnight, 9,211 came to tea, 14,056 lined up for handshakes and light refreshment at receptions, 1,320,300 visited the public rooms. She presided over the Easter Egg Rolling on the White House lawn—at which the average attendance was 53,108—during which event one year "the record shows that 180 children were lost and found; two people were sent to the emergency hospital; six people fainted and twenty-two had to be treated for small abrasions."

In addition to everything else, Franklin's "hands" also continued her writing. Eleanor Roosevelt was the first Presidential wife to continue her own independent career after becoming First Lady: having begun in the '20s, she distinguished herself before, during, and after the White House days with her prolific output as a career journalist. She worked to earn money: "I could not help the various [causes] in which I am interested if I did not earn the money which makes it possible." To publicize her concerns, Eleanor wrote books and daily, weekly, and monthly columns in a number of periodicals; she lectured constantly on her values, and in the mid-'30s developed her own radio program.

Her first major volley as First Lady was fired in 1933. In an article entitled "It's Up to the Women," Eleanor argued that, on issues of war and peace, the environment, social and civil rights, and the economic dismay left over from the Depression, that the "understanding heart" of women gives them a slant that men lack, and gives the world a hope for change in humane directions. "Mrs. Roosevelt's Page" began in 1934 in the monthly *Woman's Home Companion*. Her syndicated daily newspaper column "My Day," began in 1935. "If You Ask Me" was begun in 1942 in the monthly *Ladies' Home Journal*, and was moved in 1949 to *McCall's*. In 1937, Eleanor published the first installment of her autobiography, *This Is My Story*, which she would update and revise throughout the rest of her life. Even more than in her frequent speeches, people learned to read Eleanor's newspaper articles for trial versions of Franklin's impending policy decisions, social concerns of the New Deal, and Administration commentary on political issues and world events—flags run up ahead of time to see who would shoot and who salute. When a woman news reporter asked Eleanor about the close coincidence of her daily column and the President's policies, Eleanor responded: "You don't just sit at meals and look at each other!"

In a sense, the entire Roosevelt Administration was Eleanor's "First Lady's project." In another sense, her two pet projects were Arthurdale (an experimental—and none-too-successful—self-help subsistence community of unemployed miners at Scottsdale, West Virginia, founded to alleviate poverty in Appalachia) and the National Youth Administration. Called by the press the "inspector-general" of the NYA, Eleanor concerned herself with finding jobs for young workers and part-time jobs for students so they could continue their education; in so doing, she pitched Franklin a political "hot potato." Some of his advisors were afraid that the NYA looked too much like Hitler's Youth Movement. But Eleanor outdistanced her critics, and the NYA was ultimately well-received after giving skills training to thousands of young people.

Both through the NYA and by getting herself in as much trouble with the racists as with her other critics, Eleanor accomplished more that was not merely symbolic for Americans of African descent than any First Lady before her. "This is a time when it takes courage to live." That is what Eleanor said, and so fought the battle against race prejudice, having first overcome her own traditionally racist indifference. Eleanor said that she knew she had outgrown the race prejudice with which she had been raised the day she ran down the White House driveway to greet her friend Mary McLeod Bethune, threw her arms around her neck, and kissed her on the cheek. Eleanor's friend was the foremost black educator.

She included Mary McLeod Bethune on the advisory board of the NYA to make certain that young Americans of African descent would be included in its program. The First Lady worked with Secretary of the Interior Harold L. Ickes and with Walter White, leader of the National Association for the Advancement of Colored People, to ensure full inclusion of black citizens throughout the New Deal. In her advocacy of Negro rights, Eleanor urged Franklin to patronize anti-lynching legislation and to abolish the poll tax. The President didn't go along for political reasons, although Franklin did not oppose Eleanor's campaign to help African America.

BEHIND EVERY SUCCESSFUL PRESIDENT

In 1939, at the Southern Conference on Human Welfare when "they" would not allow Eleanor to sit on the African side of the audience at a meeting of the races in Birmingham, Alabama, she positioned her chair as close to the line of demarcation as she could; and then, throughout the session, kept scooting her chair little by little until she was fully straddling the color line.

When the Daughters of the American Revolution refused permission to Marian Anderson to sing at Constitution Hall, Eleanor resigned from the D.A.R. She and Ickes arranged, instead, for the celebrated black contralto to sing on the steps of the Lincoln Memorial before an audience of 75,000.

The First Lady invited black people to visit the White House, and she herself visited their schools and communities. She agitated for equal treatment of black military personnel and black workers in the war industries, and she took the racist flak without flinching. Eleanor had a knack for taking sides with any people under fire, and "Eleanor jokes" became common. Jokes about "Eleanor the Nigger-lover" went the rounds. But the Democrats had the last laugh: descendents of the slaves, traditionally Republican since Lincoln's day, began to join the Democratic Party in great numbers, thanks to Eleanor.

The bigots were at it again. Eleanor was called "Eleanor the Jew-lover," when the Jews of Europe were fleeing the Nazi terror, and the First Lady pressed the State Department to admit more refugees into America. When, after Pearl Harbor, American fear of foreign Japanese turned racist and took aim at Japanese Americans, it became "Eleanor the Jap-lover." She had herself photographed with a group of incarcerated West Coast Nisei and did what she could to stop their internment in "relocation camps." During Franklin's repetitively successful bids for re-election, some opponents wore campaign buttons proclaiming: "And we don't want Eleanor either." But a New England fisherman got it right in his sober comment after a tour of the White House: "She ain't stuck up, she ain't dressed up, and she ain't afeared to talk."

When Their Royal Highnesses George VI and Elizabeth visited America in 1939 to make personally visible the alliance against fascism that America had not yet affirmed publicly, Eleanor—proving that the New Englander knew what he was talking about—treated the royals to an American backyard barbecue at Hyde Park complete with hot dogs and potato chips. Kate Smith and the Coon Creek Girls from Pinchem-Tight Hollow, Renfro Valley, Kentucky, entertained. The Windsors seemed to enjoy themselves, but mother-in-law Sara Roosevelt found the hot dogs positively shocking.

It was at one of Eleanor's democratic backyard cookouts, like the one given for the royals, that the Secret Service proved unable to protect her from the only recorded "assassination attempt" on an American First Lady. While Eleanor was bending over the barbecue grill, Shirley Temple shot her in the behind with a slingshot.

Eleanor was opposed to Franklin's running for a third term in 1939, but pressures due to the war in Europe convinced her that he ought to continue in the Presidency for the good of the country. When the Democratic Convention fell into a heated wrangle over his chosen Vice Presidential running mate (Henry Wallace, a New Deal hardliner), Franklin sent in Eleanor to save the political ball game: "You know Eleanor always makes people feel right. She has a fine way with her." She made an elegantly simple speech that reunited the feuding Democrats.

BEHIND EVERY SUCCESSFUL PRESIDENT

When the next World War came, Eleanor put on her Red Cross uniform again; she also took to the air for Franklin, and made three overseas trips to visit America's allies and, especially, the troops. Packing only a single bag with two day dresses, one evening gown, one suit, some blouses, one pair of shoes for daytime and another for night, she was off in 1942 on a state visit to England and to talk with "officers and men." Eleanor got past the glitter of the brass by breakfasting with the enlisted men.

To fool the Nazis—and everyone else—she was assigned the code-name "Rover" (one of Franklin's little jokes, thought Eleanor). One of her assignments on this tour was to mend relations between British and American military personnel. Prime Minister Winston Churchill—with whose imperialist politics Eleanor heartily disagreed—praised the success of her mission: "You certainly have left golden footprints behind you."

In 1943 she dodged Imperial Japanese air raids while island-hopping across the South Pacific from New Zealand to Guadalcanal, where the air battle still raged. On her Pacific tour of duty, Eleanor traveled 25,000 miles and lost 25 pounds; saw war factories, rubbed noses with Maoris, and visited Red Cross clubs and 400,000 men—although (as she quipped) "General MacArthur was too busy to bother with a lady." In 1944, Eleanor toured the Caribbean and Latin America.

Many people thought Eleanor had far too much influence on the President, and Franklin's sense of humor contributed to the impression. He boasted about her, quoted her, and referred to her as "the missus." "My missus says . . ." he would begin in making some important point. She was his partner and his wife and he loved her. Franklin kept a picture of Eleanor hanging on his office door.

Pointing to it, he told Frances Perkins: "That's just the way Eleanor looks, you know—lovely hair, pretty eyes. And she always looks magnificent in evening clothes, doesn't she?" Franklin warned Lorena Hickok, Eleanor's friend and travel chum: "Never get into an argument with the missus, you can't win. You think you have her pinned down here . . . but she bobs up right away over there somewhere! No use —you can't win!"

Sometimes he baited her, drawing her out on issues, making every contrary argument against her he could think of, and leaving her certain that he was totally unconvinced by her advocacy—only the next day to announce his new policy to the world with the familiar preamble: "My missus told me . . ." Eleanor described his tactic:

> Without giving me a glance or the satisfaction of batting an eyelash, he calmly stated as his own the policies and beliefs he had argued against the night before! To this day I have no idea whether he had simply used me as a sounding board, as he so often did, with the idea of getting the reaction of the person on the outside, or whether my arguments had been needed to fortify his decision and to clarify his own mind.

When Franklin refused to arrange appointments with Eleanor's favorites, she got around that by inviting them to dinner.

Her acting as Franklin's "legs and eyes" was often thrown up to Eleanor as an example of her "excessive influence over the President." After one of her many lectures, this time in Republican Ohio, a crossways questioner tried to nail her by asking: "Do you think your husband's illness has affected your husband's mentality?"

Eleanor, expert at turning the hostility of her critics to

her own favor, replied with utter poise and a blinding array of teeth in the Eleanor trill: "I am glad that question was asked. The answer is Yes. Anyone who has gone through great suffering is bound to have a great sympathy and understanding of the problems of mankind." The answer was met with resounding applause.

Eleanor said that Franklin and she "thought alike;" but on matters where they disagreed, she called herself the "hair shirt" on his conscience. She favored Prohibition; he favored its repeal. She stood by the League of Nations when he, for political reasons, repudiated it. She was unable to persuade him to abandon neutrality during the Spanish Civil War.

In the words of Abigail Adams, Eleanor was always reminding Franklin to "remember the ladies."

Eleanor did not, of course, win all her points with Franklin. Although Eleanor had started out a passive female averse to women's rights and traditional in her racial theories, as her thinking matured she was generally ahead of Franklin on issues of race and gender, as well as social issues and progressive legislation. On some matters, his politics and her idealism remained permanently irreconcilable: "I'm the agitator; he's the politician." She took pride in saying that "sometimes my conscience bothered him."

After Yalta, Eleanor lamented to Franklin his bartering away of Estonia, Latvia, and Lithuania to the Soviets—by then, already absorbed into the Russian bloc. "How many people in the United States," he asked, "do you think would be willing to go to war to free Estonia, Latvia, and Lithuania?"

During Franklin's declining months in 1945, Eleanor realized that their family debate style had become too much for him. They were going at it over the issue of a peacetime military draft—Franklin, pro; Eleanor, contra—when he became visibly upset; she dropped the subject immediately. He was "no longer the calm and imperturbable person who, in the past, had always goaded me to vehement arguments when questions of policy came up."

When news of Franklin's death reached her, Eleanor sent this cable to her four sons scattered round the world, all of them in uniform: "DARLINGS: FATHER SLEPT AWAY THIS AFTERNOON. HE DID HIS JOB TO THE END AS HE WOULD WANT YOU TO DO."

The First Lady called Vice President Harry Truman to the White House. Putting her hand on his shoulder, Eleanor said: "Harry, the President is dead."

Struggling to overcome the emotions and his speechlessness, the President-designate choked out: "Is there anything I can do for you?"

Eleanor responded: "Is there anything *we* can do for *you*? For you are the one in trouble now."

A number of Eleanor's female friends were lesbian; but Eleanor resisted allowing her friendship and infatuation with "Hick darling"—Lorena Hickok—to continue to develop sexually. Eleanor wrote in a letter:

> I know you often have a feeling for me which for one reason or another I may not return in kind, but I feel I love you just the same.... Of course, dear, I never meant to hurt you in any way, but that is no excuse for having done it. It won't help you any, but I'll never do to anyone else what I did to you.

Besides Earl Miller, her Secret Service guard friend, and Hick, there were other friends, both male and female.

BEHIND EVERY SUCCESSFUL PRESIDENT

But none of them fulfilled in Eleanor what Franklin did as her reciprocally affectionate peer; and, apparently, no one at all fulfilled her in the sexual dimension of her personality. For this, Eleanor turned not to a person but to her career. Perhaps her most self-revelatory comment was a statement made in 1927, ostensibly about women in general, that "politics may serve to guard against the emptiness and loneliness that enter some women's lives after their children have grown."

Franklin's attraction to other women was something Eleanor learned to work around; and her own and Franklin's lack of mutual sexual attraction was something she chose to live with for the sake of their common Presidential achievement.

Eleanor wrote of Franklin words that apply equally, if not more so, to herself: "Through the whole of Franklin's career there never was any deviation from his original objective—to help make life better for the average man, woman and child." Reviewing that career—their common Presidential career—Eleanor concluded: "There are no regrets."

In her long, human-rights-serving career that followed FDR's death, Eleanor was heard and seen frequently. She was always in the news, especially when she guided the new United Nations committee in its drafting of the Universal Declaration of Human Rights (1948), becoming, in effect, the Thomas Jefferson of the United Nations. In so doing, she had also become, as President Harry Truman said, "The First Lady of the World." She died on November 7, 1962.

Lou Henry Hoover

Presidential Girl Scout

THE FIRST shell exploded in the backyard. Lou Hoover ran to the back door, leaving the news reporters who were staying in her house mystified. Wasn't she scared? She looked to see where the blast had dug its crater, then went into the front room that was her library, sat down, and dealt herself a hand of solitaire. Wasn't she concerned? Lou knew—and the newsmen would soon find out—that the Chinese Boxer artillery blasts came in threes and were automatically spaced: in a few seconds and at a predictable distance away, shells number two and three would explode. Lou had calculated that the explosions would not hit the library.

The second shell exploded in the street in front of the house, killing a Japanese sentry posted at the Hoover compound. The third shell detonated in the upstairs hallway of the Hoover house, hitting and exploding the newel post at the head of the stairs. The wooden column was splintered into about seventy pieces, scattered all over the room. Through the haze of smoke and disintegration of plaster dust, in the library. Lou was sitting at the table, studying her cards. "I don't seem to be getting this," she mused to one of the newsmen over her shoulder. He noticed that some cards had fallen to the floor. "But that was the last one for the present, anyhow," she continued. "Let's all go and have tea." Lou Hoover had a tight grip on her nerves, the situation, and most of her cards.

Lou Hoover had been born Lou Henry on March 29, 1874, in Waterloo, a little town in Iowa, just a few miles away—and four months apart—from Bert Hoover. The two families had not known one another; and each, independent of the other, would later move to California—Lou's family in search of a warmer, drier climate to clear up her mother Florence's chronic bronchitis. The daughter of Dr. Charles Henry, Lou had grown up her dad's sidekick, trapping rabbits and going fishing. They had lived for a while in Shell Rock, Iowa; in Texas; and in Clearwater, Kansas, before moving to Whittier, California, in 1884, when Lou was ten. At Whittier, Lou's father established the first bank, as he did in Monterey, California, six years later when the Henrys moved there.

Life in California was ideal for a bareback-bronco-riding, hiking, camping, straight-shooting sunburnt gal who gathered hazelnuts in the woods and had an independent, unconventional mind. (Lou could also ride side-saddle.) She graduated from San Jose Normal School (later San Jose State University), worked as assistant cashier in her father's bank for a while, and then taught third grade in Monterey for a year. When she heard geologist Branner's lecture on "The Bones of the Earth" in a university extension course, she decided on the spot to enter Stanford and study with the brilliant professor. Lou soon learned to put up with everybody asking her if she minded being the only girl in the Geology Department.

Tall, blue-eyed, and beautifully bony; athletic, with bobbed but luxuriant coils of brown hair and a California-girl, suntan, the eager freshperson first met Bert, the shy, tongue-tied, beetle-browed and bearded senior-class treasurer in 1894, in Professor Branner's presence. Lou and Bertie held their initial conversation over whether certain fossils in Branner's collection were carboniferous or not. After that first meeting, Bert was a little put off by the brainy Miss Henry.

Soon afterwards, Professor Branner's wife invited a quartet of students to the Branner home for dinner on Saturday night, apparently with matchmaking in mind. She assigned Bert to escort Lou. Bert, however, who said he "didn't much go for" Lou, negotiated with his chum, Bob McDonnell, to switch dates; Bob would take Lou, and Bert would take Grace Diggles. When they arrived at the Branners', and Mrs. Branner discovered her plan going agley, she did her best to correct matters.

"Mr. McDonnell," said Mrs. Branner with professional graciousness, "will you please take Miss Diggles in to supper?"

Bert was reassigned to Lou. As the evening progressed, Bob noticed that, instead of being miserable, Bert was entranced. Lou had penetrated Bert's shyness, they were enthusiastically discussing geology, were amazed to discover their common Iowa background, and were already making plans to do outdoor things together.

"Lou Henry's all right," said Bert to Bob after supper, "She not a bit snooty like I thought she was."

Bert was attracted to Lou's "whimsical mind, her blue eyes and a broad grinnish smile." Lou was not like the other girls. On field trips together, instead of waiting for him to offer a helping hand over a fence, Lou grabbed the top rail and vaulted over by herself. Moreover, she was better at baseball and basketball, skating, archery, and horse riding than Bert was; they were a match at fishing. Bert's buddies voted her a "thoroughly good fellow," though not someone you ought to slap on the back.

From the very beginning, Lou felt protective of Bertie. When Lou's sorority sisters got snooty about her dating Bert, the laundry boy (Bert, the entrepreneur, had a number of capitalistic gigs going), Lou moved out of the sorority house in a huff. The real problem Lou's sorority sisters had with Bert was his Quaker "barbarianism"—his egalitarian opposition to Greek-letter societies: he considered them undemocratic.

Lou and Bertie became informally engaged just as he graduated from Stanford and went off to mine coal for two years in Australia. Lou told her sorority chums that they would marry once Bert found a job that would allow him to settle down long enough to make a home. For the rest of their life, however, any settling down done by Lou would have to be occasional and temporary. When a prospecting job for the Chinese Engineering and Mining Company came through, Bert cabled Lou his formal proposal of marriage (and nomadism). Lou cabled back an eloquent affirmative: "Yes." Bert traveled half-way around the world to collect his bride.

On February 10, 1899, Bert, a Quaker, and Lou, an Episcopalian, were married by a Catholic priest in a civil ceremony, there being no Protestant clergy available in Monterey, California, at that time. Father Roman Mestres had been a good friend—Lou, after graduating from Stanford, had taught school in his parish hall when the public school burned down, and she had helped the padre build a baseball park in town. The ceremony took place at noon, the bride and groom dressed in brown travel suits that each had bought independent of the other; they were on the train for San Francisco by two p.m.; the next day they sailed for the Far East. Lou and Bertie's honeymoon trip was a slow boat to China; as they sailed, they read a steamer trunk full of all the books they had been able to find.

In China, at first, Bertie went out prospecting without Lou, leaving her at home in Tientsin to oversee her Chinese housekeeping—she had the language to learn and a "multitude" of fifteen servants to keep organized: cook, houseboy, gardener, maid, rickshaw boys (for transportation and message delivery), stable hands, and more. Learning the Chinese language was something Lou did far more competently than Bertie—she spent two or three hours a day in study of Chinese. Bert said that Lou left him "open to insult," because the English-speaking Chinese always spoke to Bert in English, and to Lou in Chinese.

Lou learned to live with the Chinese "squeeze" system —the institutionalized right of servants to take petty graft— a way the poorer people had of seeing that the richer people share the wealth. When Lou complained to the cook that the groceries he bought for her were costing twice as much as Mr. Hoover's secretary's groceries, the cook replied that this was only appropriate, as Mr. Hoover's salary was twice as big as his secretary's.

Lou wrote to Professor Branner in California about her fascination with ancient Chinese mining technology. She and Bert were gathering material for a book—maybe two, one on mining; the other, a general interest book about China. Both had begun a collection of Chinese books about mining—wherever they lived, they would always be collecting books about whatever subject currently fascinated them. Lou catalogued a collection of mining laws of the world for Bert to present to his Chinese employers.

Lou was a collector by nature—semi-precious stones, Chinese artifacts, books; she also started a collection of antique Chinese blue-and-white porcelains, which in time would become rare and very costly. In spare hours, the accomplished horsewoman went riding in the Chinese countryside. Shortly before the outbreak of the Boxer Rebellion, tough Lou lived through an attack of the Chinese flu, the same virus that would later carry off millions in Europe and America towards the end of World War I.

Much of the time, the newlywed team of geologists went prospecting. Together they drafted geological maps of the regions under study together, and Bert depended on Lou's work with the material on Chinese mining and international mining law. Bert's assistant engineers were aware that they were not working "just for Mr. Hoover, but for Mrs. Hoover too." They traveled in imperial splendor, because it would have been a loss of face for them and their employer, the Chinese government, were they to move about the country in less officious way. The Hoovers rode shaggy Manchurian ponies, while, alongside them, walking coolies carried the palanquins in which a high-ranking mandarin would have been carried in state—to prove to onlookers that the important Hoovers could have ridden officially on the backs of the people if they had wanted to.

In pomp and inefficiency, they made their way up dizzying mountainsides and across dreadful deserts, twenty-five miles or less per day, accompanied by a retinue of two interpreters, a number of Chinese mining officials, a staff of personal servants, a cook who insisted ritually on preparing a five-course meal every night (even when available supplies limited the menu to five different ways to cook eggs and chicken), a couple of dozen armed guards, carts and pack mules laden with too much luggage, advance runners, and banners. Lou and Bert were keen to look for industrial resources; Minister Chang, who was trying to build face for himself in the government, wanted them to look for gold. The rumors ran ahead of them that the coming "foreign mandarin" could, because he had green eyes, look through the rocks down into the earth and see gold. As they would approach a mining center, the people would come out to meet them, waving banners and popping firecrackers.

Oftimes, Lou Hoover—whom the Chinese called Hoo Loo—would, like Bert, snake herself into the cramped crawl space where the coolies did the mining—two-foot-high tunnels that no higher-ranking mining officials ever crawled through. When she surfaced, the locals would exorcise the mines with firecrackers, lanterns, and drums to get out the demons that Hoo Loo, a female, had let in. Women in China in 1900 did not go down into mines. Bertie and Lou found very little gold, but they proved that the world's greatest coal fields underlay northeastern China.

Lou wrote home about it: they slept in rude, one-room inns, where the guests had to bring their own bedding and cooking equipment; the only amenities supplied by the inn were a roof, water, and bedbugs. In Mongolia, they huddled around charcoal fires and slept on beds made of bricks warmed against the night chill. Everywhere they went, the communities turned out to greet them and crowded around to watch the gold magicians at work. Even when her husband was not seeing gold in the earth, the white lady—even when she was asleep—was a wonder just to stand and look at. Occasionally Lou awoke in the mornings to an audience—a congregation had gathered respectfully to observe Hoo Loo asleep.

Lou remembered her bridal tour scouting inland China as one of the happiest times of her life. Astride a pony or on a brick bed or as a great lady attended by servants, Lou Hoover was in her element.

The Boxer Rebellion of 1900 was a movement among religiously fanatical Chinese resentful of any foreign influence, and outraged in particular at the Western betrayal of China: the nations of Europe were getting rich by trafficking in drugs, imposing the opium trade on China. The Boxer forces believed, for a time, that they could not be hit by foreign bullets, and were wild to commit mayhem on any foreigner whom they could not chase out of the celestial empire. Lou and Bertie, with assorted other foreigners, found themselves besieged in Tientsin for 28 days, outnumbered more than one hundred to one.

Because Bert was the leading engineer, he was in charge of building defenses, organizing food distribution, and keeping the waterworks going. As the casualties mounted, Lou turned the social club of the foreign community into a hospital and its kitchen, and organized a nursing staff of herself and two others to help the one doctor. They cared for dozens of wounded each day, and on a single day, Lou found herself nursing a madhouse of two hundred wounded Chinese and assorted Westerners, each one crying out in some unknown tongue.

She raided her neighbors' stores of bedding to tear sheets into bandages. She rationed food, planned meals, and served afternoon tea to the sentries. She took charge of the cows, deciding which would be kept for milk and which would go into the stew. She fed incoming refugees: diplomats and their families, tradespeople, foreign soldiers, missionaries, Chinese Christians—anyone tinted with the West. Lou, it was said, had the best recipe for horse meat.

Above all, she helped people keep their spirits up under the daily barrage of none-too-accurate-but-still-dangerous fire from the 80,000 regular Chinese army and 300,000 Boxer force surrounding them. "I didn't see much of Bert in those days."

During a temporary letup in the fighting, the Russian Cossacks, allies almost as bad as enemies, began looting the European and American houses. One of Lou's servants, braving the danger of being abroad in daylight (any Chinese might be taken for an enemy and shot on sight), ran to the hospital to tell her. The pilferers had already cleaned out the house next door, he reported, and when one of the Chinese servants there had pleaded with them to stop, crying out that this was an "English house!"—the Russians had spitted him on a bayonet.

Lou pedaled home in a fury, her servant running alongside; and when she got there, the soldiers were just exiting, their arms loaded with Hoover loot. The enraged housewife confronted the Cossack cavalry, and by dint of her intensity of purpose caused them to drop what they were carrying. Lou failed to notice, however, that their boot tops were stuffed and their pockets bulged with every knife in her house and all her female finery—lace fichus, ribbons, embroideries, and an opera bag.

They had eaten everything they could swallow and drunk every drop they could swill. They had found her jars of strawberry jam in a closet, had emptied them with their fingers; and when they had finished licking their fingers, they had wiped their hands on the walls, the clothes, and the bedding. One Tsarist serf in a soldier suit, who either did not know what to make of a typewriter or had an antirevolutionary sense of humor, had dumped a jar of strawberry jam into Lou's writing machine.

When an opportunity arose to evacuate some of the women and children downstream, Bertie wanted Lou to board that steamer. They had been packing and were ready to go. Although their house had taken five direct hits—with two dozen more in the gardens and stables, ruining books and clothes and killing their six ponies—they had succeeded in boxing up Lou's grand collection of blue-and-white Ming and early Ching dynasty porcelains intact. In years to come, she would keep adding to her collection, until it became quite extensive and very valuable.

When they did leave China, they left together. "There were two chins in the Hoover family," the assistant engineers joked. Someone else commented that Lou had seemed positively to thrive on the excitement, enjoy the battle, and to be negligent of the danger she was constantly in.

Relief arrived in the form of Welsh Fusiliers and U.S. Marines playing "There'll Be a Hot Time in the Old Town Tonight" as they marched in. After the siege was lifted, Lou read with mock pride a glowing, three-column obituary about herself in a Beijing newspaper that greatly exaggerated the account of her death in Tientsin: "I was never so proud in my *life!*" she quipped.

After the siege, but while the Rebellion continued, Joaquin Miller, a venerable and eccentric reporter who had been one of the Hoovers' houseguests, proposed to go on to Beijing, and hired himself a ricksha for the trip. Although this journey would have taken him through Boxer-occupied territory and would have meant certain death, Lou could not dissuade him, try as she might. So, Lou, who had learned her Chinese lessons well, bribed Miller's coolie with a sizable "squeeze" to abandon him in Tientsin, thereby saving Miller's life.

During the next two busy years, more travel took Lou and Bert to London, with stopovers in Monterey, California, some time in Japan, a return to Tientsin, life in Tong Shan (where Lou was the only Western woman in that Chinese city, polyglot depot, and mining camp), and to more prospecting in China. They bought a little cottage in Monterey, so they would have a geographical anchor in America—a place to come back to, international mining explorations allowing. Next they went, among other places, to South Africa, Western Australia, and the Gold Coast (Ghana). On tramp steamers and tugboats, on horses, in buggies, and camelback, Lou and Bert traversed thousands of uncharted miles together, her geological opinions at the ready, eager for whatever new adventure cropped up, the constant delight of her husband, and a marvel of energy to the sedentary, wherever she went.

In 1902, they more or less settled near London, renting a small place in Walton-on-Thames called the White House; later that year, they also rented an apartment in London's Kensington—and here, Herbert Jr. was born. Whenever the Hoovers stayed in one place long enough to set up housekeeping, even if only for a few months, they preferred a house rather than rooms—it seemed more like a home, they thought, and the greater spaciousness allowed them to be more hospitable. They were almost never alone.

Bert's profitable mining travels continued, sometimes with Lou, sometimes not. When Bert was away, Lou stayed at their London apartment in Kensington and did a lot of auto-touring of the English and Welsh countryside. She logged 2,000 miles in 1902 alone. Five weeks after Herbert Junior was born, early in August 1903, Lou—carrying the baby in a basket—sailed out of Southampton, bound for Gibraltar and the Mediterranean. Bert joined them in Genoa, and from there the family traveled on through Suez and arrived in Kalgoorlie, Western Australia in mid-October. On December 25, they sailed from Auckland, New Zealand, for London via Monterey. Baby Hoover had traveled 31,000 miles around the world by the time he was six months old.

Late in 1905, after spending five months Down Under —during which time Lou, in and out of mines as usual, collected a number of Australian geological specimens for Professor Branner—they were returning to London through the Suez Canal, and Lou stopped off in Cairo, while Bert sailed on. For two weeks she consulted with British geologists in Egypt on Professor Branner's behalf about Red Sea geology.

In 1907, when Lou was pregnant with second son Allan, Bert was away again, although he returned on the day before the boy was born. Two months later, the traveling Hoovers, with Lou's sister Jean—who sometimes accompanied them on these excursions and kept a diary of the sisters' adventures—were off again, this time for Burma, this time carrying Allan in a basket. The Hoovers thought that "traveling with babies is easier than with most grown-ups," a truth that most new parents are too fearful to find out for themselves. It took Bert half a page in his memoirs just to list the names of all the countries he and Lou lived in between 1901 and 1908, while they were becoming wealthy mining consultants. In the year of Allan's birth, the Hoovers moved to Red House in Kensington, a grand establishment soon to become the seat of Hoover hospitality in London.

In 1908, Bert and Lou set themselves up as an independent mining consultancy, with offices in London,

New York, and San Francisco. In 1909, the Hoovers in London fostered the beginning of *The Mining Magazine*, a journal of applied geological scholarship and professional, advanced mining practice, under the editorship of T. A. Rickard. In the same year, Bert, with Lou's help, published his Stanford and Columbia lectures as a textbook, *The Principles of Mining*: Lou especially influenced the chapter on building character in budding engineers and the importance of professional ethics in mining.

The Hoovers, in spite of Bert's personal shyness, invited dinner guests to Red House who could be counted on to give them stimulating conversation for an evening. Among the numerous celebrity names on the guest list of the well-to-do and intellectual appeared the writer Joseph Conrad and the historian H. G. Wells, as well as British and American government officials and foreign dignitaries. Bertie, some said, was a bit of a "grunter," but Lou was a sparkling conversationalist who knew how to get other people talking, and often guided discussions towards topics she knew Bertie would like them to debate. Acquaintances called her "absolutely brilliant" and "the soul of gentleness," and one person said of Bertie that "he was a very fortunate man to have had the wife he had. . . . He needed explaining. She made a speciality of explaining him."

In London, when World War I broke out, Lou and Bert suddenly were presented with a snarl to be untangled by their inventive minds. The Hoovers during these years were latent Quakers who did not attend Meeting. But the plight of so many in trouble—200,000 Americans stranded in Europe by the war—springboarded them into religious helpfulness. They undertook direction of the effort to get these people home. They organized an emergency fund for those without money, and a credit fund guaranteeing payment on any American checks cashed by British banks. (Out of a total in excess of $1,500,000 in paper transactions backed by the Hoovers, they had to make good on only about $400.) They got an American Wild West Show, stripped of its gear and horses and all clothes except for the valuable feathers and beads of its Indian regalia, back on the west side of the Atlantic.

Lou was in charge of the Women's Committee, concerned primarily with clothes and food, caring for unaccompanied children, and keeping nervous tourists occupied until their passage home could be arranged. One elderly lady refused to board her steamer without a written guarantee from Lou that German submarines would not sink the ship. "We gave it to her," chuckled Bert.

Once Lou's charitable machine was working smoothly, she sailed for America with her boys on board the *Lusitania*. The Hoovers agreed that, with the war on, it was time to transplant their sons into a semi-permanent home-and-school situation. While getting them settled at Stanford, Lou also organized a musical society; but she did not stay put in California. Lou returned to England to travel with and help Bert while he directed the Allied Belgian Relief project to save the lives of a whole nation starving under Imperial German control.

In 1915, instead of returning to California, Lou kept Red House open as a "general commissariat for the men coming and going on relief [work]."

The Hoover boys returned with Lou to England and were enrolled in a "public" (which means "private") school near Oxford, straightway trading their California accents for Oxbridge ones.

The war was still on, and one night when the German Zeppelins were raining fire on London, Lou ran up to the boys' room in Red House, thinking to scurry the family to safety in the cellar. The boys had climbed out onto the roof, where Lou and Bert joined them, and all watched the searchlights rake the sky, saw the British fighting planes, and marked where a Zeppelin was downed, so they could carry out an expedition on the following day to observe the wreck and collect souvenir pieces of the broken Zeppelin. Shades of Tientsin!—Lou loved excitement. Shortly thereafter, to get their American accents back, Lou took the boys home to California again. Bert gave her credit for singlehandedly raising their sons during the war years. The family was reunited in Washington in 1917.

While Bert headed up the American Food Administration—"Food Will Win the War!"—Lou, as usual, took hold of Bert's job from her own angle and set about to make it, and him, succeed. Lou typically saw herself as helping Bert: she had majored in geology at college, but, as she liked to say, she had "majored in Herbert Hoover" ever since.

Momentarily tabling her enduring antipathy towards the media's invasion of family privacy, Lou invited the press into her kitchen. America was feeding the Allies, keeping up their strength and morale at considerable expense to the American dinner table. Not only did the fighting troops need training but also the nation's housewives had to be mustered out to keep the pledge of meatless, wheatless, sugarless days. Thus a new word came into the language: "to Hooverize." Lou Hoover, wife of the Food Tsar, showed the press that she was Hooverizing with efficiency and enthusiasm, substituting molasses and honey for sugar, and corn and rye for wheat. Moreover, she made speeches to housewives and restaurateurs, recruiting America's food army—fourteen million families, the largest volunteer army in history—to step up behind her to sign and keep the pledge of food conservation.

When the war ended in November 1918, the U.S. government promoted Bert from being "Food Tsar" in America to being "Food Regulator of the World," thus to oversee relief work and the economic reconstruction of Europe. Lou carried forward her assistance of Bert's work as head of the American Relief Administration, tearing herself away from her preferred life in California to live part time in New York with Bert.

She organized special banquets to raise money for the European relief effort: the tables were laid with tin cutlery and the guests were served plain food; an empty high chair was reserved for "the Invisible Guest," a hungry child in Europe. Lou hostessed a $1,000-per-plate dinner for 1,000 guests in New York in 1920. Not all of Lou's charity work was public or done purely as assistance to Bert. Raising funds for the Visiting Nurse Society was Lou's own idea; and her more numerous acts of private, individual, and personally implemented caring were often kept secret even from Bert. Sometimes she went incognita—at Christmas, Lou distributed treats at Washington's Children's Hospital disguised as Mrs. Santa Claus.

When Lou was not feeding children left hungry by war, she was engaged in the design and construction of her dreamhouse on San Juan Hill, high above the Stanford campus. The dwelling was an adaptation of Hopi Indian architecture, built of reinforced concrete, fireproof, and it incorporated the latest in technology—except for a refrigerator. Lou refused to buy a refrigerator, she said, because she wanted the local iceman not to lose his job! The rooms were semi-detached, connected by walks and exterior stairways across open-air patios; some of the flat roofs became terraced gardens—it was an indoor/outdoor house. Every major room and the terrace rooms all had a fireplace, because Lou liked fireplaces and so that a weiner roast or a marshmallow toast would be possible everywhere. At Allan's request, Lou instantly penciled in a swimming pool. Wide windows looked out on the Santa Clara Valley. "Our home," Lou told Allan, "must be an elastic thing, never entirely finished."

The dining room walls concealed hidden storage places where Lou kept her pewter collection, to which access was gained through secret panels. This device was intended not to foil thieves, but because Lou disliked the look of handles, hinges, and knobs. The locks were sprung through pinholes in the paneling by hatpins kept handy on the mantlepiece. Bert loved showing off the secret pewter, and claimed that it was Lou's only collection that had not cost him very much.

The one time anyone remembers Lou and Bert "having words" was over building the house. In the California fashion, she had designed the living room with indirect lighting, no lighting fixtures visible. Bert looked at it, smiled, and said: "Well, it looks kind of like early Pullman to me."

"Bert, it does not," she said, irritated.

A set of "secret stairs" led to Lou's "secret room" on the second floor. When she was in her writing room, everyone was to understand that Lou was "out." Its windows looked out on the front door, so that Lou could see who was arriving and decide whether or not to continue to be "out."

The Hoovers' outstanding service to humanity had made them both famous. At the Versailles peace conference, Bert was the U.S. representative to the Supreme Economic Council; and while he was in Paris, Lou and Allan were with him. In 1921, the Harding Administration recognized in Bert the talents that would make him useful as Secretary of Commerce, a job that he got and kept until 1927, into the Coolidge Administration. The job offer was an opportunity to trade his guaranteed income of half a million dollars per year for a government check worth a few thousand. Bert and Lou talked it over. They already had money, they agreed; what they wanted was to be able to help more people. Instead of returning to his lucrative engineering career, Bert stepped, as he said, upon "the slippery road of public life" and entered a new career in politics.

Living in Washington provided Lou, as wife of the Secretary of Commerce in the buoyant America of the Roaring Twenties, every reason to spread the table of life sumptuously. Turning her designer's eye from California Hopi to Washington Colonial, Lou redecorated their S Street home according to her special flair: everything was black and gold (an elegant complement to the boys' alligators, who slept in the bathtub); Lou's collections were scattered everywhere—Chinese boxes, carved quartz, Belgian curlicues, breakfast figurines—an exquisite litter that caused one little-boy visitor to comment that "you were always likely to bump a table and knock 25 things onto the floor, and you'd worry about what you've broken this time."

Lou became lifelong friends with the fun-loving Grace Coolidge; and during the Harding and Coolidge years, Lou also became one of the Capital's leading hostesses. There were guests for breakfast, guests for dinner, and sometimes guests for tea. Bert often brought guests home for dinner without warning, and Lou took it all in stride. Bert would keep the announced Senators and their wives busy in the library while Lou raided the icebox: "I never entertain; I just ask people to come in to see us and we enjoy each other." One year, when Grace Coolidge was under the weather,

BEHIND EVERY SUCCESSFUL PRESIDENT

Lou stood in for the First Lady and entertained 1,500 members of the D.A.R. at the S Street house: they came in through the front door, went through the receiving line, passed through Bert's den, and went out into the garden for punch and cookies, exiting by the garden gate.

Afternoons at S Street were more relaxed. It was Prohibition time. The Secretary of Commerce would come home, and tall orange juice drinks would be served on the verandah overlooking the back garden. Bert and Lou would swap their adventures of the day; the boys, the occasional guest, and a secretary or two would all join in the conversation. (The neighbors wanted the Hoovers to promise that they would not sell the S Street house to black people or Jews; but Bert and Lou refused to sign the petition.)

In 1921, eight years before she became the best-educated, most widely traveled First Lady up to her time, Lou the globetrotting linguist, scholar, geologist, social organizer, antique collector, house designer, and heroine of Tientsin, stated to the press: "I have done nothing extraordinary." Lou made this characteristically self-effacing misstatement on the occasion of her receiving from Albert, King of the Belgians, the Cross Chevalier, Order of Leopold, in recognition of her distinguished war-relief work. Lou described her wifely service too modestly, failing to verbalize that her work had been truly her own, as well:

> I have done nothing extraordinary, nor anything more than a woman should do for the man she loves. I have been deeply interested in Mr. Hoover's work and have tried to be of whatever assistance I could. My chief hobbies are my husband and our sons.

Lou's order of priorities, she said, started with

"assisting Mr. Hoover's work"; then, she listed the relief of suffering humanity as her next most important concern, and added in last place the reading of history books, biographies, and anything about "my husband's work." Lou concluded, with a clue to the complex causes that kept Lou Hoover the least-known First Lady of the 20th century: "I would like to steal away for a few months, to some place where I could have my family all to myself."

Lou's too-modest press releases belied her essence as a rugged individualist. In the Flapper Era, although Lou herself was no flapper, she was an outspoken voice of her generation advocating feminist progressivism.

Moreover, Lou began increasingly to make her feminist opinions known. She championed various women's organizations including the Campfire Girls and Girl Scouts of America, the General Federation of Women's Clubs, and the League of Women Voters. In 1923, Lou founded the women's division of the National Amateur Athletic Association.

Following the Teapot Dome scandal of the Harding Administration, Lou organized a women's conference on law enforcement, declaring that the "women of the country are tired of seeing the laws of our land ignored!" To a group of Republican women in Philadelphia, Lou proclaimed in 1923:

> Bad men are elected by good women who stay away from the polls on election day . . . Women should get into politics. They should take a more active part in civic affairs, give up some of their time devoted to pleasure for their duty as citizens. Whether we are wanted in politics or not, we are here to stay.

Lou encouraged women to follow independent careers

"even after marriage," and she waxed judgmental against any woman who used housework or mothering as an excuse to dodge involvement in the wider world. "I think she is lazy," she wrote. "The modern home is so small there is little work to do. The baby? It isn't a baby for long. There is no reason why a girl should get rusty in her profession during the five or six years she is caring for a small child."

Lou got her biggest chance to "get into politics" in 1928, when the Republicans were thinking about running Bert for President. Lou demonstrated the innate canniness required in any aspiring politico's spouse. When a news reporter called at the S Street house, hoping to get a scoop on Hoover presidential plans, and remarked on the beauty of the Hoover establishment and (with the White House in mind) commented that, next time, he might see her in an even more beautiful house, Lou responded with coy laughter: "Yes, you *must* come to see us in California!"

When Bert got the nomination, apolitical Lou was reluctant at first to hit the campaign trail; but Bert encouraged her: "I need you there. And who else should receive all the bouquets?" Just as Bert's public career had been grooming him for the Presidency, so also Lou's parallel career had been preparing her for the First Ladyship. Shunning the limelight, as usual, she echoed Bert's convincing line to a group of supporters in Palo Alto: "I enjoy campaigning, because my husband makes the speeches and I receive the roses." The artful comment, however, belies the reality: Lou was also making the occasional campaign speech off the back of the campaign train.

After Bert had won the election, but before the Inauguration, the President-elect borrowed a battleship from Cal Coolidge and set out on a diplomatic tour of Latin America, taking Lou with him, "whose California upbringing," he said, "enabled her to speak considerable Spanish."

In the Presidency, Lou is thought to have contributed to the government's increasingly equal treatment of women by influencing Bert to issue the Executive Order requiring Civil Service nominations "without regard to sex." Before the Hoover Administration, only thirteen women had held positions requiring Senate approval. Bert appointed seven others. Alice Roosevelt Longworth said (not entirely historically accurately) that Lou as First Lady was the first "to take a public part on her own." Lou's political influence remained behind the scenes.

As First Lady, Lou ran the White House as she had run her S Street house in Washington, her White and Red Houses in England, and her compound in China, only more so. "The best of everything" was her motto; and the White House became a watering hole for all the interesting people who wandered in and out of her and Bert's life, a conversational arena for lively discussion of the issues of their time, and a seat of permanent hospitality. When the bills for this lavish entertaining exceeded the amount appropriated by Congress for official fodder, the Hoovers picked up the tab. White Housekeeper Ava Long summarized Lou's Administration with a single word: "Company, company, company!" After their first three years in the Presidency, Bert and Lou reckoned that they had dined alone on three occasions only—the three February 10ths, their wedding anniversary. Lou's good times did not, however, include dancing; that, as she said in her characteristic deference to Bert's ways, was because "Daddy doesn't dance."

During the Christmas Eve party that the Hoovers gave for the children of the Mansion staff in 1929, the office area in the West Wing caught on fire. While most of the men

BEHIND EVERY SUCCESSFUL PRESIDENT

dashed off to tend the fire, Lou kept the party going while the White House smouldered. She made herself a hero with the children when she invited them up to the second floor to watch the fire!

Sometimes Lou would conduct two (and more) teas simultaneously in different state rooms, and she would circulate from gathering to gathering, enjoying them all; she and Bert expanded formal receptions into all the public rooms at once, the whole downstairs. The exasperated White House staff never knew how many to expect for a meal. Once, 500 guests showed up for a meal to which 200 had been invited: the staff scurried out to local grocery stores and emptied picnic baskets that had just been packed for an outing to Virginia. On another fabled occasion, when forty people showed up for a dinner that had been planned as chops for four, Lou went to the kitchen, ordered all the White House leftovers of ham, beef, lamb, and the aforesaid chops ground up, seasoned well, and cooked into croquettes. When one of the guests asked for the menu, Lou delivered it without a flicker and titled it with a flourish: "White House Surprise Supreme."

Hospitable Lou achieved a hitherto unparalleled expansiveness of numbers at White House gatherings. She had to hire three secretaries just to keep up with her guest lists and send the invitations. On New Year's Day 1930, the crowd was already lined up by 9 a.m., although the reception was not scheduled to begin until 11. "We can't keep all those people waiting another two hours," Lou told Bert, and opened the doors. A record nine thousand handshakes later—breaking Teddy Roosevelt's previous record of 8,513 handshakes, and three times the usual number—Lou and Bert were shook out, stiff, and sore.

Deciding that enough was enough, the Hoovers broke

with time-honored tradition the following New Year's Day. The Hoovers arranged not to be at home, and a venerable Presidential ceremony passed into the history books. Bashful Bert would gladly have done away as well with other formal receptions, but Lou was unwilling: she did not want them to be thought of as snobbish.

Lou's reputation as First Lady has been clouded by the gossip of her staff. She was considered by the White House regulars to be haughty—a reputation that she may have deserved. Lou had developed her managerial style in Tientsin and London, and she treated her thirty-two-person American staff as she had treated her English servants and as she had learned to deal with Chinese coolies on the "squeeze." Shy Bert seems to have kept his distance from the staff, rarely even looking at or speaking to them. Taking this diffidence amiss, they called him "His Majesty" behind his back. Bert, the egalitarian Quaker and man of action, rather than being haughty, felt uncomfortable being waited on like royalty.

Lou, by contrast, seemed imperious. She imposed a set of hand signals according to which she expected the staff to perform, but who mostly became confused: hand-to-hair, for example, meant "announce dinner," and a touch of her glasses meant "clear the table." Butlers, table waiters, and footmen—all exactly the same height, all in black tie by day and tails by night—were to stand at dignified attention like English butlers in disinterested silence; they were not to smile at guests' jokes or rattle the dinnerware while serving.

"Finer people never lived," commented Head Usher Ike Hoover (no relation), "but the President and Mrs. Hoover rarely broke through the barrier between those who serve and those who are served." White Housekeeper Ava Long agreed: "I found it much easier to admire the Hoovers than to like them."

The staff, however, were not the only people in the White House being regulated according to Lou's Chinese ways. Through the years, and now during the Presidency, on *"sotto voce* occasions" (as Bert called them), Lou would communicate privately with him in public by using the one hundred or so Chinese words that he had managed to retain!

A more endearing aspect of Lou's First Ladyship, of which many details are still unknown, was her parental concern for her staff and her considerable expenditure of charitable energies and funds to a long list of beneficiaries whose number and names are only now being catalogued. Lou sent food from the White House kitchen to ill staff members, and intervened with the hospitals when they were not getting proper health care. Cream delivery with the compliments of Mrs. Hoover started at the house of a butler who could not afford the prescribed dairy products for his ulcer. She offered to pay the college expenses of a White House maid. Throughout their career the Hoovers had on numerous occasions organized the feeding of whole populations: being First Lady only put Lou in a better spot to carry out her generosity. But she did it her own way—quietly, from the background, and with a firm hand. Lou required a secretary and two assistants to keep track of and implement her anonymous contributions.

Lou did her alms in secret, and she gave no interviews. But when a matter of principle required a public stance, she willingly, if painfully, became the contrary weathervane to point unturning against the wind of bigotry. In 1929, Lou invited Jessie DePriest, wife of Oscar DePriest, an African-American Congressman from Chicago, to tea at the White House. The reactionary gossips cried foul, and racist newspaper editors denounced her for "defiling" the President's House and offering "arrogant insult" to the South and the whole nation; the Texas Legislature passed a resolution condemning the "breach of public morality."

Lou was also the first to entertain Mormons at the White House and to include noticeably pregnant women in her receiving lines; but black people are more noticeable even than noticeably pregnant women and were more upsetting than Mormons.

The cruel Southern journalism, Bert remembered, "wounded her deeply. Her tears, however, did not melt her indomitable determination." Bert "diverted the lightning" by inviting R. R. Moton, president of Tuskegee Institute, to become his dinner guest—the first black person invited by the President to the Mansion since Teddy and Edith Roosevelt had invited Booker T. Washington, thirty years before. "The White House was thus 'defiled' several times during my term," Bert reminisced.

Riding out on horseback from Camp Rapidan, Lou discovered Appalachian poverty for herself; and a surprise return visit from a neighbor prompted the Hoovers, long before the invention of government social programs, to undertake improvements for the sake of the residents of Appalachia. During Bert's birthday party in 1929 at Camp Rapidan, eleven-year-old William McKinley Burraker from a nearby mountain slipped past the security guards to present the President with a birthday 'possum in a cage. Nonetheless grateful, the Hoovers declined to eat the gift (Allan turned it into the camp pet); but during a conversation with their guest, discovered that there was no school on Master Burraker's mountain. So the Hoovers funded Dark Hollow School, and hired Christine Vest, from Yosemite, Kentucky, and a graduate of Berea College, as teacher for the student body of 17.

The children marveled at water coming from a faucet, when they saw indoor plumbing for the first time; Christine took them to the Madison County Fair, their first trip off the mountain; and Lou paid for all this and clothing and Christmas presents, too.

The guest list at Camp Rapidan was a long one: Anne Morrow and Charles Lindbergh were among the most frequent visitors (Lindy liked trout fishing as much as Bert); and Winston Churchill and Thomas A. Edison also paid visits. Lou used Camp Rapidan for the new chief hobby she had taken up soon after coming to Washington—Girl Scouting. Lou wanted American girls to enjoy the contact with nature and the out-of-doors that she had known as a girl in the wilds of California: "I was a Scout years ago, before the movement ever started, when my father took me hunting, fishing and hiking in the mountains. . . . When I learned of the movement I thought, here is what I always wanted other girls to have."

Lou joined the Girl Scouts of America five years after its founding in 1917, worked with founder Juliette Low, served twice as national president, sponsored the first national GSA cookie sale in 1935, and conceived the ideas of GSA summer day camps. She held her national GSA meetings both at Camp Rapidan and at the White House. Whenever issues of etiquette came up, Lou's final appeal was to the *Girl Scout Handbook*, which she considered definitive. The Girl Scout First Lady liked nothing better than to invite a couple of hundred GSA leaders to an informal lunch or a Christmas party at the Mansion. They described her as the one woman they would most like to be with in the middle of an earthquake. During the Great War, Lou had inspired her D.C. Girl Scouts to plant "Victory

Gardens" as part of her Hooverization campaign—Girl Scouts helped to win the war by raising their own vegetables.

For Lou, Scouting was not just about the craft of the outdoors; it instilled other kinds of self-reliance, as well: ". . . how to bake a cake, darn a sock or do any of the thousand-and-one little domestic tricks their grandmothers could perform as second nature." Girl Scouting also had a leveling effect, throwing together girls from all economic levels, all wearing a common uniform. "The intimacy of the life in common with her patrol thaws out a girl's self-consciousness and helps her develop initiative and personality," said the First Lady, who possessed personality and initiative in immeasurable amounts.

Lou installed a radio lab in the White House to "improve [my] talkie technique," and began to make nationwide speeches to young people on a variety of issues. Although Lou's public speaking ability was less than captivating, her ideas still ring with challenge. "Be yourself!" was Lou's motto for "the modern woman." She advocated that women act as independent individualists, free to dress as they please, be domestic when they please, and have a career outside the home, if they please.

In defense of the much-criticized flappers, Lou made it clear that short skirts and bobbed hair bothered her not at all. "I have the greatest faith and admiration for the young people of today, even for their sensible clothes, which some people seem to think are immodest." Sometimes she aimed her gender egalitarianism at the boys: speaking coast-to-coast from Camp Rapidan, Lou praised the joys of camping, and then went on to talk about young peoples' work around the house in terms that exploded the notion that "girl's work" is different from "boy's work." Housework, said Lou, is "as much the work of boys as of girls." She said to the boys:

> Just stop a second to think what home is to you. Is it just a place where mother and the girls drudge a good part of the day in order that father and the boys may have a place to come to eat and sleep? [She told them that boys as well as girls should help] with the dishes, sweeping. Boys, remember you are just as great factors in the homemaking of the family as are the girls.

Lou took a house designer's and historian's interest in the Presidential Mansion. She added richly to its furnishings at her own expense (and she saw to it that a comfortable chair was provided for the bedroom of each staff member). Also paying for it out of her own purse, she had the Signal Corps photograph every piece of White House furniture, and, with the help especially of Dare McMullin, one of her secretaries, catalogued every item. Lou, the antiquarian, was planning publication of a book on the historic White House, a project interrupted by the Depression. Her research did lead to the production of a detailed, illustrated catalogue of the Mansion's contents, which, unfortunately, came to light only after the restoration projects of a generation later.

When the Great Depression of 1929 began to be felt, the Hoover Administration was blamed for it in the popular mind; making matters worse, Bert's habitual shyness made him seem incommunicative and uncaring. He would sit at the dinner table, saying nothing to his guests. Lou, still good at "explaining Bert," kept the conversation going. She took it as an important part of her job to surround Bert with congenial people, as he hated to be alone. "You have to hammer and hammer at him," she explained to someone who complained of his seeming aloofness. No one knew better than Lou how Bert's compassionate Quaker heart, that could still cry when he thought about the starving Belgians, was anguished now over hungry Americans. As assisting Bert had been Lou's chief hobby in the past, protecting him now became her passion—keeping his homelife sane and affectionate, a place where he could find in her and their friends respite from the abuse being piled on his sensitive, humanitarian, essentially shy soul.

Lou did all that one wealthy influential well-meaning volunteer could do to ease the Depression. She hostessed a concert by the Polish pianist Paderewski, and raised a large sum to keep the soup kitchens going. Paderewski donated his talent in reciprocity for America's having fed Poland during the war, when the Hoovers had run the Food Administration. She put the White House on economy rations. On state occasions she wore American-grown and American-spun cotton dresses, rather than foreign silks, to set a precedent among her peers. She appealed to the well-off that they not hoard cash: ". . . otherwise we throw the whole machine out of gear. If we stop buying things we need, employment will drop tremendously." She explained the Depression as the result of postwar economic conditions in Europe, not as a failure of the American system. She called on the nation to tighten its belt, keep working hard, and maintain those "activities that are essential" so that the economy could correct itself.

Lou's efforts, like Bert's, praiseworthy though they were, were not on a scope that could meet the depth of need. When the Bonus Expeditionary Force—a 12,000-man army of Depression-racked unemployed veterans—camped in demonstration against the government at Washington's Anacostia Flats in 1932, Lou sent coffee and sandwiches from the White House kitchen to the protesters. But that was the time when communication between the Commander-in-Chief and his domestic militia broke down: General Douglas MacArthur opened fire on the demonstrators; the tanks were under the command of a youthful Ike Eisenhower. Bert got the discredit.

Castigated by the press, by the Democrats, and by their Household staff, Bert got the reputation of being an uncaring conservative, instead of the tenderhearted progressive that he was; and the smear that tarred Bert with blame for the Depression also stuck Lou with a reputation for having been imperious rather than generous. The Hoovers' popularity sank so low that their enemies began stooping to cheap tricks: someone spitefully cut Lou's wires during one of her broadcasts from the White House radio lab.

When Lou took Eleanor Roosevelt on the traditional out-going First Lady's tour of the White House, and the in-coming First Lady asked to see the kitchen, Lou—hostile over the new Administration—confirmed the worst rumors of Hoover haughtiness. Drawing herself up, she said: "I'm sorry, but the housekeeper will have to show you the kitchens. *I* never go into the kitchens." So out of favor with the nation were the Hoovers at the end of their Administration, the courtesy of Secret Service protection was not extended to them after they left the White House!

After Lou's sudden heart attack and untimely death on January 7, 1944, Bert found in her desk a stack of uncashed checks. Among the many strangers and friends, indigent college students, mothers too poor to afford the necessities for their babies, and old people without food or homes, recipients of Lou's generosity, not a few had tried to repay her. Lou had kept their checks as keepsakes.